Higher and Professional Education in **InOia**

by

William J. Haggerty

Consultant

State University of New York

U.S. DEPARTMENT OF HEALTH, EDUCATION, AND WELFARE
Office of Education

ROBERT H. FINCH, *Secretary*
JAMES E. ALLEN, JR., *Assistant Secretary and Commissioner of Education*

INSTITUTE OF INTERNATIONAL STUDIES, ROBERT LEESTMA, *Associate Commissioner for International Education*

This report was made by Wm. J. Haggerty, State University, New York, pursuant to Contract No. OS–64–27 with the Office of Education, U.S. Department of Health, Education, and Welfare.

Opinions expressed in the report are those of the author and do not necessarily reflect official policy of the U.S. Office of Education.

Superintendent of Documents Catalog No. FS 5.214:14141

U.S. GOVERNMENT PRINTING OFFICE
Washington: 1969

For sale by the Superintendent of Documents, U.S. Government Printing Office
Washington, D.C. 20402 - Price $1

Foreword

The present report is another in a series of Office of Education publications on education in other countries. Confined primarily to Indian higher education (defined as postsecondary education leading to the baccalaureate or higher degree), it discusses the development of higher education against the background of both relevant political and educational history and the educational needs in a country progressing at a rapid rate economically and technically.

The author served as Educational Adviser to the Government of India in 1952–53, and subsequently revisited India to acquire information for this study. At that time he received much valuable information and many helpful suggestions from Federal and State education officials; officers of colleges and universities; the staffs of the American Embassy and the United States Agency for International Development in New Delhi; and members of the Education Commission, the Inter-University Board of India and Ceylon, and the University Grants Commission—agencies of primary importance to the development of higher education since Independence. To these persons and to many others associated with them, the author and the Institute of International Studies wish to express their appreciation.

Particular thanks are due to the following persons, identified here with their titles and positions during the time they assisted the author: the Hon. M. C. Chagla, Minister of Education and former Ambassador of India to the United States; the late Professor Humayun Kabir, Minister of Scientific Research and Cultural Affairs; Mr. Prem Kirpal, Education Secretary of the Government of India; Dr. D. S. Kothari, chairman of the Education Commission of 1964–66 and of the University Grants Commission; Mr. J. P. Naik, Adviser to the Ministry of Education and secretary-member of the Education Commission of 1964–66; Dr. Olive Reddick, director of the United States Educational Foundation in India; Dr. K. G. Saiyidain, Education Commission member and former Educational Adviser to the Government of India; and Dr. M. S. Thacker, education member of the Federal Planning Commission.

ROBERT LEESTMA

Associate Commissioner
for International Education

iii

A university stands for humanism, for tolerance, for reason, for progress, for the adventure of ideas and for the search for truth. It stands for the onward march of the human race towards even higher objectives. If the universities discharge their duty adequately, then it is well with the nation and the people. But if the temple of learning itself becomes a home of narrow bigotry and petty objectives, how then will the nation prosper or a people grow in stature?

A vast responsibility, therefore, rests on our universities and educational institutions and those who guide their destinies. They have to keep their lights burning and must not stray from the right path even when passion convulses the multitude and blinds many amongst those whose duty it is to set an example to others.

Jawaharlal Nehru, in a speech
at Allahabad University,
December 13, 1947

Contents

Part III.   Background of Higher Education

Part IV.   The Universities

Appendixes

Tables

Charts

Maps

Introduction

The educational system of the Republic of India reflects both its ancient culture and its recent social awakening. In the past, education was for the select few; today, India's educators and political leaders strive not only to educate the majority but also to adapt education to the country's social needs.

Although the form and content of Indian education have been the theme of countless studies and reports for two centuries, Indian higher education came of age as late as 1857, when the British Government established universities in Bombay, Calcutta, and Madras. Patterned after the University of London, these three universities affiliated most of the 20 existing Indian colleges; and in most cases prepared students to fill Indian Civil Service positions under the British Government.

Since Independence in 1947, Indian political and educational leaders have faced the tremendous task of rapidly providing meaningful educational opportunities for children and adults at all levels, out of minimum economic resources, for an enormous population, and in an expanding economy. The story of their progress, particularly at the level of higher education, forms the central part of this report.

To United States citizens the Indian educational system should be of particular interest. In contrast to India, the United States developed mass education at the same time that its economy and population were expanding. Nevertheless, the educational philosophy and accomplishments of the two countries are similar. Both India and the United States, committed to a democratic form of government and society, realize that its success requires universal education. Both countries follow a similar pattern of organization, financing, and control of education, with public education primarily the responsibility of the States rather than of the Federal Government; [1] although in both countries the Federal Government's educational expenditures are increasing to supplement those of the States. Since Indian Independence, educational collaboration between India and the United States has progressed on many fronts, under both public and private auspices, and will probably and hopefully continue with mutual benefit to the educators and to the people of both nations.

---

[1] For clarity, this publication uses the term "Federal Government." In India, the term is generally "Union Government" or "Central Government."

Part I.

India as a Nation

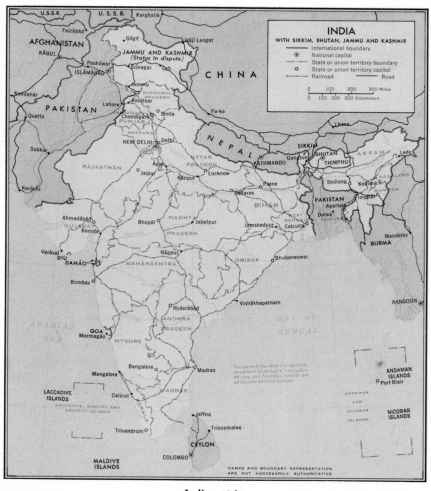

India: 1968

1. Geographical Setting

India is shaped like a kite, its northern end embedded in the Himalayan mountains and the Asian land mass, and its southern tip extending 2,000 miles south to within 8° north of the Equator. From west to east across its northern borders lie West Pakistan, Afghanistan, China, Tibet, Nepal, Sikkim, Bhutan, Burma, and East Pakistan. About a third of the distance south from India's northern tip and at the place of its greatest width (1,850 miles), its two coast lines begin, descending on a converging course to Cape Comorin at the southern tip of the country. At the west coast is the Arabian Sea, at the east coast, the Bay of Bengal, and below are the Indian Ocean and the island nation of Ceylon. Two groups of islands belong to India—the Andaman and Nicobar Islands in the Bay of Bengal and the Laccadive, Minicoy, and Amindivi Islands in the Arabian Sea.

Within this peninsula, sometimes referred to as the subcontinent of Asia, are found the highest mountains of the world, forests, deserts, and tropical areas like the Malabar Coast in the southwest. Many great rivers originate in the Himalayan mountains or in the high plains of the Deccan plateau and flow to one side or the other. Temperatures vary greatly from the frigid areas of the northern mountains to some of the hottest regions of the world, such as the Rajasthan desert and the Deccan plains. Rainfall ranges from well over 400 inches a year in the northeast to 4 inches or less in the northwest. The monsoon brings life-sustaining rain to most parts of the country for a few months each year; but if it comes too late or lasts too short a time crops may fail and cause famine, and if it produces too great a torrent, it may damage crops and sweep away people and houses in the floods.

Although India is the second largest nation of the world in population, and seventh geographically, it covers an area only about one-third that of the United States.

2. History

Ancient Civilizations

To this land of contrasts and extremes, uncounted thousands of visitors, travellers, invaders, and traders have come during the last 40 to 50 centuries. Earlier, human beings whose origins are unknown—pre-Dravidians —lived in the southern region. Current archeological studies indicate that by 3000 B.C. several areas in the northern and northwestern regions contained civilizations equal in sophistication to the early civilizations of Egypt and Mesopotamia. Excavation of the cities of Harappa, Mohenjodaro,[1] and others have revealed similarities to the city of Sumer, although whether there was any contact between the Indians and Sumerians is unknown. The early Indian civilizations had developed substantial cities with wide streets, two-level brick houses, water systems, and some of the amenities often lacking in parts of rural India today. Archeologists have found in good condition ceramic utensils, sundried bricks, seals with as yet undeciphered writing, and sculptured images of men and animals.

The cause of the decline and disappearance of the early Indian centers of civilization has not been ascertained. Professor George Dales of the University of Pennsylvania, heading an archeological project in the region, has advanced the theory that the Indus River, through the uprising of a natural mud-and-sand dam, created a lake of silt and swamp which inundated the cities of Mohenjodaro, Harappa, and probably others located near the dam. Such flooding followed by subsequent rebuilding may have happened several times.[2] This theory contrasts with earlier ones that Harappa, Mohenjodaro, and other cities of the same period had been overrun and defeated by Aryan invaders from the north and west about 2000 B.C.

Through the 35 to 40 centuries since that date, until the arrival of the British toward the end of the 16th century, historians have recorded at least 26 invasions. Countless people of many races have come to India. Some, such as the Chinese and Greeks, came as scholars to learn about the land and people, and have written accounts of their travels and dis-

---

[1] Harappa and Mohenjodaro are now within the borders of Pakistan.
[2] *Scientific American*. May 1966. p. 93–100.

coveries; some came to explore; some were in search of wealth; and others came to conquer. Persians, Greeks, Parthians, Scythians, Huns, Turks, Afghans, Arabs, Mongols, and Europeans (Portuguese, Dutch, Danes, French, and British) filed through the mountain passes along the northern, northwestern, and northeastern frontiers, or landed on the eastern and western coasts to the south.

Origins of Hinduism and Buddhism

The first Aryans to come to India were probably cultivators and cattle raisers who had mastered the use of iron. The Vedas, the oldest religious hymns of India and the basis of the Hindu faith, are associated with these early Aryan settlers in the north. The caste system originated before 1000 B.C. as an aspect of Hinduism. Based on four major occupational groups, it produced a rigid hereditary classification of persons, with the Brahmins or priestly class dominant. The Sanskrit epic *Ramayana* tells in epic poetry the story of the life and religious beliefs of these early times.

Two powerful revolts against the religious and social strictures of reactionary Hinduism took place approximately during the sixth century B.C. The revolt of the Jain sect, led by Vardhamana Mahvira, fostered a belief in nonviolence so extreme that Jains even today take every precaution to avoid killing anyone or anything, even the smallest insect. The other revolt was led by Gautama Buddha. He preached nonviolence as a way of life; taught that evil could be overcome by good; and proposed an eight-point code for human conduct whereby a person could learn to live at peace with his fellowmen and ultimately achieve a perfect state of peace within himself. Buddhism not only expanded to a far greater extent in India than did Jainism, but also became in various forms a major religion of Ceylon, China, Korea, Japan, and many other Asian countries, where it still exerts a powerful influence.

Gupta Period

About a century and a half after Buddha's death, in the year 326 B.C., Alexander invaded India. He brought with him scholars who, having learned of India through Hecataeus and other Greek historians, wanted to extend their knowledge and understanding. Alexander not only captured territory, but also established communities, leaving followers in many locations. He reached the Indus river valley, sailed down the Jhelum (a tributary of the Indus), and after a 2-year sojourn returned to Babylon.

During the next century, Chandragupta Maurya established in the north the Mauryan empire, which his grandson Asoka (272–232 B.C.) extended throughout most of the country. Asoka supported and extended Buddhist influence in India and surrounding countries. After the decline of the Mauryan empire came invasions by Greeks, Bactrians, Parthians, and others. War and violence were prevalent for several centuries.

The Gupta period brought a system of law and order that permitted the development of agriculture and commerce. Frequently known as the golden age of Indian history, the Gupta period was a time of enlightenment

3

and tolerance. Hindu art, literature, music, science, and sculpture flourished. Kalidasa, the famous Sanskrit scholar and dramatist who wrote the play *Shakuntala,* may have lived at the court of the Guptas. During this period the Government extended its contacts and influence in many directions through expanded trade and through diplomatic missions to foreign capitals. Although Buddhism remained the dominant religious philosophy, Hinduism was regaining strength and adopting many aspects of Buddhist thought. The Gupta period ended about 480 A.D.

During the fifth and sixth centuries the Huns, after conquering the Persians and Afghans, invaded and gained considerable control over India, only to lose it after a defeat by the Turks at the Oxus river. The Huns gradually became absorbed by the Hindus, adding another strain to the expanding population. During the first half of the seventh century, an Indian monarch by the name of Harsha established an empire in the north. Interesting accounts of this period were written by Hiuen Tsang, a Chinese pilgrim who visited India. Following Harsha, who died in 648, more invasions brought people from central Asia and Turkey, many of whom had Mongolian backgrounds. The Parsees, who followed the religion of Zoroaster, came to India in the eighth century and have remained a small but influential group, particularly in the Bombay area.

Coming of the Muslims

Although the Muslims came to India as early as the seventh century, it was about the year 1000 that the Muslim conqueror Mahmud of Ghazni extended his father's empire from Persia to the valleys of the Ganges, led armies to many parts of northern India more than a dozen times, and converted many persons to the Muslim religion in the Punjab and elsewhere.

The Muslims occupied Delhi in 1193, ruling a sultanate there until in 1526 Babar established the first Mughul empire. Babar was succeeded by Humayun (1530–56); Akbar (1556–1605); Jehangir (1605–27); Shah Jahan (1628–58), who built the Taj Mahal at Agra, the Red Fort in Delhi, and other still famous places; and Aurangzeb (1659–1707). These Mughul emperors extended Muslim influence throughout parts of northern and central India. At times they exhibited a degree of religious tolerance towards the Hindus; at other times they destroyed Hindu temples, erecting mosques either on top of the ruined temples or with the materials salvaged from them. After the death in 1707 of Aurangzeb, Muslim leaders remained on the throne until the Indian revolt against the British in 1857; but during these years the Muslims left little mark on Indian history.

Early European Explorers and Settlers

The first western Europeans made contact with India 28 years before the Mughul rule began with Babar in 1526. In 1498 Vasco de Gama, leading a Portuguese expedition, landed at Calicut on the Malabar coast. The Portuguese reached Goa in 1510, remaining in control there and in other small enclaves (Daman, Diu, Dadra and Nagar-Haveli) on the west coast of India for more than 4½ centuries, until in 1961 the Indian Government absorbed these Territories. During most of the 16th century the Portuguese dominated sea trade with India.

At the beginning of the 17th century, the Dutch and then the British began to dispute the Portuguese for Indian trade. The United East India Company of the Netherlands was formed in 1602, bringing together many private Dutch companies already established in the northern Provinces of India. On December 31, 1600, Queen Elizabeth chartered The Governor and Company of Merchants of London Trading into the East Indies, later known as the East India Company. The first expedition of the Company did not go to India, but to Sumatra in 1602. In 1608, a British sea captain by the name of Hawkins, representing the Company, traveled inland to Agra to meet the Mughul Emperor, Jehangir, and by 1611 the British had established a settlement at Masulipatam on the east coast. Rivalry with both the Portuguese and the Dutch occupied British attention in Asia for many years. Ultimately, preoccupied with Southeast Asia, the Dutch left India, and the Portuguese maintained only their small enclaves on the west coast.

Denmark and France also were involved with India during the 17th century. About 1620 the Danes began to explore India, settling in a few places in small numbers for more than 200 years; the East India Company bought these settlements in 1845. A French company, backed by Louis XIV, founded Pondicherry in the Madras region in the latter part of the 17th century, keeping it until in 1954 France voluntarily returned it to India.

Britain, having finally won the European competition for supremacy in India, maintained a dominant influence there until Independence in 1947.

The East India Company

The East India Company, to which the Queen had granted exclusive trade rights, included China and Southeast Asia in its sphere of operations in 1600, but after only a few years and a defeat by the Dutch in Indonesia in 1623, it restricted its activities to India (which for the British included Burma and Ceylon). In its primary search for raw materials and wealth, the Company operated under its charter from the Crown, but in many respects independently of the British Government. The Company was generally managed by a Court of Directors which chose its administrative and executive leaders.

Although the Company developed slowly in its early decades, its efforts to expand and dominate the country forced it into military actions, not only against its European rivals but against the Indians themselves in one part of the country after another. It received some assistance from the Royal Navy beginning in 1685 and from the Army in 1754.

The first three settlements, other than trading posts and factory sites, were at Madras (Fort George) in 1639, Bombay in 1668, and Calcutta in 1690. The Company acquired the seacoast site of Madras from a local Indian ruler; the site of Bombay from King Charles II who had received it as part of his dowry when he married Princess Catherine of Portugal;

and the site of Calcutta from the Mughul Emperor Aurangzeb in 1679, although military conflicts continued between the Company and Mughul troops until 1690. The areas for which these three sites served as focal points and administrative centers became known as the "Presidencies" of Madras, Bombay, and Calcutta.

The large operations of the East India Company inevitably raised issues affecting both domestic and foreign policies in London. In 1773 and 1774, acts were passed which gave the British Government a considerable degree of control over the Company. Henceforth a Government agency, the Board of Control shared both authority and responsibility with the Company's Court of Directors. Additional regulating acts were passed in 1813, 1833, and 1853.

As the activities of both the Company and the British Government expanded, military conflicts arose leading to wars with the French, the Maharattas, the Gurkhas, the Burmese, the Afghans, and the Sikhs. Territorial annexation of Sind, Oudh, and other areas of India by the British created a growing resentment which prompted Lord Canning in succeeding Lord Dalhousie as Governor-General of India in 1856, to prophesy: "I wish for a peaceful term of office. But I cannot forget that in the sky of India, serene as it is, a small cloud may arise, no larger than a man's hand, but which, growing larger and larger, may at last threaten to burst and overwhelm us with ruin." [3]

Revolution of 1857

In 1857, revolution brought great changes in the British position in India. Indian troops of the British military establishment (Sepoys) revolted in northern Provinces of India, from Bengal to Punjab, and sought to reinstate the ex-Mughul emperor of Delhi on his throne. The conflict raged for months from place to place with slaughter on both sides. As peace was gradually restored, the British began to allow the Indians greater representation and participation in the management of their own affairs, and the Indians began a slow but persistent campaign for national independence.

The British Government in India

In 1858, the British Government passed the Act for the Better Government of India, which transferred all power from the Company to the Crown. Lord Canning, the first viceroy of India, proclaimed the changes intended by the Crown and granted amnesty to many who had revolted.

During the following decades, successive British viceroys established an effective and extensive Indian Civil Service; instituted a pervasive judicial system including some of the provisions of western jurisprudence which safeguard individual rights; and initiated communications by rail, road, and telegraph. Service in India became a career and a way of life for many Britishers in both civilian and military roles.

---

[3] Quoted in *Encyclopaedia Britannica* (14th edition). 12:96.

In the field of education, British efforts were almost nonexistent during the early years of the East India Company and only sporadic until the time of the revolution (part III, chapters 1 and 2). In 1835, however, Lord Bentinck proposed "the promotion of European literature and science among the natives of India" [4] in the English language. For the most part the British, during their almost 350-year tenure in India, developed educational institutions which were modeled on the educational system in England and which trained students for those jobs in government and industry for which Indians were eligible. A few wealthy and socially favored Indians attended universities in England.

Development of Indian Nationalism

Meanwhile, from 1857 to 1947, successive Indian leaders, particularly those of the Congress Party, had been spurring the thoughts and feelings and demands of the people for freedom.

Western ideas of liberty, freedom, and democracy combined with Hindu reform movements to arouse nationalist feelings. Raja Ramohan Roy (1772–1833) in 1828 founded the Brahmo Samaj, a society which, seeking to blend Hinduism with Western thought and with Christianity, was active particularly among English-speaking people in Bengal. The Arya Samaj, founded somewhat later by Swami Dayanada (1824–1883), attempted to eliminate the caste idea and some narrow Hindu concepts. Swami Vivekananda (1862–1902), following in this tradition, helped to foster the growth of Hindu nationalism. The Muslims took no part in this movement, although it was in no sense anti-Muslim.

As the effects of British suppression of the Indians after the revolt of 1857 began to wear off, new nationalist ideas gained strength, particularly among the small but increasingly influential upper classes of Indian society. The Indian National Congress Party, founded in Bombay in 1885 primarily to champion the desires of the upper economic groups, at first did not oppose the British, but rather sought to obtain concessions and modifications in the more restrictive Government policies. For several decades the Congress Party represented that minority of Indians who came from the upper economic classes, were mostly Hindu, and had been educated through the medium of the English language. Early Congress Party leaders included Dadabhai Naoroji, who first used the word Swaraj (freedom) to describe the goal of the Congress Party movement; Mrs. Annie Besant, an English devotee of Theosophy, an admirer of Gandhi, and the first woman president of the Congress Party; Gopal Krishna Gokhale, president of the Congress Party in 1905; and Bal Gangadhar Tilak (1856–1920).

Tilak represented the more radical group, and in 1907 when the moderates under Gokhale won Congress Party leadership, many of the radical leaders including Tilak were sent to prison by the British. At a meeting in Lucknow in 1916, the two branches of the Congress Party arrived at a compromise, but shortly afterwards the moderates left the fold. At the

[4] Quoted in J. P. Naik and Syed Nurullah. *A History of Education in India* (2d edition). Bombay: Macmillan and Company, 1951. p. 139.

same meeting the predominantly Hindu Congress Party and the All-India Muslim League agreed that the future national constitution would reserve a certain percentage of seats for the Muslim minorities. The Congress Party still represented only the small minority at the top of the economic scale.

After the end of World War I major changes took place that brought a fresh spirit and a new direction to the Congress Party and the Independence movement. Labor had begun to organize in unions. The middle classes, including Muslims and Sikhs as well as Hindus, had become aroused to their intolerable living and working conditions. Meanwhile, expectations of greater freedom and better conditions to be granted by the British rulers were not fulfilled; instead, restrictive legislation in the Rowlatt Bills gave the Government power to arrest and keep persons in jail without trial. Agitation grew.

At this stage Mohandas Karamchand Gandhi (1869–1948) came rather suddenly to national prominence. He had been well known in India for a long time, both because of his almost 20 years of active work in South Africa combating racial discrimination, and because of his support of the oppressed people in Bihar and Gujarat following his return to India in 1915. Gandhi's methods and his philosophy (that of Satyagraha—nonviolent cooperation and civil disobedience) were known to the Indians, but mainly through reports of his activities elsewhere.

The year 1919 was a crucial one. Gandhi was organizing his Satyagraha campaign among those who were ready to break particular laws, considered unjust, and to take the consequences. On the sixth of April a nationwide demonstration took place in India for the first time, against the Rowlatt Bills. One week later a British officer gave the command to fire on a large mass of defenseless civilians, thus starting the massacre in the Jallianwal Bagh in Amritsar. This incident aroused the country. The following year the Congress Party officially adopted Gandhi's Satyagraha movement and nonviolent resistance continued. Disagreements among the Congress Party leaders, growing difficulties between the Hindu and Muslim communities, and Gandhi's imprisonments delayed the movement from time to time, but with Gandhi as its main leader it gradually gained strength and exerted a strong influence on British policy.

In 1928 the Simon Commission came from London to investigate conditions in India and to recommend changes, but, including no Indians, it created little hope for improvement. Round Table Conferences were held in London in 1930 and 1931 to discuss Indian problems, but although Gandhi attended the second session very little occurred to satisfy the Indians. Civil disobedience spread.

Finally in 1935 the British Government passed the Government of India Act, which provided for Provincial elections and a measure of Provincial authority. As a result of such elections, the Congress Party in 1937 gained a majority of seats in seven of the 11 Provinces. At Congress Party meetings there was much discussion as to whether complete independence or dominion status should be the goal.

World War II to Independence

The coming of World War II increased the demand for independence. As a price for participating in the war, the Indians asked for and were refused freedom from British rule. The Congress Party then adopted its 1942 "Quit India" resolution, which told the British to depart. The British Government under Churchill promised independence to India, and the Labor Party in power in Britain after the war upheld this promise by sending Lord Louis Mountbatten to India in March of 1947 to arrange for Indian independence.

By then both the Indians and the British realized that freedom would require the establishment not of one but of two countries, for the Hindus and Muslims could not agree on a government structure. Muhammad Ali Jinnah, head of the Muslim League, had long sought a separate Muslim state, and the Hindu-Muslim conflict was growing so bitter that communal riots were occurring in many places. Finally Mountbatten, then Governor-General of India, and Gandhi agreed to partition and transfer of power from the British Crown.

Burma had been separated from India in 1937, as far as British rule was concerned, and along with Ceylon was to secure its independence in 1948.

The British Parliamentary Indian Independence Act, which came into force on August 15, 1947, partitioned India into the two independent Dominions of India and Pakistan. India retained 14 British Provinces and 535 Indian States, the latter ruled more or less independently by maharajas and lesser princes. India remained within the British Commonwealth, but as an independent Dominion with the right to dissolve that relationship.

The bitterness between Hindus and Muslims did not cease with independence and partition. As Muslims sought to reach Pakistan, and Hindus and Sikhs to reach India, massacre and slaughter were rampant. Gandhi, the apostle of nonviolence, started his last of many fasts to induce both sides to cease killing. Promises of many leaders to use their influence to bring about peace led Gandhi to give up his fast; but violence continued. On the 30th of January 1948, Gandhi, known to millions as the Mahatma, or great soul, and foremost leader of India's struggle for independence, was killed. Migrations continued until refugees numbered an estimated 15 million, causing great hardship and problems of resettlement for both countries. During the months after the day of Independence, the Indian Constituent Assembly wrote, enacted, and on November 26, 1949, ordained a new Constitution for the new nation, effective January 26, 1950.

3. Present Conditions[1]

Cultural Diversity

India is striving for unity and integration to fulfill its national purposes. With a heritage of 50 centuries of human civilization and a long history of absorbing countless immigrations of persons of many backgrounds and from many places, India today is characterized not by unity but by cultural and social diversity. No Gupta king, no Mughul emperor, and no European power was able to unify the country. The long movement for independence had its unifying influences, as did the reaction to the Chinese threat of 1962, but attachment to local and regional cultural traits is so strong that the Federal Government has at times conceded to regional cultural demands.

Language

The most striking example of this concession is in the area of language. The Constitution, recognizing the existence of large and powerful groups, each unified by a common language, declares the right of each group to speak and write in its own language:

> Any section of the citizens residing in the territory of India or any part thereof having a distinct language script or culture of its own shall have the right to conserve the same.[2]

One complete section (part XVII) of the Constitution is devoted to language problems, defining the official language (Hindi in the Devanagri script), the use of regional languages, and the language of the courts; and setting forth special plans for safeguarding the rights of small linguistic minorities and directives for promoting the spread of Hindi. Any one or more of the languages in use in a State, or the Hindi language, may be adopted by a State for official use. The Constitution also lists 15 regional

---

[1] Except as indicated, the source of the statistics in this chapter is a series of fact sheets prepared by the Ministry of Information and Broadcasting for a document called *India in Perspective*, published in 1966.
[2] *The Constitution of India* (As modified up to the 1st September, 1967). Part III, article 29 (1). Subsequent citations will be listed simply as *The Constitution of India*.

languages, each of which must be represented on a commission charged with making language policy recommendations to the President of India. Those languages are Assamese, Bengali, Gujarati, Hindi, Kannada, Kashmiri, Malayalam, Marathi, Oriya, Punjabi, Sanskrit, Sindhi, Tamil, Telugu, and Urdu.[3] The Constitution in 1950 listed only 14 regional languages, Sindhi being added in the 1967 modification.

Although the Constitution designates Hindi in the Devanagri script as the official language of India, it also states that "for a period of fifteen years from the commencement of this Constitution, the English language shall continue to be used for all official purposes of the Union for which it was being used immediately before such commencement." [4] In 1963, Parliament passed the Official Language Bill authorizing the continued use of English for the same purposes. In 1965, Prime Minister Shastri made a clarifying statement in Parliament in which he both urged the progressive use of Hindi and named English as an associate official language. No date has been fixed for the designation of Hindi as the sole official language of India.

In addition to the 14 regional languages listed in the 1950 Constitution, the 1960 census lists 36 languages, each with over 100,000 adherents; and of these 36 at least 11 each have more than a million adherents.

The multiplicity of languages in India has created serious problems, both in providing education and in delimiting State boundaries. As described later in this study, the "medium-of-instruction" problem in Indian education is a vexing one, which practically every committee and commission dealing broadly with education has tried to solve.

The factor of language in determining State boundaries has been crucial. Of the original 14 regional languages, Sanskrit had been included "on grounds of national sentiment" and Urdu "to safeguard the interests and placate the feelings of Muslims." [5] Of the remaining 12 languages, nine became official State languages, with Hindi the natural choice for several States. Only three language groups were not assigned linguistically based States—those speaking Telugu, Gujarati, and Punjabi. The agitation of these groups then led to fasts and demonstrations in which some people were killed. Finally, for the benefit of Telugu speakers the State of Andhra was formed from most of Hyderabad and parts of Mysore and Madras; for Gujarati speakers the State of Gujarat was formed by a division of the State of Bombay into Gujarat and Maharashtra (the latter having Marathi as its official State language) ; and in 1966, when the old State of Punjab was divided into the new States of Punjab and Haryana, Punjabi became the official language for the new State of Punjab (and Hindi the official language for Haryana).

The importance of national and international communication on the one hand, and the extremely strong attachment to local and regional languages on the other, have created a situation in which most Indians may need to become trilingual, particularly if they continue in their education as far as the college level.

[3] Ibid. Eighth schedule.
[4] Ibid. Part XVII, chapter 1, article 343 (2).
[5] *The Constitution of India, With Introduction and Notes by K. Santhanam.* Delhi: The Hindustan Times, 1951. p. 274. These citations are part of the author's notes, not part of the Constitution.

Religion

In religion as in language, modern India accommodates many groups. The 1961 census reports the following religious division of India's 439 million people:

Total	439,000,000
Buddhists	3,000,000
Christians	11,000,000
Hindus	366,000,000
Jains	2,000,000
Muslims	47,000,000
Parsees, Jews, and others	2,000,000

India is a secular state. The Constitution clearly proclaims "freedom of conscience and the right freely to profess, practise and propogate religion" [6] as well as the freedom to manage religious institutions and affairs. Religion, race, caste, or language may not bar any citizen from admission or attendance at any institution partially or wholly supported by the state. In India's history, periods of religious tolerance have alternated with periods of religious strife, particularly associated with political issues. Government policy is to permit each religious group to promote its interest and growth but to discourage the coming of foreign missionaries.

The "Fundamental Rights" section of the Constitution went far beyond freedom of religion. Discrimination by the state with regard to use of public places on the grounds of religion, race, caste, sex, or place of birth is expressly forbidden. The Indian Constitution resembles the Bill of Rights of the United States Constitution in that it specifies not only such rights as freedom of speech and expression, peaceful assembly, and freedom to form associations, but also property rights, rights of minorities, right to constitutional remedies, and protection of life and personal liberty.

For the minority of the Indian population that belongs to "scheduled castes and tribes," the Constitution has provided special educational opportunities, has safeguarded claims for public employment, and has reserved a number of seats proportionate to population both in the Federal House of the People and in State legislative bodies.

Although discrimination on the basis of caste was officially abolished, the caste system has been so interwoven with the personal, family, and social life of the Hindus that it cannot be totally and immediately eliminated, despite Government efforts. The spread of education, the trend toward industrialization, and the migration toward urban centers are all leading towards greater opportunities in employment and in other areas of life where the caste system had enforced rigid restrictions.

Science and Technology

In science and technology also, India presents a diversified pattern. On the one hand, there is the typical farm, a small plot of land irrigated by

---

[6] *The Constitution of India.* Part III, article 25 (1).

water that the farmer has pulled up in a bucket from a shallow well, and plowed with a sharpened piece of metal; on the other hand there is the well-tended farm, irrigated by a modern and effective irrigation system, cultivated by modern tractors, and producing crops from seeds nourished by synthetic fertilizers from a new fertilizer plant.

India still makes and uses both the ancient bullock cart and also airplanes and jet engines. The atomic energy establishment manufactures its own uranium, thorium, and plutonium; operates three reactors; and is constructing atomic power plants. India's first computer was built jointly by Jadavpur University and the Indian Statistical Institute.

Literacy

The rate of literacy varies greatly among the States of India, from 11 percent in Jammu and Kashmir to over 50 percent in Delhi (table 1). From 1951 to 1961, the rate for the country as a whole rose from 16.6 percent to 24.0 percent, reflecting the substantial efforts made to expand education at all levels (including the adult level). Population density figures (table 11) in combination with those for literacy rates in the States show that the two States ranking highest in literacy (Delhi and Kerala) also rank highest in population density; and the four States ranking lowest in literacy (Jammu and Kashmir, Madhya Pradesh, Rajasthan, and Uttar Pradesh) also rank lowest in population density.

Table 1.—*Literacy rate, by State or Territory: 1951 and 1961*

[_____ indicates source did not show any figures]

State or Territory [1]	Percent		Rank	
	1951	1961	1951	1961
Average for country	16.6	24.0		
Males	24.9	34.4		
Females	7.9	12.9		
Andhra Pradesh	13.1	21.2	11	11
Assam	18.3	27.4	8	7
Bihar	12.1	18.4	12	12
Gumarat	23.1	30.5	4	4
Jammu and Kashmir		11.0		17
Kerala	40.7	46.8	1	2
Madhya Pradesh	9.8	17.1	15	15
Madras	20.8	31.4	6	3
Maharashtra	20.9	29.8	5	5
Mysore	19.3	25.4	7	8
Nagaland	10.4	17.9	14	13
Orissa	15.8	21.7	9	10
Punjab [2]	15.2	24.2	10	9
Rajasthan	8.9	15.2	16	16
Uttar Pradesh	10.8	17.6	13	14
West Bengal	24.0	29.3	3	6
Delhi	38.4	52.7	2	1

SOURCE OF DATA: *Census of India.* 1961.

[1] Three Federal Territories (Andaman and Nicobar Islands—33.6, Manipur—30.4, and Pondicherry—37.4) ranked higher than the national average in 1961; five Territories (Dadra and Nagar Havelli—9.5, Himachal Pradesh—17.1, Laccadive, Minicoy, and Amindivi Islands—23.3, and NEFA—7.2) ranked lower than the national average in 1961. Data for Goa, Damon, and Diu are not available.

[2] Divided in November 1966 into two States, Punjab and Haryana.

13

Although more than seven out of every 10 Indians are illiterate, the publishing of books and periodicals increases substantially each year. Of the approximately 7,800 periodicals being published, 1,600 are in English, 1,650 in Hindi, and the rest in the other major Indian languages. One of the top film producing countries of the world, India in 1964 produced more than 300 films in 14 different languages.

Governmental Structure

India is a sovereign democratic republic established by the people, from whom all power and authority are derived. The preamble to the 1950 Constitution is very similar to that of the United States Constitution, declaring as its goal the securing of justice, liberty, equality, and fraternity. The system of government that it established borrows from the constitutions and national systems of several other democratic countries. The President of India is the Head of State, but, as in Britain, the powerful executive leadership resides in the Prime Minister, who represents the leadership of the dominant political party. As in the United States, a strong Federal Government unites a system of State governments, with executive, legislative, and judicial branches at both levels. In some cases at the State level there is a unicameral Legislative Assembly, and in others there is both a Legislative Assembly and a Legislative Council. At the national level, the lower house of the Union Parliament (the Federal legislative body) is called the Lok Sabha, or House of the People, and the upper house the Rajya Sabha, or Council of States.

Two provisions give the Federal Government more authority, in relation to the States, than it has in the United States. When a State Governor reports to the President of India that the State government can no longer function in accordance with the Constitution, the President by proclamation may take over all of the duties of the State government as well as the powers of the Governor. In this situation, the powers of the State legislature come under authority of Parliament. Also, any residual powers not allocated to the Federal Government or the States reside with the Federal Government, whereas in the United States such powers reside with the States.

At the time that the proposed Constitution was being considered, a plan was worked out to amalgamate into the new country the 535 Territories ruled by the maharajas and other princes, a very large proportion of the total subcontinent. Sardar Vallabhbhai Patel, a forceful Indian leader, was largely responsible for persuading the local princes to give up their territorial sovereignty in exchange for an annual privy purse from the Federal Government. One of the princes, however, a Muslim with the title Nizam, protested to the United Nations the taking of his Territory of Hyderabad, but finally succumbing to pressure from New Delhi, relinquished his sovereignty to the Indian Government. His Territory in 1950 became the State of Hyderabad, one of the largest in India. It was later divided, most of it being included in the new State of Andhra.

Elections

India is the most populous democracy in the world. Suffrage is universal and there are no property or literacy requirements. Four general elections have been held since Independence—in 1951–52, 1957, 1962, and 1967 (table 2). In 1962 the largest election in world history up to that time took place in India, with 216 million persons voting.

Women make use of their political rights. In the 1962 election, 47.8 million women voted; 146 women were elected to State Legislative Assemblies; and 35 women won seats in the House of the People (7 percent). Not only have there been women members in the Union Cabinet and in most of the State cabinets, but several women have been elected State Governors. In January 1966, Mrs. Indira Gandhi, daughter of former Prime Minister Jawaharlal Nehru, became Prime Minister.

Population

India is second in population among the nations of the world. The total population of India, as of the 1961 census, was 439,235,000 (table 1). According to estimates for 1967, the total population was 511,114,900; [7] and seven States had more than 35 million people, making each of them larger than any one of 100 member states of the United Nations. One out of every seven human beings lives in India, and one out of every three persons lives in India or in India's neighbor, China. As in all industrializing countries, people move from rural to urban areas—the 1961 census reported 18 percent of the population in urban areas, whereas the 1921 census reported 11 percent.

Table 2.—*Number and percent of seats in the House of the People, by political party: 1962 and 1967*

[———————— indicates source did not show any figures]

Political party	Percent		Number [1]	
	1962	1967	1962	1967
Total	100.00	100.00	494	512
Communist	5.87	8.00	29	41
Congress	73.08	54.89	361	281
Dravida Munnetra Kazhagam (Madras)	1.42	4.88	7	25
Independents	4.05	5.47	20	28
Jan Sangh (Hindu)	2.83	6.83	14	35
Praja Socialist	2.43	2.55	12	13
Republican	————	0.20	————	1
Socialist	1.21	4.49	6	23
Swatantra (Conservative)	4.45	8.59	22	44
Others	4.66	4.10	23	21

SOURCE OF DATA: Figures for 1962 from Ministry of Information and Broadcasting. A series of fact sheets for *India in Perspective.* 1966.

Figures for 1967 from *India Briefing.* New York: India Council, Asia Society, 1967. No. 16.

[1] The number of seats may differ each year with population changes, because the ratio of the number of seats to population must be approximately the same for all States, with a total of not more than 525 seats.

[7] The estimated population as of October 1968 was 527 million. Planning Commission. *Fourth Five-Year Plan Draft: 1969–74.* Section 17.16.

Table 3.—*Population of India, by State or Territory: 1961*

Total	439,235,000
State	
Andhra Pradesh	35,983,000
Assam	11,873,000
Bihar	46,456,000
Gujarat	20,633,000
Jammu and Kashmir	3,561,000
Kerala	16,904,000
Madhya Pradesh	32,372,000
Madras	33,687,000
Maharashtra	39,554,000
Mysore	23,587,000
Nagaland	369,000
Orissa	17,549,000
Punjab [1]	20,307,000
Rajasthan	20,156,000
Uttar Pradesh	73,746,000
West Bengal	34,926,000
Territory	
Andaman and Nicobar Islands	63,000
Dadra and Nagar Haveli	58,000
Delhi	2,659,000
Goa, Daman, and Diu	627,000
Himachal Pradesh	1,351,000
Laccadive, Minicoy, and Amindivi Islands	24,000
Manipur	780,000
North Eastern Frontier Area (NEFA)	337,000
Pondicherry	369,000
Tripura	1,142,000

SOURCE OF DATA: *Census of India.* 1961.
[1] Divided in November 1966 into two States, Punjab and Haryana.

India's leaders are disturbed by the increase during this century of the rate of population growth:

Year	Population in millions	Percent increase during decade
1901	238	—
1911	252	5.8
1921	251	0.0
1931	279	11.9
1941	319	14.3
1951	361	13.1
1961	439	21.6

The Government has allocated about $200 million to population control through free family planning centers, which distribute intrauterine and other mechanical devices and encourage sterilization. Most of the 17,000 centers are in rural areas. The goal is to lower the birthrate from 40 per thousand to 27 per thousand by 1975–76, and to 18 by 1985–86. Such a decrease in birthrate would in part offset the population increase caused by the drop in mortality rates, due to improved health conditions and medical services. If this goal is reached, in 1975–76 the population will be 605 million instead of 650 million (figured on the present annual rate of increase), and in 1985–86 it will be 693 million instead of 880 million.

Economic Factors

Most recent indexes of economic conditions in India show definite improvement for the nation. Because of the constant population increase, however, the per capita income has not risen at an equal rate. The economic well-being of the people depends upon limiting their number.

16

Agriculture, in which 70 percent of the population (or more than 300 million persons) find their occupations and which accounts for approximately 50 percent of the national income, showed a 62-percent production growth between 1951 and 1965. This growth resulted from a doubling of the number of irrigated acres and an increase of more than eightfold in the use of fertilizer.

Although modern industrial production went up 150 percent during the last 15 years, it accounts for only 10 percent of the national income. India is still largely rural and much of its production comes from rural artisans and cottage industries. More than four times as many persons (20 million) are employed in cottage industries as in factories (4.5 million). For example, the number of persons employed in handweaving alone approximately equals the total number employed in all of the manufacturing and mining industries together. Most of India's industry, including almost all of the small industry, is privately owned.

Energy sources have increased and rural electrification is being fostered. Mineral resources are being explored and ore production facilities have been built. Communication facilities are being expanded. Railways move 10,000 trains, five million passengers, and one-half million tons of goods every day. Highway mileage has doubled since Independence. Shipping, aviation, and the postal and telegraphic systems are all expanding.

Planning and Goals

The Planning Commission of India, which is responsible for continued planning and evaluation for the Executive and the Parliament, has developed a series of Five-Year Plans covering all major aspects of Indian life.[8] Both the Ministries at the Federal and State levels and also, through consultation, the private sector have participated in this planning. The Commission has set goals for all kinds of agricultural and industrial production, for improvement in health and education, and for expansion and extension of most facilities and services.

Since Indian Independence much progress has been made: Millions of new jobs have been created; life expectation has been greatly lengthened; total income and per capita income have risen, the latter from $52 to $66 per year; major diseases have been eradicated or their prevalence has been greatly reduced; and education is available for larger proportions of the population.

---

[8] The first plan was for 1951–56, the second for 1956–61, and the third for 1961–66. The fourth plan, originally for 1966–71, was interrupted by drought and the war with Pakistan; several annual plans were substituted, and the new Fourth Five-Year Plan set for 1969–74.

Chart 1. The Educational Pattern: 1966

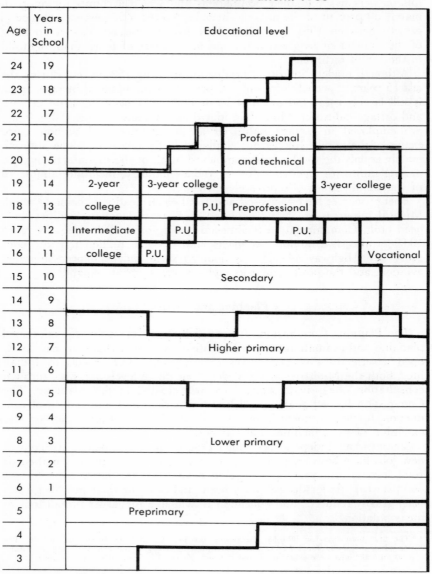

Age	Years in School	Educational level				
24	19					
23	18					
22	17					
21	16			Professional		
20	15			and technical		
19	14	2-year	3-year college			3-year college
18	13	college		P.U.	Preprofessional	
17	12	Intermediate	P.U.			P.U.
16	11	college	P.U.			Vocational
15	10	Secondary				
14	9					
13	8					
12	7	Higher primary				
11	6					
10	5					
9	4					
8	3	Lower primary				
7	2					
6	1					
5		Preprimary				
4						
3						

Key: Heavy line = division between levels (varying among States).
Double line = year when the student achieves a first-level degree (varying among States).
P.U. = pre-university year.

18

Part II.

The Educational System

1. National Policies and Goals

The broad educational purposes of any nation are found in its basic national documents, in the reports and pronouncements of national organizations, in the considered statements of its leaders, and in its educational accomplishments. Thus, in its Constitution, India affirms its educational purposes.

The Constitution

In the section on "Fundamental Rights", the Constitution states:

> No citizen shall be denied admission into any educational institution maintained by the State or receiving aid out of State funds on grounds only of religion, race, caste, language or any of them.[1]

> All minorities, whether based on religion or language, shall have the right to establish and administer educational institutions of their choice.[2]

In Part IV, entitled "Directive Principles of State Policy," the Constitution states:

> The State shall, within the limits of its economic capacity and development, make effective provision for securing the right . . . to education . . . .[3]

> The State shall endeavour to provide, within a period of ten years from the commencement of this constitution, for free and compulsory education for all children until they complete the age of fourteen years.[4]

Although the provisions in this part of the Constitution are not enforceable in court, "the principles therein laid down are nevertheless fundamental in the governance of the country and it shall be the duty of the State to apply these principles in making laws."

Five-Year Plans

The Five-Year Plans have also emphasized that education is vitally important both to the success of India's self-government and also to the attain-

---

[1] *The Constitution of India.* Part III, article 29 (2).
[2] Ibid. Part III, article 30 (1).
[3] Ibid. Part IV, article 41.
[4] Ibid. Part IV, article 45.

ment of her national goals. The following statements are from the first, second, and third plans, respectively:

> In a democratic set-up the role of education becomes crucial, since it can function effectively only if there is an intelligent participation of the masses in the affairs of the country.[5]

> The system of education in a country has a determining influence on the rate at which economic progress is achieved and the benefits which can be derived from it.[6]

> Education is the most important single factor in achieving rapid economic development and technological progress and in creating a social order founded on the values of freedom, social justice, and equal opportunity. . . . In all branches of national life, education becomes the focal point of planned development. . . . At all stages of education the aim must be to develop both skill and knowledge and a creative outlook, a feeling of national unity which stands above religion, caste, and language, and an understanding of common interests and obligations.[7]

University Education Commission: 1950 Report

The University Education Commission's 1950 report stated succinctly the political importance of education: "Democracy depends for its very life on a higher standard of general, vocational, and professional education." [8] The Commission further pointed out its economic as well as political importance:

> We have now a wider conception of the duties and responsibilities of universities. They have to provide leadership in politics and administration, the professions, industry, and commerce . . . . They must enable the country to attain, in as short a time as possible, freedom from want, disease, and ignorance, by the application and development of scientific and technical knowledge.[9]

Humayun Kabir, a leader of contemporary thought in India, wrote: "If . . . democracy is to function properly, at least general education must be spread among all citizens. Provision of such education for the people is as much an obligation of the state as the maintenance of law and order." [10]

University Grants Commission: 1965 Report

In 1965, the University Grants Commission called attention both to the need of a study of human values as part of a technical and utilitarian education, and also to the two major aims "applicable to all universities in the world," namely: (1) "the transmission of existing knowledge to

---

[5] Planning Commission. *First Five-Year Plan 1951–56*. Delhi: Government of India, 1952. p. 525.

[6] Planning Commission. *Second Five-Year Plan 1956–61. A Draft Outline*. Delhi: Government of India, 1956. p. 183.

[7] Planning Commission. *Third Five-Year Plan 1961–66*. Delhi: Government of India, 1961. p. 573.

[8] Ministry of Education. *Report of the University Education Commission* (Reprint of 1950 edition). Delhi: Manager of Publications, 1962. I:66.

[9] Ibid. p. 33.

[10] Humayun Kabir. *Education in New India* (2d edition). London: George Allen and Unwin, Ltd., 1959. p. 102.

new generations," and (2) "the advancement of the frontiers of knowledge by research." Its report further stated:

> First of all, we should see that every student who passes out of an Indian university takes with him some understanding of India's cultural heritage, its past achievements and triumphs in the field of art, philosophy, science and so on. He should, in other words, know what he is heir to.
>
> . . . it is also essential to develop in our universities a critical approach to the values and schools of thought which have come down to us from the past, by subjecting them to critical examination and adaptation.
>
> . . . it should be considered obligatory on the part of the university to make an intensive study of problems that beset its neighbourhood for the purpose of finding practical remedies for them.
>
> It is expected of every university in India that it will exercise a wholesome influence on the thinking and planning activities of government and other agencies for bringing into being a society based on the secular and ethical principles embodied in our Constitution.
>
> One of the most pressing problems facing our country is the development of a national outlook over-riding parochial, religious, and linguistic considerations. In this task the universities can and should play a decisive part.
>
> Universities in India have also to be internationally minded. . . . In the pursuit of truth and excellence to which all universities are committed, there is neither east nor west, north nor south.[11]

Education Commission: 1966 Report

In 1966, the Education Commission stated that "education should be developed so as to increase productivity, achieve social and national integration, strengthen democracy, accelerate the process of modernization and cultivate social, moral and spiritual values." [12]

The same report lists the functions of universities as follows:

> . . . to seek and cultivate new knowledge, to engage vigorously and fearlessly in the pursuit of truth, and to interpret old knowledge and beliefs in the light of new needs and discoveries; to provide the right kind of leadership in all walks of life, to identify gifted youth and help them develop their potential to the full by cultivating physical fitness, developing the powers of the mind and cultivating right interests, attitudes and moral and intellectual values; to provide society with competent men and women trained in agriculture, arts, medicine, science and technology and various other professions, who will also be cultivated individuals imbued with a sense of social purpose; to strive to promote equality and social justice and to reduce social and cultural differences through diffusion of education; and to foster in the teachers and students, and through them in society generally, the attitudes and values needed for developing the 'good life' in individuals and society. . . . [13]

Universities "must learn to strive to serve as the 'conscience of the nation'," and become a "forum for a critical assessment of society." [14]

---

[11] University Grants Commission. *Report on Standards of University Education.* Delhi, 1965. p. 2–7.
[12] Ministry of Education. *Report of the Education Commission: 1964–66.* 1966. p. 613.
[13] Ibid. p. 274–75.
[14] Ibid. p. 275.

The report further recommends that Indian universities perform two specific functions: (1) develop university extension, by correspondence courses and inservice education programs for professional workers of all kinds, and by general adult education programs "to create a unity of outlook and faith between the masses and the intelligentsia";[15] and (2) improve education through courses, institutes, and the development of new curricula, textbooks, and teaching materials.

Indian leaders and educators have asked the universities to concern themselves with values and attitudes, to promote equality and social justice, to help solve social problems, to aid in increasing productivity and economic development, and to extend their many services to the community at large. They have asked the universities to act as the conscience of the nation—certainly a challenge to any educational system.

---

[15] Ibid. p. 276.

2. Organization

Constitutional Provisions

The Constitution of India defines, more clearly than that of the United States, the educational responsibility of both the Federal and State Governments. The Union List of governmental powers describes those functions for which the Federal (or Union) Government is responsible; the State List, those for which State governments are responsible; and the Concurrent List, those for which responsibility is divided between the State and Federal Governments.

Although "education, including universities" [1] is a function on the State List, the States' responsibility is modified by the item "vocational and technical training of labour" [2] on the Concurrent List, and by the following items on the Union List:

- 63. The institutions known at the commencement of this Constitution as the Banaras Hindu University, the Aligarh Muslim University and the Delhi University, and any other institution declared by Parliament by law to be an institution of national importance.

- 64. Institutions for scientific or technical education financed by the Government of India wholly or in part and declared by Parliament by law to be institutions of national importance.

- 65. Union agencies and institutions for—(a) professional, vocational or technical training, including the training of police officers; or (b) the promotion of special studies or research; or (c) scientific or technical assistance in the investigation or detection of crime.

- 66. Co-ordination and determination of standards in institutions for higher education or research and scientific and technical institutions. [3]

Because of the political and economic power of the Federal Government and the extent to which education is becoming a matter of national interest, the Federal Government in India (as in the United States) will probably increasingly support and influence educational development, particularly in the field of higher education. Naik ably describes this trend in India,

---

[1] *The Constitution of India.* Seventh schedule, list II, no. 11.
[2] Ibid. Seventh schedule, list III, no. 25.
[3] Ibid. Seventh schedule, list I, no. 63–66.

pointing out three main developments partly, if not largely, responsible for "undermining" the States' educational responsibility: (1) the desire, partly initiated by Gandhi, to develop "a national system of education for the country as a whole"; (2) the revival of appropriations in the form of grants to the States, by the Federal Government to help finance public education; and (3) "the adoption of centralized planning and the creation of the Planning Commission"[4] at the national level. Naik points out that experience and rpacticality show "education . . . to be more of a joint responsibility than an exclusive preserve of the states."[5]

Many proposals have been made to put higher education on the Concurrent List by amending the Constitution. The Federal Minister of Education,[6] the Parliament's Committee on Higher Education,[7] and the University Education Commission in its 1950 report [8] have all recommended such action.

State Educational Organization

The main responsibility for education rests with the States. State legislatures must pass enabling acts to create universities, and State governments are a major source of revenue for all educational levels. Organization for the administration and supervision of education is similar from State to State, although variations have increased with individual efforts to develop all educational levels rapidly.

In each State an Education Minister heads the educational structure; in some of the large States a Deputy Minister may assist him; and in every State an Education Secretary is in immediate charge of the Education Department.[9] The whole structure is usually divided into a small secretariat, which serves as a policymaking and coordinating agency; and a larger directorate of education, which handles mainly elementary and secondary education and is responsible for supervising, regulating, and inspecting schools. In some States, special directorates within the education department deal with higher and technical education; and in others, technical education is the responsibility of a department of industry or a department of public works.

The great increase of educational activity during the last 2 decades has brought about not only an expansion in the size and complexity of the State educational organization, but also several important new developments. Some States have—

• Passed laws making primary and secondary education compulsory.

• Established boards for secondary education.

---

[4] J. B. Naik. *The Role of Government in Indian Education.* Delhi: National Council of Educational Research and Training, Ministry of Education, 1962. p. 1–17. (Educational Studies and Investigations, Vol. 1).

[5] Ibid. p. 32.

[6] Inter-University Board of India and Ceylon. *University News.* February-March 1964. p. 1.

[7] *Report of the Committee of Members of Parliament on Higher Education.* Government of India, 1964. p. 44.

[8] Ministry of Education. *Report of the University Education Commission* (Reprint of 1950 edition). Delhi: Manager of Publications, 1962. I:435.

[9] This description of the State educational organization is largely based on Ministry of Education. *Education in Eighteen Years of Freedom.* 1965.

- Initiated school services related to audiovisual aids, curriculum planning, evaluation, guidance, textbooks, and other matters.

- Established advisory bodies on education, with both official and unofficial representation.

- Decentralized the supervising and inspecting functions of State education departments to district offices and inspectors.

- Increased local control and support of primary education, consistent with a national effort to organize, strengthen, and stimulate local self-government.

In 1966, the Education Commission made several recommendations for State educational organizations. The primary ones were that States should:[10]

- Reorganize their education departments to:
  1. Develop and implement a program of school improvement.
  2. Prescribe and enforce standards.
  3. Provide and train teachers.
  4. Take responsibility for inspection and revitalized supervision of schools.
  5. Provide extension services.
  6. Maintain quality institutions.
  7. Coordinate secondary vocational and technical education.

- Establish State institutes of education to:
  1. Provide inservice training for department staff.
  2. Improve teacher education.
  3. Improve textbooks, guidance programs, and research and evaluation programs.

- Establish an autonomous State Evaluation Organization.

- Establish State boards of school education with broad powers to supervise all primary and secondary education, including external examinations at the end of the lower and higher secondary stages.

- Establish a National Board of School Education in the Federal Ministry of Education to advise the Federal Government on all elementary and secondary education. Such a board should define, revise, and evaluate standards at all levels, advise State education departments, and collaborate with universities and the University Grants Commission.

State universities have considerable freedom in internal administration. Although they depend for financial support upon State legislatures, most government control is exercised indirectly, through use of one of the following circumstances:[11]

- The State Governor is usually ceremonial head of a university, with power to approve or veto the appointment of a vice-chancellor. (He seldom vetoes a duly chosen person.)

- The State government has the power to veto statutes passed by governing bodies of a university. (It sometimes exercises this power.)

- The State government may have the final decision as to which colleges a university affiliates.

---

[10] Ministry of Education. *Report of the Education Commission: 1964–66.* 1966. p. 643–45. For a discussion of the University Grants Commission, see part III, chapter 3, under the section University Grants Commission: 1953, 1956 (of this report).

[11] B. P. R. Vithal. "University Autonomy and Internal Democracy." *Journal of University Education.* 1:85. December 1962.

- Heads of State government departments are ex-officio members of a university's supreme governing body.

- The State government may nominate members to the governing bodies of a university.

- All university accounts are subject to annual audit by the State government.

National Educational Organization

The Federal Government discharges its educational responsibilities primarily through its Ministry of Education. Other ministries, however, have main responsibility for education in their respective fields—such as the Ministry of Agriculture for agricultural education, and the Ministry of Health for medical education. A total of 18 ministries in 1963 reported education and training activities.[12]

The Minister of Education has full cabinet rank in the Government of India. Under him are two deputy ministers, two secretaries, one additional secretary, two joint secretaries, and two joint educational advisers. Each of 12 divisions is headed by a deputy secretary or a deputy educational adviser. The additional secretary supervises higher education through the University Education Division, headed by one deputy educational adviser, and through the Division of Technical Education, headed by three deputy educational advisers. Several other divisions are partially concerned with aspects of higher education such as scholarships.

The total budget of the Ministry for 1965–66, according to its annual report, was more than $255 million. Of this, about $1.67 million was spent on the secretariat, a fact indicative of the size and complexity of the Ministry. Of the $79.38 million spent for higher education, over $35 million went to the University Education Division (more than $32 million of the $35 million channelled through the University Grants Commission), and over $44 million to the Division of Technical Education.

For 1969–70, the Ministry estimates that it will spend for higher education over $66 million, of which over $42 million will go to the University Education Division (about $32 million of the $42 million to be channeled through the University Grants Commission) and over $24 million to the Division of Technical Education.[13]

The duties of the Ministry of Education include:[14]

- Primary responsibility for the 13 institutions of higher education which have been declared "of national importance."

- Varying degrees of responsibility for 61 attached or subordinated offices and autonomous organizations, including the University Grants Commission, the Indian Institutes of Technology, the Indian Institute of Science at Bangalore, and the Birla Institute in Pilani (all degree-granting institutions of higher education).

---

[12] Ministry of Education. *Educational Activities of the Government of India: 1963.* 1963. passim.

[13] Ministry of Education. *Annual Report: 1968–69.* 1969. p. 36–37, 45–46. Figures for years through 1965–66 have been converted from rupees to dollars on a 5-to-1 basis; for years after 1965–66 on a 7.5-to-1 basis.

[14] Ministry of Education. *Annual Report: 1965–66,* 1966. passim.

- Responsibility for 40 national laboratories, research stations, institutes, and museums.

- Financing and operating, through a "Central Schools Organization," 89 central schools primarily for children of Federal Government employees. (These schools often include some of the best features of higher secondary schools.)

- Sponsoring 39 advisory boards, councils, conferences, and committees within the Ministry and its many agencies.

- Issuing 300 publications, including statistical reports and regularly published journals. (Most of these are in English, but several are in Hindi and the other regional Indian languages.)

The Ministry has also formulated a plan to develop an Indian Educational Service, consisting of all Federal and State administrative positions and divided into a General Education Branch and a Technical Education Branch. The upper house of Parliament approved a draft constitution of the new Service in 1965, all State governments have agreed in principle to such a Service, and final plans are being worked out between Federal and State agencies.

Although the Constitution places primary responsibility for education with the States rather than with the Federal Government, the latter through its Ministry of Education has become involved with State educational activities at all levels, increased its grants to the States, and expanded its own educational activities, offices, and organizations. It is in a position to play a major role in the planned development of Indian education.

3. The Educational Ladder

The pattern of the Indian educational system has been shifting rapidly since 1947. As each State has sought to develop its own educational system, variations have occurred between States (chart 1). Successful efforts to extend the total years of schooling have led to lengthening the duration of some levels and to forming new ones.

Many questions have been raised concerning the advisability of pre-primary education, the duration of each level, and the point of separation between levels. Extensive conferences, discussions, pronouncements, reports, and studies have gradually produced a growing consensus as to the best educational structure. The consensus is that:

- Preprimary education of 1 to 3 years is advisable.

- Lower primary education of 4 to 5 years should begin at age 6.

- Higher primary and secondary education of 7 to 8 years (sufficient with the number of lower primary years to equal 12 years) should be required for college entrance.

- Undergraduate college education of 3 years should lead to the bachelor's degree.

The 2-year intermediate college followed by a 2-year college (shown at the left of chart 1) is disappearing in response to many recommendations. The University Grants Commission reported: "Excepting for Bombay University and the State universities in U.P. (Agra, Allahabad, Gorakhpur, and Lucknow), all other universities which are providing undergraduate courses in arts, sciences, and commerce have adopted the 3-year degree course pattern." [1]

The pre-university course (shown at the center of chart 1) is usually a 1-year program offered by colleges and universities for students considered insufficiently prepared for undergraduate studies. The Education Commission recommends that this 1-year program be dropped from higher education and incorporated in secondary education.

The Education Commission and many others have strongly advised a major shift toward "vocationalization" at the secondary level. Such voca-

---

[1] University Grants Commission. *Annual Report: 1964-65.* 1966. p. 23.

tional programs would begin at age 13, 14, or 16 (grade 8, 9, or 11) and continue for 1 to 3 years as necessary (shown at the right of chart 1).

In Uttar Pradesh and Kerala, secondary education is generally completed by the end of grade 10. The recent development of 2-year junior colleges in Kerala, however, enables students to begin their 3-year college course after 12 years of schooling.

Preprimary Education

In India, preprimary education, which is education below the primary level for children under 6 years of age, usually has been provided by private agencies located in urban areas and supported by fees. The number of preprimary schools receiving little or no government assistance has been increasing.

The Federal Government provides preprimary education in *balwadis,* which "offer creche and pre-school facilities for infants and maternity service, craft training and recreational and cultural programs for women and children." [2] In 1958–59, the Federal Government through the Central Social Welfare Board maintained about 4,000 *balwadis;* [3] by 1966, it maintained 20,000 *balwadis* with a total enrollment of about 600,000.[4]

In the Third Five-Year Plan, the Federal Government provided $6 million for strengthening *balwadis* and for intensive pilot projects for child welfare. At the same time, the States initiated several model preprimary schools at various educationally strategic centers.

Preprimary education is also available in the many small private schools established by teachers trained in India by Dr. Maria Montessori during World War II.

Enrollment in preprimary schools has been increasing: [5]

Year	Number	Percent of age group
1950–51	5,177	18.3
1955–56	7,135	21.3
1960–61	8,612	22.3
1965–66	11,773	26.7

Elementary Education

The Constitution requires the States to "endeavor to provide . . . free and compulsory education for all children until they complete the age of fourteen years." [6] Although the age at which such education must first be provided has not been stated, the Federal and State Governments have interpreted the Constitution to mean that it is required for children from the age of 6 to the age of 14 years. This 8-year period of schooling is classified as "elementary education," with the first 5 years called "lower primary education" and the next 3 "higher primary" (other terms are sometimes used).

---

[2] Ministry of Education. *Report of Educational Development: 1967–68.* 1968. p. 43.
[3] Ministry of Education. *Review of Education in India: 1947–1961.* 1961. p. 50.
[4] Ministry of Education. *Report of the Education Commission: 1964–66.* 1966. p. 148.
[5] Ibid. p. 589.
[6] *The Constitution of India.* Part IV, article 45.

Although the Constitution expressed the hope that by 1960 all children within the age group 6–14 would be in school, it soon became evident that this goal would not be reached. It was decided, therefore, to concentrate first on providing free and compulsory education for all children for the age group 6–11. The intense activity by both the Federal and State Governments to achieve this goal has produced impressive results (table 4).

One of the uniquely Indian concepts of elementary education is basic education, placed before the country in 1937 by the leader of the Independence movement, Mahatma Gandhi. The philosophy of this concept may be summarized as follows: The education formerly available to Indians had weaned them away from their cultural and physical environment and encouraged them to leave their villages for Western-oriented urban centers; the education that should be available would help them both to strengthen the unique aspects of India's age long culture and also to improve tangibly their own physical and social environment.

Basic education appealed to the national leaders. Started on an experimental basis in the Provinces where Education Ministries were composed of Indians (under the 1935 Government of India Act), basic education was abandoned when the Ministries resigned after disagreements with the British Government. After Independence, the Federal and State Governments declared a long-term goal of converting all elementary schools to the basic pattern.

Under the basic pattern, the elementary school approach is changed from one of exclusive concern with the teaching of the three R's to one which emphasizes their relevance to the child's life in his community—which for most Indian children is the village. School projects such as

Table 4.—*Number of pupils in grades 1–5, 6–8, and 9–11; and the percent this number represents of the total school-age population normal for those grades, by selected school years: 1901–02—1971–72*

[————————— indicates source did not show any figures]

School year	Grades 1–11 Percent	Grades 1–5 Number	Grades 1–5 Percent	Grades 6–8 Number	Grades 6–8 Percent	Grades 9–11 Number	Grades 9–11 Percent
1901–02	———	3,564,122	———	180,670	———	82,312	———
1906–07	———	4,336,154	———	205,429	———	109,625	———
1911–12	———	5,494,416	———	276,401	———	141,695	———
1916–17	———	6,404,200	———	385,372	———	216,160	———
1921–22	———	6,897,233	———	434,810	———	218,606	———
1926–27	———	9,120,458	———	713,939	———	277,970	———
1931–32	———	10,427,980	———	980,514	———	344,758	———
1936–37	———	11,465,709	———	1,142,254	———	432,038	———
1941–42	———	13,105,618	———	———	———	1,698,874	———
1946–47	———	14,105,418	35.0	2,036,100	9.0	870,812	4.2
1950–51	25.4	19,154,457	42.6	3,119,958	12.7	1,180,149	5.3
1955–56	32.1	25,167,013	52.9	4,113,301	16.5	1,857,384	9.4
1960–61	39.9	34,300,000	61.1	6,290,000	22.8	2,910,000	11.5
1965–66	50.1	51,467,000	78.5	11,033,000	32.4	5,376,000	17.8
1971–72 (est.)	———	70,467,000	93.1	19,033,000	47.4	———	———

SOURCE OF DATA: Figures for 1901–02—1960–61 from National Council of Educational Research and Training. *Review of Education in India (1947–1961).* 1961. p. 132.

Figures for 1965–66 and estimates for 1971–72 from Ministry of Education. *Report: 1965–66.* 1966. p. 3. Percents of girls in 1965–66: *grades 1–5*—56.4 percent; *grades 6–8*—17.0 percent; *grades 9–11*—7.7 percent. Percents of girls for 1971–72 (est.): *grades 1–5*—81.5 percent; *grades 6–8*—29.6 percent.

cleaning the village and maintaining vegetable gardens are initiated. Every child is taught some useful crafts such as leatherwork, spinning, or weaving. Such activities are not considered extracurricular because the subjects of the curriculum are to be taught through them. For example, in a spinning lesson the teacher might explain the arithmetical concept of average (on the basis of total yarn spun and number of students spinning) and then illustrate the sources of cotton in India as a lesson in geography.

Although many educationists believe that basic education will spread all over the country, others are somewhat skeptical. The major criticisms of the basic pattern for India today are that:

- The concept in practice is too costly at this stage of India's development.

- The kind and amount of knowledge that can be imparted through craft activities is limited.

- The basic approach is probably not the right and most effective one for a nation set on rapid industrialization.

- Basic education would maintain or even widen the gap between the urban and rural populations, thereby thwarting some of India's democratic goals.

- The basic approach requires a very high order of imagination and intelligence which many teachers may not possess.

In spite of these criticisms, faith in the basic education concept is strong. The Ministry of Education, committed for many years to the adoption of a basic education system, stated that "the pattern of basic education has been accepted for the country as a whole and as a consequence of this decision all elementary schools as soon as may be practicable, are to be converted to the basic pattern."[7] The number of basic schools is increasing—from 32,000 in 1950–51 to an estimated 170,000 in 1965–66.[8]

Some compromise will probably be achieved. The best features of the older non-basic schools may be continued with greater emphasis on the practical aspects of education stressed by the new philosophy.

Secondary Education

In 1953, the Indian Government appointed—for the first time in India's history—a high-level commission to study the problems of secondary education throughout the entire country. That commission's report formed the basis for a reconstruction of secondary education. The goal (similar to that of basic education at the elementary level) was to serve the national need by increasing the efficiency and everyday usefulness of secondary education.

To attain this goal, the Secondary Education Commission strongly recommended that multipurpose schools be established,[9] combining general and vocational education in a wide variety of courses for students of different abilities and vocational interests. By 1966, however, few multipurpose schools offered more than three alternative courses.[10]

---

[7] Ministry of Education. *Annual Report 1965–66*. 1966. p. 9.
[8] Ibid.
[9] Ibid. p. 30.
[10] Ibid. p. 186.

Since 1953, the following steps have been taken to improve secondary education:

1. Extracurricular activities have been introduced.
2. Multipurpose schools have been established (374 during the First Five-Year Plan and almost 4,000 by 1965).
3. New textbooks have replaced obsolete ones.
4. Science education has been strengthened.
5. Student achievement tests of an objective and dependable kind have been introduced in many schools.
6. Teachers' colleges have received financial and technical assistance from the Federal Government to start extension departments providing inservice teacher education.

Despite these improvements, secondary education is still far from its goal:

- Progressive measures have not been sufficiently widespread to have made a decisive impact on secondary education.

- Most States have not yet reorganized their secondary education to include the first year of intermediate education, as the Education Commission of 1964-66 recommended.

- The number of unemployed secondary school graduates has increased.

- Although secondary level enrollment has been increasing, the percent of children of the appropriate age attending school in the higher grades remains less than the percent of children of the appropriate age in the lower grades (table 4).

Implications for Higher Education

Education at the elementary and secondary levels closely affects higher education. In the first place, because the number of students completing the lower levels has increased, the number seeking a university or higher technical education has also increased, crowding college and university facilities and jeopardizing educational quality. If secondary education becomes a satisfactory terminal stage for many students, fewer will seek higher education and its quality can be maintained or increased. In the second place, because the quality of education at the lower levels largely determines the ability of students entering colleges and universities, it also determines the quality of education such institutions may offer them. In the third place, because fewer girls than boys receive lower level education, fewer women than men take advantage of higher education.

Adult Education

Social education is the phrase frequently used in India to denote adult education because the latter has become associated almost wholly with the adult literacy effort. Social education promotes not only literacy, but also "education in health, understanding of science as applied to everyday life, acquisition of information and skills that would improve vocational efficiency, development of hobbies, and organization of cultural and recreational programmes." [11]

---

[11] Ministry of Education. *Review of Education in India, 1947–1961.* 1961. p. 40–41.

Although social education involves more than the spread of literacy, the achievement of many of its goals depends on the existing degree of literacy. Of the total population, more than 24 percent are literate; of the males, more than 34 percent; of the females, less than 13 percent. Wide variation exists among the States, from Delhi with more than 50 percent literate to Jammu and Kashmir with only 11 percent (table 1).

To extend adult literacy, appropriate teaching materials are necessary. Literacy materials for adults must be as basic as those for children but their content must be geared to adult learning processes. When good materials have been produced in one language, they must be translated into other languages. Books for a newly literate adult must be written so that when he has learned to read he will have the incentive and opportunity to remain literate and acquire further education.

India's leaders recognize that social education is a necessity for giving its people an understanding of the basic ideas of a democratic society and the concepts behind India's plans to improve health and modernize agriculture and industry. The Ministry of Community Development and Cooperation has developed social education programs. Both the Federal and State Governments have sponsored centers for training social education workers. Centers to develop and produce literacy materials have been established. Prize competitions for books for neoliterates have been sponsored.

The United Nations Educational, Social, and Cultural Organization (UNESCO), cooperating with India's literacy and social education programs, has also sponsored competitions for new adult reader books.

Part III.

Background of Higher Education

1. Before 1857

Ancient Indian Education

In ancient and medieval India, several types of higher education centers existed. One consisted of a single teacher, or *guru*, who instructed his pupils in a particular Veda or in a subject such as grammar or logic. Another was run by legally constituted assemblies of scholars who were specialists in the Vedas and Dharma Sutras. These assemblies may well have been the forerunners of the later Brahminic universities, the most important and famous of which were in Taksasila (also spelled Taxila)—now in Pakistan—and Nalanda, near Patna in northern India. Brahminic universities originated in the 7th century B.C. and flourished for almost 1,000 years. They had highly developed curriculums in several fields such as astrology, astronomy, medicine, surgery, and Vedic philosophy; and enrolled as many as 10,000 students, for their fame attracted students from nearby countries. Fa Hien and Hiuen Tsang of China, for example, have recorded much about the organization and course of instruction in Taksasila and Nalanda.

A number of Islamic colleges (*madrasahs*) also existed in urban centers such as Allahabad, Delhi, Lahore, and Lucknow. Although the language of instruction was always Arabic, the curriculum paralleled the European *trivium* (grammar, logic, and rhetoric) and *quadrivium* (arithmetic, astronomy, geometry, and music).

There was little connection, however, between the ancient and medieval institutions and modern Indian education, which began slowly during the latter part of the 18th century.

Education Under the East India Company

Until 1793 the British had established in India only three educational institutions: an Islamic college, founded in Calcutta in 1781 by Warren Hastings; an Asiatic Society of Bengal, founded in Calcutta in 1784 by Sir William Jones; and a Sanskrit college, founded in Banaras in 1792 by Jonathan Duncan.

When the House of Commons in 1792–93 considered renewing the East India Company's charter, a debate concerning higher education arose.

William Wilberforce argued that Parliament should take steps to provide useful knowledge to the inhabitants of British India. One of the Court of Directors of the Company, however, is reported to have observed: "We have just lost America from our folly, in having allowed the establishment of schools and colleges, and it will not do for us to repeat the same act of folly in regard to India." [1] This opinion prevailed at that time, but not for long. In 1797, Charles Grant, a director of the East India Company, urged the Government to provide English-language instruction for Indians as a way of opening a new world of ideas to them; and in 1811 Lord Minto expressed his regret at the neglect of literature and science by the Government in India.

In 1813, when the Company's charter again came up for renewal, the House of Commons provided (in the Charter Act of 1813) that Company duties would include education of the Indian people. The Company was to put aside $20,000 annually to revive and improve literature and to introduce and promote scientific knowledge among the Indians. Until about 1823, however, the Company's Court of Directors did not effectively act upon the provisions for encouraging education. [2]

Meanwhile in 1817, as a result of the initiative of a number of Indians led by Raja Rammohan Roy, Hindu College was established in Calcutta to make European knowledge available to Indians. In the following year, the Bishop of Calcutta founded an institution to train young Indian Christians as preachers and to teach English to Hindus and Muslims.

Finally, from 1823 to 1833, prompted by influential Englishmen such as Lord Moira and Charles Metcalfe, the Company increased its educational activity. The Calcutta Madrasah and the Banaras Hindu College were reorganized; and a Sanskrit college was founded in Calcutta, oriental colleges in Agra and Delhi, and (in 1834) Elphinstone College in Bombay.

Macaulay's Minute of 1835

The increasing popularity of the English language and Western knowledge created a controversy as to whether English or the traditional languages— Arabic and Sanskrit—should be used for instruction and encouraged. Thomas Babington Macaulay, in 1835 both president of the General Committee of Public Instruction and law member of the Executive Council of the Governor-General, discussed the controversy in the famous Minute of February 2, 1835, [3] a document of great significance to Indian education. Macaulay opposed the spending of Government funds to preserve and spread Sanskrit and Arabic, eulogized the virtues of the English language, and expressed his strong belief that both the English nation and the Indian people would gain by adopting English as the language of instruction in India.

The Governor-General at that time, Lord William Bentinck, adopted Macaulay's point of view. The subsequent Government resolution stated

[1] Quoted in Inter-University Board of India and Ceylon. *Universities' Handbook, India and Ceylon: 1964.* Delhi, 1965. p. ix.

[2] J. P. Naik *and* Syed Nurullah. *A History of Education in India* (2d edition). Bombay: Macmillan and Company, 1951. p. 88.

[3] Ibid. p. 135–38.

that "His Lordship in Council is of the opinion that the great object of the British Government ought to be the promotion of European literature and science among the natives of India and that all the funds appropriated for the purpose of education would be best employed on English education alone." [4] Thereafter every attempt was made to establish English as the language of instruction.

Because Macaulay has been heavily criticized for swinging the Government in favor of the Anglicists, it ought to be noted that he foresaw and welcomed the eventual consequences of introducing English education in India. "It may be that the public mind of India may expand under our system until it has outgrown that system . . . that having become instructed in European knowledge, [the Indians] may, in some future age, demand European institutions. Whether such a day will ever come I know not. Whenever it comes, it will be the proudest day in English History." [5]

Wood's Despatch of 1854

As Macaulay's Minute turned the tide of modern Indian education toward use of the English language, so the Despatch of Sir Charles Wood to the Court of Directors decided the superstructure of that education. The Despatch, called the Magna Charta of English education in India, is a long document of 100 paragraphs about important issues such as the aims of the Company's educational policy, the medium of instruction, the need to create a network of elementary and secondary schools, the principle of grant-in-aid, teacher training, and the education of women.

Of principal interest, however, is the recommendation of the Despatch that Indian universities should be modeled after the University of London, which at that time did not instruct but only examined candidates from affiliated institutions of higher education and awarded degrees to the successful candidates. The Despatch further recommended that Indian universities should:

- Be governed by a chancellor, vice-chancellor, and senate.
- Provide detailed examination regulations.
- Send Government inspectors to visit their affiliated institutions.
- Institute professorships "for the purpose of the delivery of lectures in various branches of learning, for the acquisition of which, at any rate in an advanced degree, facilities do not now exist in other institutions in India." [6]

The Despatch specifically recommended that universities be established in Bombay and Calcutta, and expressed the hope that universities might be created in Madras or in any part of India where the number of higher institutions required an examining and degree-conferring university.

---

[4] Ibid. p. 139.
[5] Ibid. p. 142.
[6] Ibid. p. 207.

2. From 1857 to Independence in 1947

In 1857 the incorporation and founding of affiliating universities in Bombay, Calcutta, and Madras brought modern Indian university education into formal and legal existence. An affiliating university is itself primarily an examining authority, with actual instruction offered only in the colleges that it affiliates. Because most of the universities established after 1857 followed this pattern, it greatly influenced the development of higher education and even the secondary school curriculum.

Report of the Indian Universities Commission: 1902

After the establishment of the three universities of Bombay, Calcutta, and Madras, the number of colleges steadily increased. However, there was no new university until in 1882 when the University of Punjab was founded to relieve the University of Calcutta of some of its affiliated colleges, spread throughout almost all of northern India and even Burma.[1] In 1887, the University of Allahabad was established. These five universities were the only ones in India until 1916.

In 1902 the Governor General of India, Lord Curzon, appointed the Indian Universities Commission

> . . . to inquire into the condition and the prospects of the Universities established in British India; to consider and report upon any proposal which . . . may be made for improving their constitution and working, and to recommend to the Governor General in Council such measures as may tend to elevate the standard of university teaching, and to promote the advancement of learning.[2]

Several of the Commission's recommendations were incorporated in the Universities Act of 1904, which enabled the existing five universities to consolidate and improve their organization, to supervise their affiliated colleges more effectively, and to encourage research. The most important outcome, however, was that Indian universities, at least in token fashion, began to take on teaching in addition to administrative duties.

---

[1] This university was located in Lahore, which in 1947 became part of the new nation of Pakistan. After partition, the colleges in the Indian portion of the Punjab became affiliated to a newly founded Punjab University at Chandigarh.

[2] Indian Universities Commission. *Report: 1902.* Simla: Government Central Printing Office, 1902, p. 1.

Government Resolution on Education: 1913

In 1913, the Government Resolution on Education both recognized that India would probably have to retain the affiliating type of university—despite its limitations—for a long time, and also decided

> . . . to restrict the area over which the affiliating universities have control by securing . . . a separate university for each of the leading provinces in India, and . . . to create new local teaching and residential universities within each of the provinces . . . .[3]

Implementation of the 1913 Resolution was frustrated in great part by the absorption of the Government of India's energies in the First World War. However, four universities—Banaras Hindu (1916), Mysore (1916), Patna (1917), and Osmania (1918)—were established as either teaching or teaching-and-affiliating universities by 1918.

Michael Sadler Commission: 1919 Report

In 1917 the Government of India appointed the Calcutta University Commission (often called the Sadler Commission because its president was Sir Michael Sadler) to make a comprehensive study of the problems of Calcutta University and to submit suitable recommendations. The Commission's report, published in 1919, without hedging the issue, stated:

> The Calcutta University Commission find that the present system of university education is wholly inadequate to the modern needs of the Presidency.[4]

It then suggested two very important changes in basic university structure: (1) universities should no longer offer the 2 years of postsecondary education leading to the Intermediate Certificate, but concentrate on the advancement of higher learning; and (2) they should be residential and unitary (having all departments on one campus) rather than affiliating.

Although the University of Calcutta did not act upon these recommendations immediately, universities in other parts of the country did. For example, in 1921 Aligarh Muslim University and Lucknow University were founded in United Provinces (now Uttar Pradesh) as unitary and residential institutions; and in 1922 Allahabad University in the same State changed its constitution to convert the university from an affiliating to a unitary institution. In addition, three States—United Provinces (now Uttar Pradesh), Rajaputana (now Rajasthan), and Central Provinces (now Madhya Pradesh)—created separate boards of secondary and intermediate education to relieve universities of intermediate instruction.

Inter-University Board of India and Ceylon: 1924 to Date

As the number of universities slowly but steadily increased,[5] the wisdom of another recommendation of the Sadler Commission—that there should

---

[3] J. P. Naik *and* Syed Nurullah. *A History of Education in India* (2d edition). Bombay: Macmillan and Company. 1951. p. 500.

[4] Calcutta University Commission. *Report: 1917–19.* 1919. 6:1. The term "Presidency" was applied to the areas for which the East India Company's first three settlements (in Bombay, Calcutta, and Madras) continued to serve as administrative centers (part I, chapter 2).

[5] Between 1916 and 1930, a total of 13 universities were established—Agra, Aligarh, Andhra, Annamalai, Banaras, Dacca, Delhi, Lucknow, Mysore, Nagpur, Osmania, Patna, and Rangoon.

be coordination and cooperation between Indian universities—began to be recognized widely. The Lytton Committee on Indian students in England expressed the hope that a properly constituted organization representing Indian universities could secure uniformity in the recognition abroad of their degrees. The recommendations of this committee led to the establishment in 1924 of the Inter-University Board of India and Ceylon at the first All-India Conference of Indian Universities at Simla.

The functions of the Inter-University Board of India and Ceylon are as follows:

1. Act as an interuniversity organization and bureau of information.
2. Serve as an authorized channel of communication and help to coordinate university work.
3. Facilitate exchange of professors.
4. Assist Indian universities to obtain foreign recognition of their degrees, diplomas, and examinations.
5. Appoint or recommend when appropriate one or more Indian representatives at Imperial or international conferences on higher education.
6. Act as an appointment bureau for Indian universities.
7. Perform any other duties assigned by Indian universities.

Membership on the board is not automatic; to be a member a university must:

1. Be chartered under an act, statute, or other legal instrument in conformity with the general principles governing universities in respect to administration, autonomy, and academic standards.
2. Comply with accepted standards for universities as educational centers.
3. Offer several fields of study.
4. Adopt an open admission policy, irrespective of caste, creed, and nationality.
5. Have functioned for at least 1 year before being considered for membership.
6. Be recommended for membership in a report to the board by two members after an inspection of the university; and then be accepted by the board.

Although, as Naik and Nurullah point out, the authority of the Inter-University Board is not above that of the universities but emanates from them,[6] it has begun to play an active and positive role in coordinating the academic programs of Indian universities. With a membership of 70 in February 1969, the Board (1) has been holding annual meetings since 1925 to discuss problems of Indian university education; (2) has organized quinquennial university conferences to discuss the most important issues in Indian higher education; and (3) has published a monthly newsletter called *University News,* the *Universities Handbook of India and Ceylon* (1951 and 1964), annual reports, and occasional studies on particular aspects of Indian higher education.

(Continued from p. 43)

The University of Rangoon was withdrawn from the list of Indian universities when Burma was separated from India in 1936, and the Universities of Punjab and Dacca were withdrawn with the partition of India in 1947.

[6] Naik *and* Nurullah. op. cit. p. 634.

Hartog Committee: 1929 Report

The increase in students and the unorganized growth of educational institutions in the second decade of the 20th century brought into focus many of the problems of Indian education. There was a general feeling that quality of education was being sacrificed for quantity.[7] The report of the Auxiliary Committee of the Indian Statutory Commission—popularly known as the Hartog Committee[8]—deplored the incapability of Indian universities to produce the kind of leadership the country needed; and criticized the low academic standards of many colleges and universities, the large percentage of failures in university examinations, the lack of adequate library facilities, and the unhealthy competition for candidates between neighboring universities. This report, however, did not offer comprehensive, detailed, and realistic solutions.

The Sargent Report: 1944

The Ministry of Education refers all major educational problems to the Central Advisory Board of Education, whose chairman is the Minister of Education. Since its reactivation in 1935, the Board has made comprehensive reviews of almost every aspect of Indian education. In 1944, encouraged by the official attitude toward national planning, the Board published a master plan for education development in post-World War II India—often called the Sargent Report because Sir John Sargent, at that time Educational Adviser to the Government of India, was the moving spirit behind it. The Report's summary of the main conclusions of its university education chapter was the following:

(a) Indian Universities, as they exist to-day, despite many admirable features do not fully satisfy the requirements of a national system of education.

(b) In order to raise standards all round, the conditions for admission must be revised with the object of ensuring that all students are capable of taking full advantage of a University Course. The proposed reorganization of the High School system will facilitate this. Adequate financial assistance must be provided for poor students.

(c) The present Intermediate course should be abolished. Ultimately the whole of this course should be covered in the High School but as an immediate step the first year of the course should be transferred to High Schools and the second to Universities.

(d) The minimum length of a University degree course should be three years.

(e) The tutorial system should be widely extended and closer personal contacts established between teachers and students.

(f) The importance of establishing a high standard in post-graduate studies and particularly in pure and applied research should be emphasized.

(g) Steps should be taken to improve the conditions of service, including remuneration, of University and College teachers where those now in operation are not attracting men and women of the requisite calibre.

---

[7] From 1930 to 1945, only two universities were established—Kerala in 1937 and Utkal in 1943.
[8] Sir Philip Hartog, chairman of the commission, had served as a member of the Calcutta University Commission and as vice-chairman of Dacca University.

(h) An Indian University Grants Committee should be constituted for the purposes and with the terms of reference set out in this chapter.

(i) To provide for the increased number of able and well-prepared students which a national system of High Schools may be expected to produce, approximately 240,000 places, or double the existing number, should be available in Universities.

(j) The estimated total net annual cost of the scheme for University Education set out in this chapter when in full operation is Rs. 6,72 lakhs.[9]

It is significant that the Sargent Report viewed university education in India for the first time in terms of compulsory primary education and a newly diversified secondary education, "the top storey of the national educational structure . . . ."[10]

University Grants Committee: 1945–47

Having pointed out that the Inter-University Board could not influence Indian university education because "it is not invested with any power of the purse,"[11] the Sargent Report suggested that a University Grants Committee be established by and under the Federal Government to exercise

> . . . a general supervision over the allocation of grants to universities from public funds with the object of ensuring that universities are in a position to meet the demands which may be made upon them.[12]

The Federal Government accepted this recommendation and in 1945 established the University Grants Committee. Although originally the Committee's jurisdiction was limited to the three federally administered universities of Aligarh, Banaras, and Delhi,[13] in 1947 it was extended to include all higher education institutions, with the understanding that it would act similarly to the University Grants Committee of the United Kingdom. At Independence in 1947, the University Grants Committee in India ceased to exist, but in 1953 the University Grants Commission was established and in 1956 given statutory powers by an Act of Parliament (part III, chapter 3 under University Grants Commission: 1953, 1956).

---

[9] Ministry of Education. Central Advisory Board of Education. *Post-War Educational Development in India* (5th edition). 1947. p. 32–33. This is the Sargent Report.

[10] Ibid. p. 26.

[11] Ibid. p. 31.

[12] Ibid. p. 32.

[13] These universities are termed "central universities." The word "central" in India is often used to mean Federal. Central universities have been established by Federal legislation, are supported almost wholly by Federal funds, and are subject to Federal control. Visva Bharati became the fourth central university when it was "declared of national importance" by an act of Parliament in 1951.

3. Post-Independence Developments

When India became an independent nation on August 15, 1947, its leaders were keenly aware of the importance of education to the well-being and progress of their country. One of the first acts of the new Federal Government was to elevate the Department of Education to the status of a Ministry.

Since Independence, the number of universities has risen rapidly. From 1946 to 1960, a total of 29 universities were established; and during the 1960's alone 39 more have been established (chart 2).

University Education Commission: 1950 Report

In December 1948 the Government appointed a University Education Commission "to report on Indian University Education and suggest improvements and extensions that may be desirable to suit present and future requirements of the country." [1] The chairman of the Commission was Dr. Sarvepalli Radhakrishman, Vice-President and later President of India until May 1967, and all other Commission members were distinguished educators. Two U.S. educators (Dr. Arthur E. Morgan and Dr. John T. Tigert) and one English educator (Sir James F. Duff) served on the Commission. After extensive observations of current practices in Indian higher education, the Commission in August 1950 submitted a report dealing with every important problem in the field. Because its recommendations have served as guidelines for new policies and practices since 1950, a summary of the most important ones appears in appendix A, under the following headings: administration, courses of study, educational quality, examinations, finance, postgraduate training and research, religion, student activities and welfare, teachers, and women's education. Specific reference will be made to the Commission's recommendations in subsequent chapters.

---

[1] Ministry of Education. *Report of the University Education Commission* (Reprint of 1950 edition). Delhi: Manager of Publications, 1962. I:1.

University Grants Commission: 1953, 1956 to Date

Following the recommendation of the University Education Commission in 1950 that a coordinating and fund-granting agency be established,[2] the Federal Government proposed a Central Council of University Education. Adverse reactions from representatives of various universities, State governments, and educational conferences led to the abandonment of the Government proposal and the adoption in 1952 of a resolution establishing as of December 1953 a more independent and autonomous organization, the interim University Grants Commission.

In 1956, Parliament finally established the Commission by an act based on the Constitution which gives the Federal Government authority and responsibility for "coordination and determination of standards in institutions for higher education or research and scientific and technical institutions." [3] The Commission is legally responsible to the Federal Government through the Ministry of Education, but in accordance with the 1956 University Grants Commission Act, the Commission exercises a good measure of autonomy.

The Commission's membership, drawn from the Government, the universities, and the public, gives it a broad, representative character. The Government appoints for 6-year terms nine members—not more than three university vice-chancellors, two Federal Government officers, and the remainder from established educators or persons with high academic distinctions—and designates as chairman a member who is neither a Federal or State Government officer.

The Commission can influence greatly the development of Indian higher education because of the broad scope of its powers and functions as specified in the University Grants Commission Act (appendix B). It has authority to—

- Advise universities and the Federal and State Governments.

- Define qualifications of university faculty members.

- Inspect universities and require reports.

- Make or withhold financial grants.

- Regulate the maintenance of standards and the coordination of work and facilities in all universities.

The act also provides that:

> The right of conferring or granting degrees shall be exercised only by a University established or incorporated by or under a Central Act, a Provincial Act or a State Act, or an institution deemed to be a University under Section 3, or an institution specially empowered by an Act of Parliament to confer or grant degrees.[4]

No institution may associate the word "University" with its name unless it has been established by a Federal, Provincial, or State act.

---

[2] The University Grants Committee, a similar organization, functioned from 1945–49 (part III, chapter 2).

[3] *The Constitution of India.* Seventh schedule, list I, no. 66.

[4] University Grants Commission. *University Grants Commission Act, 1956.* (As modified up to January 1, 1963). Delhi: Manager of Publications, 1963. Section 22.

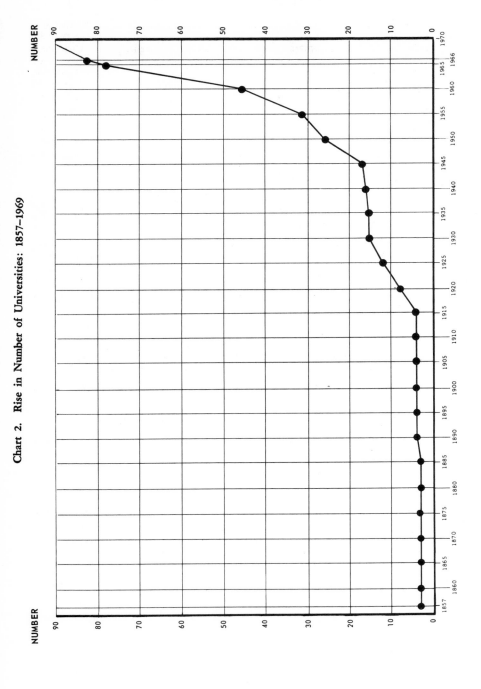

Chart 2. Rise in Number of Universities: 1857–1969

49

The increase in the amount of money spent annually by the Commission is evidence of its growing importance: [5]

1956–57	$ 6,800,000
1957–58	7,000,000
1958–59	12,000,000
1959–60	16,000,000
1960–61	16,600,000
1961–62	22,400,000
1962–63	23,400,000
1963–64	25,800,000
1964–65	28,600,000
1965–66	35,400,000
1966–67	21,987,000
1967–68	25,293,000

Since 1956, the University Grants Commission has made grants to:

1. Aid in expanding and improving university programs in agriculture, engineering, humanities, medical science, and science. (Science is by far the largest financial grant category.)

2. Construct and provide equipment for health centers, laboratories, libraries, non-resident student centers, staff quarters, and student and teacher hostels.

3. Develop Centers of Advanced Study (part IV, chapter 6).

4. Help defray costs of extending the bachelor's degree course from 2 to 3 years in certain institutions.

5. Maintain the constituent and affiliated colleges of Delhi University.

6. Provide aid for extension lectures, fellowships, and scholarships; publications and seminars; and foreign exchange authorization to purchase equipment abroad. (Grants for these purposes were smaller than for others.)

7. Raise faculty salaries toward minimum standard pay scales set by the Commission.

8. Recognize approximately 30 colleges for having served 100 years or more.

9. Support the four central universities (Aligarh, Banaras, Delhi, and Visva Bharati).

10. Support institutions "deemed to be universities."

11. Support special projects at the central universities.

The Commission also (1) makes an annual report to the Government of India; (2) undertakes studies and activities through such committees as those on area studies, centers of advanced studies, general education, medium of instruction, review committees (of university syllabuses and courses), standards of university education, and university and college libraries; and (3) publishes addresses of eminent educators and of others interested in higher education, the *Handbook of Universities in India,* results of educational investigations and conferences (many sponsored by its committees), and statistical reports about Indian higher education.

---

[5] These figures come from the annual reports of the University Grants Commission. Figures for years through 1965–66 have been converted from rupees to dollars on a 5-to-1 basis; for years after 1965–66 on a 7.5-to-1 basis, with rounded figures.

Three major areas of professional higher education—agricultural, engineering, and medical—are not wholly within the purview of the Commission, although strong recommendations have recently been made to give it greater responsibility in these areas. All indications are that the Commission will become even more influential in shaping and coordinating the growth and improvement of higher education in India in the years ahead.

Education Commission: 1966 Report

In 1964 M. C. Chagla, Education Minister of the Federal Government and former Indian Ambassador to the United States, appointed an Education Commission, under the chairmanship of Dr. D. S. Kothari, chairman of the University Grants Commission, and composed of 11 Indian and 5 foreign members (two from England and one each from France, Japan, the United States and the Union of Soviet Socialist Republics). The Commission's task was "to make a thorough evaluation of education today and tomororw bearing in mind the roots of our culture and civilization and the need to develop education on scientific lines." [6] The specific assignment was to survey the entire field of Indian education and then recommend to the Government national education patterns, principles, and policies to develop education at all stages and in all fields (except legal and medical).

The Education Commission engaged in wide-ranging activities. For example, the Commission—

- Authorized more than 20 special studies.

- Consulted many foreign educators and leading Indian citizens, in and out of government and the field of education.

- Established 12 task forces on: adult education, agricultural education, educational administration, educational finance, higher education, manpower, new techniques and methods, school education, science education and research, student welfare, teacher training and teachers' status, and technical education.

- Held many meetings with various individuals and groups.

- Organized discussion on seven topics: implications of the Constitution for education, implications of socialism for education, moral and spiritual values, national integration, Sanskrit education, secularism, and sociology of education.

- Set up seven working groups on: education of the backward classes, pre-primary education, school buildings, school community relations, school curriculum, statistics, and women's education.

- Visited all of the States of India.

In the final 1966 report of more than 700 pages, three chapters deal entirely, and several others in part, with higher education. The large amount of data accumulated will in itself be useful. The Education Commission's impact, however, will depend primarily upon the extent to which the appropriate authorities consider and implement its far-reaching

---

[6] Inter-University Board of India and Ceylon. *University News*. February-March 1964.

recommendations. Subsequent chapters of this report refer specifically to many of the Commission's suggestions and recommendations; excerpts from the report's summary of recommendations appear in appendix C under the following headings: administration, course of study, educational quality, examinations, finance, language, postgraduate training and research, religion, student activities and welfare, student assistance, teachers, and women's education.

Part IV.

The Universities

1. System of Higher Education

In this report, higher education is defined as postsecondary education leading to a recognized degree, and a university as an institution legally authorized to grant such a degree. The activities of Indian postsecondary institutions that are neither authorized to grant degrees nor affiliated with a university are for the most part not discussed in this report.

Universities

Authority to Grant Degrees

Since Indian Independence in 1947 and the adoption of the Constitution in 1950, the decision as to which institutions can grant degrees rests exclusively with the Federal and State Governments (part II, chapter 2 under section Constitutional Provisions). The 1956 University Grants Commission Act (part III, chapter 2 under section University Grants Commission: 1953, 1956) specified three categories of such institutions:

1. State universities (established by State legislatures).

2. Institutions "deemed to be universities" (by the Federal Government).

3. Institutions "declared of national importance" (either by the Constitution [1] or an act of Parliament).

As of 1969, there are 93 universities in India, of which 70 are State universities, 10 are institutions "deemed to be universities," and 13 are institutions "declared of national importance" (table 5).

State universities.—Of the 93 universities in existence in 1969, 70 receive legal status from their State governments. Whether the act creating a university was passed by a Province under British rule (as was the United Provinces Act No. V, of 1920) or whether it was passed by a State after Independence (as was the Marathwada University Act of 1959 by the State of Bombay), each act specifies the powers of the university, its

---

[1] The institutions "declared of national importance" by the Constitution (Seventh schedule, list I, no. 63) are Aligarh Muslim, Banaras Hindu, and Delhi Universities.

Table 5.—*Number of universities by category of degree-granting status and by State or Territory: 1969*

[_____ indicates source did not show any figures]

State or Territory	Total	Category		
		State universities	Institutions "deemed to be universities"	Institutions "declared to be of national importance"
Total	93	70	10	13
Andhra Pradesh	4	4	---	---
Assam	2	2	---	---
Bihar	7	6	1	---
Gujarat	7	6	1	---
Haryana	1	1	---	---
Jammu and Kashmir	1	1	---	---
Kerala	2	2	---	---
Madhya Pradesh	9	9	---	---
Madras	4	3	---	---
Maharashtra	9	7	1	1
Mysore	5	4	1	1
Nagaland	---	---	---	---
Orissa	4	4	---	---
Punjab	4	3	---	1
Rajasthan	4	3	1	---
Uttar Pradesh	15	9	2	4
West Bengal	9	6	---	3
Delhi	6	---	3	3
Other Federal Territories	---	---	---	---

officers with their duties and responsibilities, the university's territory of jurisdiction, and a non-discriminating admission policy; and prescribes the procedures for enacting university statutes and ordinances, for affiliating colleges, and for preparing and administering examinations.

Because the pattern for State acts establishing universities no longer met the changing conditions in India, the Ministry in 1961 appointed a committee to propose a "Model Act for Universities." Issued in 1964, the committee's report carefully analyzed the current situation and recommended that: "The main Act of a University should lay down the structure and organization in broad terms and the relevant details may be prescribed by statutes and ordinances." [2]

Institutions "deemed to be universities".—Privately or publicly controlled, the 10 institutions "deemed to be universities" tend to specialize in a particular field. Dr. D. S. Kothari, chairman of both the University Grants Commission and the Education Commission (of 1964–66), described such institutions as follows:

> Perhaps, some distinction can be made between a "university" and an "institution deemed to be a university." A university, if it is to justify its name and fulfill its responsibilities, must cover a reasonable range of studies, and it cannot turn itself into an institution devoted to only one profession or subject. The characteristic of a university is the wide range of disciplines and special studies that it covers, and the opportunities it provides for contact and cross-fertilization between students and staff members cultivating different specialisms. On the other hand, an institution "deemed to be a university" may deal with only one specialism or a narrow spectrum of subject, but its level of work must conform to proper university standards. [3]

---

[2] Ministry of Education. *Report of the Committee on "Model Act for Universities."* 1964. p. 4.
[3] D. S. Kothari. *Education and the Universities.* (Address delivered at the Vice-Chancellors' Conference, Delhi, 1961.) Delhi: University Grants Commission, 1962. p. 27.

The Indian Institute of Science was in 1958 the first institution "deemed to be a university" (table 6). Many of the institutions so honored, however, had long been known for their excellence both nationally and internationally. Examples are the Indian Agricultural Research Institute (founded at Delhi in 1905), the Indian Institute of Science (founded at Bangalore in 1909), and the Tata Institute of Social Sciences (founded at Bombay in 1936).

Institutions "declared of national importance".—Among the most important of the 13 institutions "declared of national importance" by Parliament, are the five Indian Institutes of Technology, located at Bombay, Delhi,

Table 6.—*Date of founding, city, and State of institutions "deemed to be universities" or "declared to be of national importance": 1969*

Institution	Date of founding [1]	City	State
"Deemed to be a university"			
Birla Institute of Technology and Science	1946 (1964)	Pilani	Rajasthan
Gujarat Vidyapeeth	1920 (1963)	Ahmedabad	Gujarat
Gurukul Kangri Vishwavidyalaya	1900 (1962)	Hardwar	Uttar Pradesh
Indian Agricultural Research Institute	1905 (1958)	Delhi	Delhi
Indian Institute of Science	1909 (1958)	Bangalore	Mysore
Indian School of International Studies	1958 (1961)	Delhi	Delhi
Indian School of Mines	1968 (1968)	Dhanbad	Bihar
Jamia Millia Islamia	1920 (1962)	Delhi	Delhi
Kashi Vidyapeeth	1921 (1963)	Varanasi	Uttar Pradesh
Tata Institute of Social Sciences	1936 (1964)	Bombay	Maharashtra
"Declared to be of national importance" *By Constitution of India*			
Aligarh Muslim [2]	1921 (1950)	Aligarh	Uttar Pradesh
Banaras Hindu [2]	1916 (1950)	Varanasi	Do.
Delhi [3]	1922 (1950)	Delhi	Delhi
By Act of Parliament All India Institute of Medical Sciences	1956 (1956)	Delhi	Delhi
Hindi Sahitya Sammelan	1910 (1962)	Allahabad	Uttar Pradesh
Indian Institute of Technology	1958 (1961)	Bombay	Maharashtra
Indian Institute of Technology	1961 (1963)	Delhi	Delhi
Indian Institute of Technology	1959 (1961)	Kanpur	Uttar Pradesh
Indian Institute of Technology	1950 (1956) and (1961)	Karagpur	West Bengal
Indian Institute of Technology	1959 (1962)	Madras	Madras
Indian Statistical Institute	1931 (1959)	Calcutta	West Bengal
Postgraduate Research Institute in Medicine	1968 (1968)	Chandigarh	Punjab
Visva Bharati [2]	1921 (1951)	Santiniketin	West Bengal

[1] Date in parenthesis indicates the year in which the institution was either "deemed to be a university" by the Federal Government (in accordance with the University Grants Commission Act of 1956) or "declared to be of national importance" (in accordance with an Act of Parliament pursuant to Item 63 of the Union List in the Seventh Schedule of the Constitution of India).

[2] A unitary university.

[3] One of India's two federal universities.

Kanpur, Kharagpur, and Madras, respectively. Authorized by Parliament according to the 1961 Institutes of Technology Act, these institutes represent five attempts to evolve a modern plan for educating the scientific and engineering personnel urgently needed for India's industrial development. The Indian Government in giving these institutes degree-granting powers has indicated clearly the importance it attaches to scientific education.

Relationship to Colleges

The relationship of a parent university to its colleges is classified as: (1) affiliating, (2) unitary, or (3) federal (table 7). Of the three categories of postsecondary institutions authorized to grant degrees, only State universities have colleges affiliated with them.

Table 7.—*Date of founding, city, State, and major type of relationship to colleges of State universities: 1969*

University	Date of founding	City	State	Major college relationship
Agra	1927	Agra	Uttar Pradesh	Affiliating
Allahabad	1887	Allahabad	do.	Unitary
Andhra	1926	Waltair	Andhra Pradesh	Affiliating
Andhra Pradesh Agricultural	1964	Rajendranagar	do.	Unitary
Annamalai	1929	Annamalainagar	Madras	Do.
Awadesh Pratab Singh	1968	Rewa	Madhya Pradesh	Affiliating
Bangalore	1964	Bangalore	Mysore	Do.
Baroda	1967	Baroda	Gujarat	Unitary
Berhampur	1949	Berhampur	Orissa	Affiliating
Bhagalpur	1960	Bhagalpur	Bihar	Do.
Bihar	1952	Muzzaffarpur	do.	Do.
Bombay	1857	Bombay	Maharashtra	Federal
Burdwan	1960	Burdwan	West Bengal	Affiliating
Calcutta	1857	Calcutta	do.	Do.
Calicut	1968	Calicut	Kerala	Do.
Dibrugarh	1965	Dibrugarh	Assam	Do.
Gauhati	1948	Gauhati	do.	Do.
Gorakhpur	1957	Gorakhpur	Uttar Pradesh	Do.
Gujarat	1949	Ahmedabad	Gujarat	Do.
Gujarat Ayurveda	1968	Jamnagar	do.	Do.
Indira Kala Sangeet Vishwavidyalaya	1956	Khairagarh	Madhya Pradesh	Do.
Indore	1964	Indore	do.	Do.
Jabalpur	1957	Jabalpur	do.	Do.
Jadavpur	1955	Calcutta	West Bengal	Unitary
Jammu and Kashmir	1948	Srinagar	Jammu and Kashmir	Affiliating
Jawaharlal Nehru Krishi Vishwavidyalaya.	1964	Jabalpur	Madhya Pradesh	Unitary
Jiwaji	1964	Gwalior	do.	Affiliating
Jodhpur	1962	Jodhpur	Rajasthan	Unitary
Kalyani	1960	Kalyani	West Bengal	Do.
Kameshwara Singh Darbhanga Sanskrit	1961	Darbhanga	Bihar	Affiliating
Kanpur	1966	Kanpur	Uttar Pradesh	Do.
Karnatak	1949	Dharwar	Mysore	Do.
Kerala	1937	Trivandrum	Kerala	Do.
Kurukshetra	1956	Kurukshetra	Haryana	Unitary
Lucknow	1921	Lucknow	Uttar Pradesh	Do.
Madras	1857	Madras	Madras	Do.
Madurai	1966	Madurai	do.	Do.
Magadh	1962	Gaya	Bihar	Do.
Maharashtra Krishi Vidyapeeth	1968	Rahuri	Maharashtra	Do.
Marathwada	1958	Aurangabad	do.	Do.

*See footnotes at end of table.

58

University	Date of founding	City	State	Major college relationship
Meerut	1966	Meerut	Uttar Pradesh	Do.
Mysore	1916	Mysore	Mysore	Do.
Nagpur	1923	Nagpur	Maharashtra	Do.
North Bengal	1962	Siliguri	West Bengal	Do.
Orissa University of Agriculture and Technology	1962	Bhunbaneswar	Orissa	Unitary
Osmania	1918	Hyderabad	Andhra Pradesh	Affiliating
Panjabi	1962	Patiala	Punjab	Unitary
Patna	1917	Patna	Bihar	Do.
Poona	1949	Poona	Maharashtra	Affiliating
Punjab	1947 (1882 at Lahore)	Chandigarh	Punjab	Do.
Punjab Agricultural	1962	Ludhiana	do.	Unitary
Rabindra Bharati	1962	Calcutta	West Bengal	Affiliating
Rajasthan	1947	Jaipur	Rajasthan	Do.
Ranchi	1960	Ranchi	Bihar	Affiliating
Ravi Shankar	1964	Raipur	Madhya Pradesh	Do.
Roorkee	1949	Roorkee	Uttar Pradesh	Unitary
Sambalpur	1967	Sambalpur	Orissa	Affiliating
Sardar Vallabhbhai Vidyapeeth	1955	Vallabh Vidyanagar	Gujarat	Do.
Saugar	1946	Saugar	Madhya Pradesh	Do.
Saurashtra	1965	Ahmedabad	Gujarat	Do.
Shivaji	1962	Kolhapur	Maharashtra	Do.
S.N.D.T. Women's [1]	1916	Bombay	do.	Do.
South Gujarat	1965	Surat	Gujarat	Do.
Sri Venkateswara	1954	Tirupati	Andhra Pradesh	Do.
Udaipur	1962	Udaipur	Rajasthan	Unitary
University of Agricultural Sciences	1964	Bangalore	Mysore	Do.
Utkal	1943	Bhubaneshwar	Orissa	Affiliating
Uttar Pradesh Agricultural	1960	Pantnagar	Uttar Pradesh	Unitary
Varanaseya Sanskrit Vishwavidyalaya	1958	Varanasi	Uttar Pradesh	Affiliating
Vikram	1957	Ujjain	Madhya Pradesh	Do.

[1] Official name is Shreemati Nathibai Damodar Thackersey Women's University. The University was given statutory recognition in 1951.

Affiliating.—The oldest universities in modern India—those in Bombay, Calcutta, and Madras—were purely affiliating for several decades. They gave recognition to colleges scattered over a large area, provided courses of study, examined students prepared by these colleges, and awarded degrees to those who passed the examinations. The universities themselves did no teaching.

Although the majority of Indian universities today are affiliating, none is purely so. Every affiliating university has at least a few teaching or research departments of its own; and it may also have "university colleges"—integral parts of the university, more directly under its control than affiliated colleges, and usually on the university's main campus.

Unitary.—Primarily teaching and residential, the unitary university centers its activities on one campus. Its colleges, usually concentrated on the same campus with the parent university, are for the most part under its direct and complete control.

Federal.—In a federal university, the related colleges are scattered throughout the metropolitan area of the city where the university is located. The term federal does not imply Government control or support, but rather refers to the relationship of the colleges to the university, which is one of federation, giving them more independence than constituent colleges but less than affiliated ones. The Ministry of Education lists only two federal institutions—Bombay University, within Greater Bombay, and Delhi University, within Greater Delhi.

Colleges

Relationship to Universities

Indian colleges, in their relationship to parent universities, fall into two broad classes: (1) affiliated and (2) nonaffiliated.

For affiliated colleges, the parent university's function is largely examining and supervisory: it sets general university policy, prepares examinations, and awards degrees to successful candidates. Affiliated colleges are not under the direct and complete control of the parent university.

In contrast, nonaffiliated colleges are for the most part under the direct and complete control of the parent university. They are variously called university, constituent, and associated colleges, but the distinctions between these terms are minor and often vary with the user. The United States Educational Foundation in India (USEFI) attempts to clarify the terms as follows:

> The colleges in India today fall into several classifications. Where a unitary university has been established it frequently has grown around an old college as a nucleus and this college may be known as the University College. Or, in a large city, as in the case of Delhi University, the colleges although scattered over the urban area will be considered "constituent" colleges of the University. Sometimes such colleges are called "associated" colleges. These words, which are applied to similar institutional relationships, mark off the colleges closely associated with the new unitary universities from the affiliated colleges which still exist in large and increasing number.[4]

Throughout this report, any college related to a university but not affiliated with it will be termed a constituent college.

Number of Colleges

It is difficult to obtain accurate information about the number of colleges at any given time not only because of the rapid increase in that number but also because the university relationship of many colleges is not permanent. A college may have a temporary affiliation status that is later withdrawn; a new university may take over some or all of the affiliated colleges within an area previously under the jurisdiction of one or more older universities; or a State government may even affiliate certain colleges to particular universities "without the knowledge or concurrence of the university concerned." [5]

---

[4] *Handbook of Indian Universities.* Compiled by U.S. Educational Foundation in India. Delhi: Allied Publishers Private, Ltd., 1963. p. 4.
[5] Ministry of Education (*and* University Grants Commission). *Proceedings of the Vice-Chancellors' Conference held on October 28-29, 1961.* 1962. p. 45.

In 1968–69, a total of 2,942 colleges had been founded, well over 10 times the 248 in existence in 1935–36, and over three times the 837 in 1955–56.[6] Between 1960–61 and 1968–69, more than 1,400 new colleges were founded: [7]

Year	Total	Affiliated colleges	Constituent colleges
1960–61	1,537	99	1,438
1961–62	1,783	107	1,676
1962–63	1,938	133	1805
1963–64	2,111	128	1,983
1964–65	2,360	147	2,213
1965–66	2,565	...	...
1966–67	2,749	...	...
1967–68	2,899	...	...
1968–69	2,942	...	...

As of 1965–66, available data showed that there were approximately: [8]

- Three times as many colleges under private as under Government control.

- Three times as many colleges offering work only through the bachelor's degree as through a postgraduate degree.

- Thirteen times as many affiliated as constituent colleges at the undergraduate level.

- Twice as many affiliated as constituent colleges at the postgraduate level.

Many more colleges specialize in arts, commerce, and science (offering degrees in one or two of these areas) than in any other field of study. For example, such colleges constituted almost two-thirds of the total number of colleges in 1960–61 and 1964–65 (table 8). The greatest increase during this period occurred in the number of colleges devoted to music and fine arts, each almost tripling.

The postsecondary educational institutions not related to universities are almost all vocational, technical, or both; and lead to a certificate below the level of the bachelor's degree (table 9).

Problems

There is some concern that many colleges are too small to provide an adequate educational environment. In 1964–65, almost 16 percent of university-related colleges had less than 100 students and almost 60 percent had less than 500 (table 10). The Education Commission recommended a minimum of 500 students and an increase to 1,000 students in as many colleges as possible.

Another matter of concern is that some universities have too many related colleges. In 1965–66, for example, the 59 universities with such colleges together had a total of 2,565 (table 11). The highest six uni-

[6] Inter-University Board of India and Ceylon. *Universities' Handbook, India and Ceylon, 1964.* 1965. passim.
[7] These figures come from the annual reports of the University Grants Commission and from the Ministry of Education's *Report on Educational Developments in India: 1967–68.* 1968. p. 25.
[8] University Grants Commission. *List of Colleges under Section 2 (f) of the University Grants Commission Act.* Delhi, 1965.

Chart 3. Rise in Number of University-Related Colleges: 1825-1965

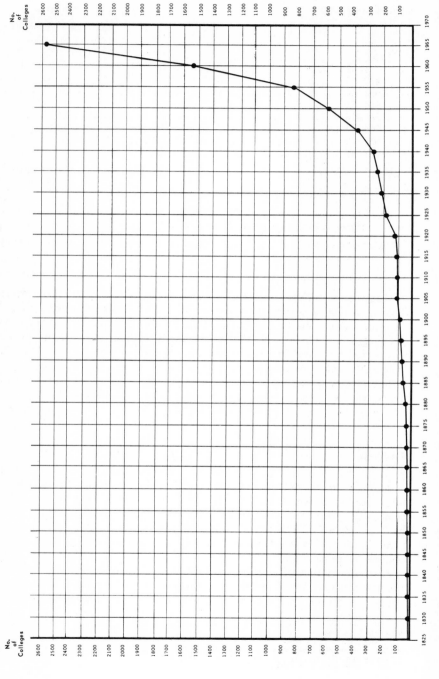

versities had 882 colleges.[9] The range among the entire 59 was from 168 (Calcutta University) down to 2 (Jodhpur University).

Other problem areas—such as laboratory and library adequacy, staff preparation, staff salaries, staff and student housing, and student-staff ratio—will be discussed in later chapters.

Table 8.—*Number of colleges in various fields of study: 1960–61 and 1964–65; and increase in number between those school years*

[_____ indicates source did not show any figures]

Field of study	1960–61	1964–65	Increase
Total	1,537	2,360	823
Agriculture	37	48	11
Arts, commerce, and science	1,094	1,615	521
Education	121	168	47
Engineering, technology	72	98	26
Home science	4	(1)	4
Law	39	63	24
Medicine	76	115	39
Ayurveda [2]	_____	10	10
Dental	5	8	3
Nursing	3	7	4
Pharmacy	2	2	_____
Western medicine	66	88	22
Music and fine arts	16	59	43
Oriental learning	54	167	113
Physical education	5	7	2
Social work	1	(1)	1
Veterinary sciences	18	20	2

SOURCE OF DATA: Figures for 1960–61 from University Grants Commission. *Statistical Digest.* September 1962. 1:1:4.

Figures for 1964–65 from University Grants Commission. *Annual Report: 1964–65.* 1966. p. 44.

[1] No explanation in source for not listing home science and social work in 1964–65. For purposes of total and increase, it has been assumed that there were no colleges in these fields of study.

[2] A traditional Hindu system of medicine based largely on homeopathy and naturopathy. For further details on Ayurvedic medicine, see part IV, chapter 5, under the section The Medical Fields.

Table 9.—*Number of institutions of postsecondary education not related to universities, by field of study: 1961*

Field of study	Number
Total	581
Agriculture and dairying	14
Banking, commerce, and cooperation	11
Domestic science	9
Engineering, technology, and industry	255
Forestry	3
General [1]	6
Marine training	1
Medicine and public health	83
Music and fine arts	36
Needle work	1
Oriental learning and theology	45
Physical education	16
Rural education [2]	13
Social science	5
Statistics	2
Teachers' training	78
Veterinary science	3

SOURCE OF DATA: National Council of Educational Research and Training, Ministry of Education. *Review of Education in India (1947–1961).* 1961. p. 163.

[1] Nonprofessional.

[2] Rural institutes generally include adult education programs in agriculture, health, and village industries.

[9] These are the universities of Calcutta, with 168 colleges; Madras, with 157; Punjab, with 149; Agra, with 143; Kerala, with 140; and Gujarat, with 125.

Enrollment	1961–62		1963–64 [1]		1964–65 [2]	
	Number	Percent	Number	Percent	Number	Percent
Total_____	1,579	100.0	1,707	100.0	2,056	100.0
Less than 100_____	276	17.4	282	16.5	320	15.6
100–499_____	705	44.6	714	41.8	898	43.6
500–999_____	342	21.7	397	23.2	457	22.2
1,000–1,999_____	220	13.9	268	15.7	328	16.0
2,000 and over_____	37	2.4	46	2.8	53	2.6

SOURCE OF DATA: Figures for 1961–62 from University Grants Commission. *University Development in India. A Statistical Report: 1961–62.* 1962. p. 19.
Figures for 1963–64 from University Grants Commission. *Annual Report: 1963–1964.* Delhi, 1965. p. 18.
Figures for 1964–65 from University Grants Commission. *Annual Report: 1964–1965.* Delhi, 1966. p. 1.
[1] Only 1,707 of the 2,111 related colleges furnished the relevant information.
[2] Only 2,056 of the 2,360 related colleges furnished the relevant information.

Standards and Autonomy

The University Grants Commission, the university vice-chancellors in annual meetings, and the Education Commission have all pointed to the need for common college standards. The major difficulty is that responsibility in this area is spread in an overlapping fashion among the Federal Government, the State legislatures, and the universities; the Federal Government is responsible for "coordination and determination of standards in institutions for higher education";[10] each State legislature has legal authority for granting affiliation within its boundaries, and the affiliating university determines the conditions under which a college can secure and maintain its affiliated status.

At present the universities have established such standards as do exist in the conditions they have laid down for affiliating colleges.

Andhra University has the following 11 requirements: [11]

1. Appointment and tenure procedures adequate for the instruction offered.

2. Appropriate student-teacher ratio.

3. Endowment of $60,000 jointly in the name of the university and $5,000 more for each science subject offered.

4. A laboratory or museum.

5. Land of 10 acres plus playing fields.

6. A library.

7. Provision for the physical welfare of students.

8. A regularly constituted governing body.

9. Staff qualifications of a high order.

10. Student housing supervision.

11. Suitable, well-lit, and ventilated buildings.

[10] *The Constitution of India.* Seventh schedule, list I, no. 66.
[11] University Grants Commission. *Report on Standards of University Education.* Delhi, 1965. p. 247–51.

Table 11.—*Number of colleges related to universities, increase in number of universities and related colleges since 1961–62, and other selected data, by State or Territory: 1965–66*

[----------- indicates source did not show any figures]

State or Territory [1]	Universities	Number of related colleges	Increase from 1961–62		Area in square miles	1965 population in thousands (est.)	Population density per square mile	University enrollment per million population	Total number of universities
			Universities	Colleges					
1	2	3	4	5	6	7	8	9	10
Total		**2,656**	[2] **31**	**782**	**1,261,421**	**469,800**	**372**	**2,806**	[3] **83**
Andhra Pradesh	*Total*	*156*	*1*	*21*	*106,052*	*38,360*	*362*	*2,051*	*4*
	Andhra	61							
	Andhra Agricultural	6							
	Osmania	61							
	Sri Venkateswara	28							
Assam	*Total*	*109*	*1*	*69*	*47,098*	*13,070*	*275*	*3,688*	*2*
	Dibrugarh	34							
	Gauhati	75							
Bihar	*Total*	*195*		*50*	*67,198*	*50,180*	*745*	*2,272*	*5*
	Bhagalpur	44							
	Bihar	44							
	Kameshwara Singh Darbhanga Sanskrit	28							
	Magadh	34							
	Patna	10							
	Ranchi	35							
Gujarat	*Total*	*144*	*1*	*60*	*72,154*	*22,580*	*313*	*3,711*	*4*
	Baroda	6							
	Gujarat	125							
	Gujarat Vidyapeeth	-------							
	Sardar Vallabhbhai Vidyapeeth	13							

See footnotes at end of table.

Table 11.—*Number of colleges related to universities, increase in number of universities and related colleges since 1961–62, and other selected data, by State or Territory: 1965–66* (continued)

State or Territory [1]	Universities	Number of related colleges	Increase from 1961–62 Universities	Increase from 1961–62 Colleges	Area in square miles	1965 population in thousands (est.)	Population density per square mile	University enrollment per million population	Total number of universities
1	2	3	4	5	6	7	8	9	10
Jammu and Kashmir	Total	34	--	1	86,744	3,730	43	3,491	1
	Jammu and Kashmir	34							
Kerala	Total	140	--	56	15,003	18,360	1,224	4,545	1
	Kerala	140							
Madhya Pradesh	Total	258	4	119	171,210	35,150	205	2,540	8
	Indira Kala Sangeet Vishwavidyalaya	32							
	Indore	17							
	Jabalpur	21							
	Jawaharlal Nehru Krishi Vishwavidyalaya	8							
	Jiwaji	30							
	Ravi Shankar	44							
	Saugar	67							
	Vikram	39							
Madras	Total	157	2	44	50,132	35,630	717	2,478	4
	Annamalai	--							
	Indian Institute of Technology	--							
	Madras	157							
	Madurai	--							
Maharashtra	Total	284	3	105	118,884	43,060	361	3,863	8
	Bombay	58							
	Indian Institute of Technology	--							
	Marathwada	28							
	Nagpur	84							
	Poona	46							
	Shivaji	51							

State	Institution								
	S.N.D.T. Women's	17							
	Tata Institute								
Mysore	*Total*	150	*3*	*50*	*74,122*	*25,470*	*344*	*2,814*	*5*
	Bangalore	31							
	Indian Institute of Science								
	Karnatak	53							
	Mysore	63							
	University of Agricultural Science	3							
Orissa	*Total*	75	*1*	*34*	*60,162*	*18,880*	*316*	*1,441*	*2*
	Orissa Agricultural	3							
	Utkal	72							
Panjabi [4]	*Total*	167	*2*	*22*	*23,084*	*24,480*	*974*	*3,551*	*4*
	Kurukshetra	4							
	Panjabi	9							
	Punjab	149							
	Punjab Agricultural	5							
Rajasthan	*Total*	88	*2*	*16*	*132,150*	*22,170*	*167*	*1,831*	*4*
	Birla								
	Jodhpur	2							
	Rajasthan	75							
	Udaipur	11							
Uttar Pradesh	*Total*	309	*6*	*64*	*113,454*	*79,390*	*178*	*1,563*	*15*
	Agra	143							
	Aligarh	4							
	Allahabad	6							
	Banaras	18							
	Gorakhpur	41							
	Gurukul Kangri Vishwavidyalaya								
	Hindi Sahitya Sammelan								
	Indian Institute of Technology								
	Kanpur								
	Kashi Vidyapeeth	18							
	Lucknow								
	Meerut								
	Roorkee	4							
	Uttar Pradesh Agricultural	75							
	Varanaseya Sanskrit Vishwavidyalaya								

See footnotes at end of table.

Table 11.—*Number of colleges related to universities, increase in number of universities and related colleges since 1961–62, and other selected data, by State or Territory: 1965–66* (continued)

State or Territory [1]	Universities	Number of related colleges	Increase from 1961–62		Area in square miles	1965 population in thousands (est.)	Population density per square mile	University enrollment per million population	Total number of universities
			Universities	Colleges					
1	2	3	4	5	6	7	8	9	10
West Bengal	Total	258	6	64	33,928	38,200	1,126	4,698	9
	Burdwan	43							
	Calcutta	168							
	Indian Institute of Technology	-							
	Indian Statistical Institute	-							
	Jadavpur	-							
	Kalyani	-							
	North Bengal	19							
	Rabindra Bharati	20							
	Visva Bharati	8							
Delhi	Total	41	5	6	573	3,140	5,479	9,691	6
	All-Indian Institute of Medical Sciences	-							
	Delhi	41							
	Indian Agricultural Research Institute	-							
	Indian Institute of Technology	-							
	Indian School of International Studies	-							
	Jamia Millia Islamia	-							

SOURCE OF DATA: Population figures for 1965 from Inter-University Board of India and Ceylon. *University News.* January 1966. p. 11.
Number of universities and colleges for 1965–66 from University Grants Commission. *Some Facts and Figures.* 1966. p. 5–6.
Number of universities and colleges for 1961–62, used to compute increase to 1965–66, from University Grants Commission. *University Development in India, A Statistical Report: 1961–62.* 1962. p. 9.

[1] Nagaland and all Federal Territories except Delhi have been omitted because no universities are located in them.
[2] Reflects an increase of 23 State universities, 5 institutions "deemed universities," and 3 institutions "declared of national importance."
[3] Includes 62 State universities, 9 institutions "deemed universities," and 12 institutions "declared of national importance." For figures as of January 1969, see table 4.
[4] Divided in November 1966 into two States, Punjab and Haryana. Kurukshetra University is in what is now Haryana.

Delhi University has the following three requirements: [12]

1. Endownment of at least $60,000 (for a constituent college, $100,000.)

2. Land of 5 to 8 acres.

3. Suitable buildings.

Madras University has the following nine requirements: [13]

1. Faculty qualifications set by the university.

2. Endowment of at least $100,000.

3. Hostels for 60 to 80 students.

4. Laboratory equipment for science courses.

5. Land of 20 acres for an urban college and of 40 acres for others.

6. A regularly constituted governing body of no more than nine, with the principal and a university syndicate representative as ex-officio members.

7. Staff quarters (if possible).

8. Staff salaries equal to Government pay scales.

9. Suitable buildings.

Because each university determines its own affiliation requirements according to the State legislative act establishing it, and because each State's acts reflect its own philosophy of higher education, it is difficult for the Federal Government to carry out its constitutional responsibility for "coordination and determination of standards." To alleviate this difficulty, the Education Commission has recommended that the University Grants Commission, in consultation with the universities and State governments

> . . . should examine this question of classification of colleges in terms of level of achievement and make use of it in the allocation of grants to colleges under the fourth five-year plan.[14]

The Education Commission further recommended that the University Grants Commission, in classifying colleges, consider the following: [15]

1. Examination results.

2. Laboratory facilities for science students.

3. Library facilities.

4. Performance of the college's graduates in national scholarship examinations.

5. Research output.

6. Staff—number and quality.

7. Students—number and general quality.

8. Student discipline.

9. Teaching procedure innovations.

---

[12] Ibid.
[13] Ibid.
[14] Ministry of Education. *Report of the Education Commission 1964–66.* 1966. p. 648.
[15] Ibid.

Colleges ranking high might be rewarded with special and "merit" financial grants on either an outright or a matching basis.

The function suggested here—of developing clearly defined criteria of institutional excellence, measuring a college's performance against those criteria, and arriving at a rating of institutional excellence for that particular college—is exactly the function performed in the United States by regional accrediting associations. Voluntary and nongovernmental, these associations through sanctions exert a power and influence equal in many ways to that of government, and in some cases they have withstood encroachment upon the integrity of a particular university or college. The experience of the United States' regional accrediting associations could provide some pertinent suggestions for the current situation in India, particularly because that situation is similar to the one in the United States during the period when these very associations were being formed. The principle on which they are based is that groups of colleges and universities working together can define for themselves criteria of excellence in higher education, can encourage member institutions to improve in line with these criteria, and can through voluntary action enforce on themselves minimum standards of higher education.

There is a growing recognition not only of the need for college standards but also of the desirability of greater autonomy for worthy colleges. The Education Commission stated:

> Where there is an outstanding college (or a small cluster of very good colleges) within a large university, which has shown the capacity to improve itself markedly, consideration should be given to granting it an autonomous status. This would involve the power to frame its own rules of admission, to prescribe its courses of study, to conduct examinations, and so on. The parent university's role will be one of general supervision and actual conferment of the degree.[16]

The Commission further suggested that universities amend their constitutions to provide for recognizing such autonomous colleges and that they inaugurate a plan for periodic review of them. It estimated that at least 50 colleges should be able to qualify for autonomous status by 1972.[17]

Geographical Distribution

As higher education expands at a rapid rate in India, the location of colleges and universities in relation to their natural clientele becomes increasingly important (map 2).

Universities vary considerably in terms of the students they serve. Because the total program or one aspect of it is unique, or because its reputation is outstanding, a university may tend to become a national institution in the sense that it draws students from all parts of the country. Another university may be more regional, drawing students from a smaller area. For instance, Aligarh Muslim University and Banaras Hindu University are national centers for the study of the Muslim and Hindu cultures. The Indian Agricultural Research Institute in Delhi, the Indian Statistical Institute in Calcutta, and the Tata Institute of Social Sciences in Bombay

---

[16] Ibid. p. 648.
[17] Ibid. p. 309.

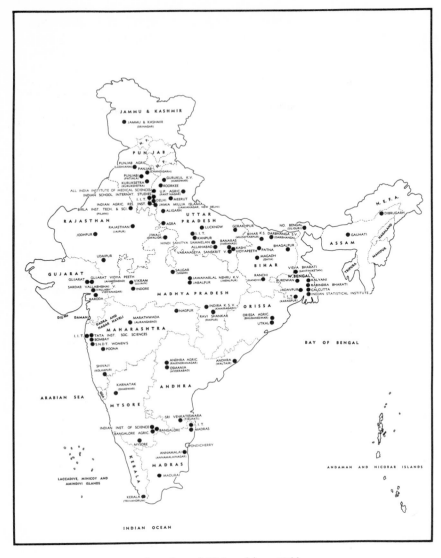

Location of Universities: 1966

are further examples of specialized national institutions. In contrast, the agricultural universities and institutes of technology (for example) are primarily regional in character.

The location of universities affects the pattern of territorial jurisdiction set up throughout India for affiliating universities. Territorial jurisdiction is the term used to indicate a university's authority to affiliate colleges within and only within a particular area prescribed by either the Federal or State Government. Areas of jurisdiction overlap only in the rare instance in which a particular type of university is given authority to affiliate the same

71

type of college, such as an agricultural university having authority to affiliate agricultural colleges in some areas over which other universities have general jurisdiction.

In 1857, Calcutta University exercised territorial jurisdiction over most of northern India. In pre-Independence days, other universities have had jurisdiction beyond their Province, although now few of a regional character have this authority beyond the borders of their States. Some universities have very restricted territorial jurisdictions, such as Allahabad, Annamalai, and Baroda Universities, each of whose jurisdiction extends only 10 miles from a central point on its campus; and Aligarh and Banaras Universities, each of whose jurisdiction extends 15 miles from a particular point, the University Mosque at Aligarh and the Main Temple at Banaras, respectively. Other universities have much larger territories, such as Jammu and Kashmir University, which has its entire State; and Madras University, which has all of the State of Madras except the area of Annamalai University (only 10 miles in radius). The Shreemati Nathibal Damodar Thackersey Women's University (S.N.D.T. Women's University) has jurisdiction over all of India, and the Varanaseya Sanskrit Vishwavidyalaya has not only all of India but also Nepal. Bombay and Delhi Universities have jurisdiction over their respective metropolitan regions.

The pattern of jurisdictions changes every time a new affiliating university is established. In 1964, the new Bangalore University took the region around Bangalore and its 27 colleges from Mysore University. In 1962, the new Udaipur University (under the name of Rajasthan Agricultural University) received jurisdiction throughout the State of Rajasthan primarily for agricultural colleges, taking 11 colleges from Rajasthan University. For the Education Commission's 1966 recommendations for new universities, see appendix C, section I.

A complicated situation arises not only when new universities are established, but also when a State is partitioned or a new State made from parts of older States. A recent instance occurred when the Federal Government partitioned Punjab State into two States—the new Punjab (where Punjabi is the common language) and Haryana (where Hindi is the common language). Chandigarh, the capital of the old State of Punjab, became the federally administered capital of both new States. Punjab University, located at Chandigarh, had had affiliating jurisdiction over the old State of Punjab and over the Territory of Himachal Pradesh (except for the areas belonging to the Universities of Kurukshetra and Panjabi); after partition, Punjab University relinquished jurisdiction in both new States, confining its affiliations to Chandigarh and to the Territory of Himachal Pradesh. The 149 colleges in the old Punjab that had been affiliated with Punjab University were divided between the two new States on the basis of final line demarcation, and are now affiliated either to the Kurukshetra University in the State of Haryana, or to the Panjabi University in the new State of Punjab.

Chart 4. Rise in University Enrollment: 1916–17—1964–65

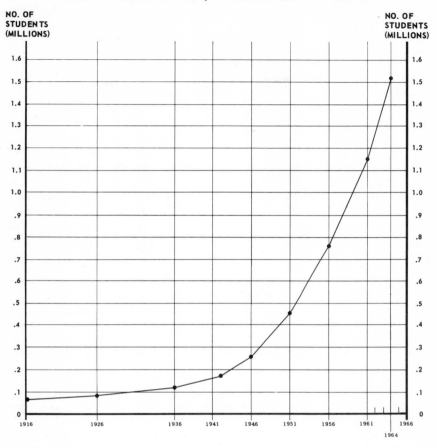

NO. OF
STUDENTS
(MILLIONS)

NO. OF
STUDENTS
(MILLIONS)

Enrollment

The number of higher education students has risen rapidly (chart 4), with an increase in each decade since 1936 of well over 100 percent: [18]

Year	Number of students	Increase Number	Percent
1946–47	265,844	139,473	110.4
1956–57	769,468	503,624	189.4
1966–67	1,949,012	1,179,544	153.3

Enrollment increases vary greatly among levels, with only a small increase at the intermediate and a large increase at the undergraduate level, indicating a decline of intermediate programs in favor of the 3-year degree

---

[18] Based on figures from table 15.

73

Table 12.—*Total number of students by higher education level: 1961–62 and 1964–65—1967–68; and number of students by level and by field of study: 1964–65*

[_____ indicates source did not show any figures]

Field of study	Total	Pre-university	Pre-professional	Inter-mediate	Under-graduate	Post-graduate	Research	Diploma or certificate
1	2	3	4	5	6	7	8	9
1961–62 Total_____	1,155,380	250,352	9,382	231,985	571,485	67,610	5,249	19,317
1964–65 Total_____	1,528,227	320,566	12,989	244,395	835,804	84,201	7,104	23,168
Agriculture_____	44,228	1,272	1,454	19,599	18,831	2,900	129	43
Arts, including oriental learning_____	641,186	144,429	--------	109,199	328,607	47,211	3,428	8,312
Commerce_____	147,789	29,096	--------	20,467	89,061	7,906	236	1,023
Education_____	29,528	--------	--------	--------	24,962	1,717	116	2,733
Engineering and technology_____	78,114	--------	5,786	--------	66,099	1,540	179	4,510
Law_____	32,000	--------	--------	--------	30,302	983	53	662
Medicine_____	61,742	--------	5,628	--------	49,847	3,101	75	3,091
Science_____	478,702	145,742	--------	89,060	222,416	18,392	2,850	46
Veterinary science____	5,711	--------	121	--------	5,070	346	26	148
Others_____	9,227	27	--------	6,070	609	105	12	2,404
1965–66 Total_____	1,728,773	369,373	15,231	277,285	944,015	91,830	8,633	22,406
1966–67 Total_____	1,949,012	430,954	18,860	308,485	1,053,750	101,798	9,668	25,497
1967–68 Total_____	2,218,972	485,271	19,633	343,807	1,211,083	117,250	11,479	30,449

SOURCE OF DATA: Figures for 1961–62 and 1965–66—1967–68 from the annual reports of the University Grants Commission.

Figures for 1964–65 from Inter-University Board of India and Ceylon. *University News.* September 1965. p. 10.

program adopted by most States and universities (table 12).[19] Although various commissions have recommended that the intermediate and pre-university courses be dropped (appendix C, section II), many students still enroll in them, particularly in the fields of the arts, agriculture, commerce, and science. In 1967–68, over one-third of all higher education students were in intermediate and pre-university courses.

Universities vary greatly in enrollment size. Calcutta University, with more than 120,000 students in 1963–64, is one of the largest universities in the world; in contrast, in the same year the Rabindra Bharati University had only 182 students, and six other universities had fewer than 1,000 students each (table 13). Along with the Calcutta University at the high end of the scale are Madras, Kerala, Punjab, Agra, Gujarat, and Bombay Universities, in descending order, each with more than 50,000 students. Approximately 90 percent of all students in the State and the four central universities (excluding intermediate colleges) in 1963–64 attended universities of more than 10,000 students, and approximately 40 percent attended universities of more than 50,000 (from calculations based on table 13).

[19] For a discussion of educational levels, see part II, chapter 3, under the section The Educational Ladder.

By level, the largest higher education enrollment occurs in the undergraduate courses leading to a first degree. In 1967–68 the division of students by courses was as follows (from table 12) :

	Number	Approximate percent
Total	2,218,972	100
Leading to a first degree	2,059,794	93
Leading to a diploma or certificate	30,449	1
Postgraduate and research	128,729	6

By field of study, the largest enrollments at all levels occur in arts, commerce, and science (table 12). In 1964–65 the division of students among the level of greatest enrollment (undergraduate leading to a first degree) was as follows (from table 12) :

	Number	Approximate percent
Total	1,413,754	100
Arts, commerce, and science	1,178,079	83
Engineering and technology	71,867	5
Other professions	163,808	12

Although enrollments in arts, commerce, and science overshadow those in professional fields, in 1963–64 the number of engineering and technology students was larger than that of students in arts, commerce, or science in three universities—Aligarh Muslim, Baroda, and Jadavpur (table 13). Of the professional fields, engineering and technology had the largest enrollment in 22 universities, and medicine the largest in 13 universities. Total professional enrollments showed engineering and technology first in number, followed by medicine, agriculture, law, education, and veterinary science, in that order.

By State, enrollments in the different fields of study show some interesting variation (table 14). For 1964–65, over 67 percent of higher education students in Delhi were enrolled in arts courses and less than 11 percent in science. In Andhra, Kerala, and Madras, on the other hand, almost 50 percent of the students in each were enrolled in science and only about 30 percent in arts. A comparison of State enrollments in individual fields shows the percent of commerce students higher in Gujarat, Maharashtra, Rajasthan, and West Bengal than in other States—probably because of the large metropolitan centers in those States; the percent of agriculture students higher in Orissa, Rajasthan, and Uttar Pradesh; of medical students in Andhra, Madras, Mysore, and Orissa; and of law in Gujarat, Madhya Pradesh, and Maharashtra.

The percent of Indian students choosing particular fields of study has not changed much from year to year, but certain trends are evident (table 15). During the 51 years from 1916–17 to 1967–68, the percents of students choosing engineering and technology, commerce, and agriculture each have risen considerably; the percent choosing medicine was comparatively constant; and the percents choosing arts, science, and law each have declined. India's successive Five-Year Plans for growth and develop-

75

Table 13.—*Number of students in each field of study in intermediate colleges and in universities, with individual totals for the latter: 1963–64*

[------- indicates source did not show any figures]

Institution	Total	Agriculture	Arts, including oriental learning	Commerce	Education	Engineering and technology	Law	Medicine	Science	Veterinary science	Other
1	2	3	4	5	6	7	8	9	10	11	12
Grand total	1,384,697	41,116	579,049	130,578	26,727	73,015	29,571	54,708	435,925	5,624	8,384
Intermediate colleges [1]											
Total	*200,000*	*17,800*	*93,000*	*15,600*	-------	-------	-------	-------	*68,000*	-------	*5,600*
Universities [2]											
Total	*1,184,697*	*23,316*	*486,049*	*114,978*	*26,727*	*73,015*	*29,571*	*54,708*	*367,925*	*5,624*	*2,784*
Agra	58,189	4,450	26,943	4,909	2,217	523	1,792	620	16,186	549	-------
Aligarh Muslim	5,148	-------	1,192	251	89	1,529	210	409	1,451	-------	17
Allahabad	9,662	217	5,135	605	28	517	604	162	2,394	-------	-------
Andhra	34,065	598	7,254	2,077	512	1,998	136	2,806	18,513	-------	171
Annamalai	3,522	274	738	245	194	937	-------	-------	1,037	-------	97
Banaras Hindu	8,732	400	2,840	548	148	2,103	186	383	1,869	-------	255
Baroda	11,191	-------	2,139	1,604	325	3,133	490	732	2,078	-------	690
Bhagalpur	20,286	365	12,680	1,067	-------	672	300	-------	5,302	-------	-------
Bihar	30,694	290	17,952	1,446	141	536	709	834	8,779	-------	7
Bombay	55,669	-------	18,640	6,569	633	1,801	3,449	3,419	20,986	172	-------
Burdwan	24,083	-------	12,332	2,806	113	591	-------	52	8,152	-------	37
Calcutta	120,829	36	57,146	20,497	1,520	2,590	3,645	4,378	30,809	171	37
Delhi	26,932	-------	18,374	1,688	184	740	690	2,173	3,068	-------	15
Gauhati	46,239	329	31,931	2,706	306	983	486	999	8,253	246	-------
Gorakhpur	16,800	2,683	8,144	695	1,293	103	563	-------	3,285	-------	34
Gujarat	54,744	314	22,654	7,281	554	1,955	2,957	2,509	16,492	-------	-------
Indira Kala Sangeet Vishwavidyalaya [3]	91	-------	-------	-------	-------	-------	-------	-------	-------	-------	91
Jabalpur	11,628	385	3,706	1,497	317	1,524	330	646	2,962	261	-------
Jadavpur	3,956	-------	791	-------	-------	2,600	-------	-------	565	-------	-------
Jammu and Kashmir	11,407	312	4,982	213	434	782	-------	635	4,049	-------	-------
Jodhpur	5,384	-------	1,520	718	155	1,208	237	-------	1,546	-------	-------
Kalyani	662	384	35	-------	116	-------	-------	-------	108	-------	19
Kameshwara Singh Darbhanga Sanskrit [3]	5,216	-------	5,216	-------	-------	-------	-------	-------	-------	-------	-------
Karnatak	21,606	503	7,884	1,527	590	1,645	572	1,338	7,747	-------	-------
Kerala	66,323	281	17,451	4,701	2,409	3,922	462	2,317	34,444	318	18
Kurukshetra	1,301	-------	551	-------	400	-------	-------	69	281	-------	-------
Lucknow	15,767	-------	6,127	962	205	-------	1,618	3,665	3,166	-------	24

University											
Madras	70,671	701	17,563	4,392	1,916	4,540	1,195	5,451	34,060	705	148
Magadh	24,021	—	14,899	1,068	177	455	320	641	7,222	512	—
Marathwada	10,912	340	3,366	1,505	759	5,983	310	2,749	4,118	—	—
Mysore	46,476	431	8,092	4,504	1,107	745	1,351	905	22,246	361	26
Nagpur	34,805	985	11,772	10,346	220	404	563	—	7,202	154	—
North Bengal	8,305	—	4,817	592	—	—	—	—	2,002	—	—
Orissa University of Agriculture and Technology	986	748	—	—	—	—	—	—	11,149	238	143
Osmania	27,536	418	6,675	2,444	510	2,371	1,079	2,443	345	304	236
Panjabi	4,124	—	1,311	170	512	848	—	702	1,980	—	—
Patna	10,946	—	5,796	571	272	644	473	1,210	—	—	—
Poona	27,808	990	9,211	4,245	638	1,420	413	1,594	9,296	—	1
Punjab	61,534	659	31,263	853	3,557	5,693	699	3,422	15,264	365	124
Punjab Agricultural	1,399	1,034	—	—	—	—	—	—	—	—	—
Rabindra Bharati	182	179	61	—	—	—	—	1,494	7,729	—	121
Rajasthan	31,309	289	13,363	5,808	851	1,274	611	482	4,493	111	—
Ranchi	22,788	—	10,384	1,679	100	4,756	494	—	80	—	—
Roorkee	2,333	—	—	—	—	2,253	—	—	—	—	—
Sardar Vallabhbhai Vidyapeeth	7,381	823	2,064	792	252	1,100	—	589	2,350	—	19
Saugar	25,080	408	10,474	3,605	971	1,702	1,051	28	6,261	—	6
S.N.D.T. Women's	4,624	—	3,881	43	220	—	—	—	446	—	—
Sri Venkateswara	11,471	267	2,199	288	300	1,141	—	909	5,890	434	43
Udaipur	1,116	924	—	—	—	—	349	—	—	192	—
Utkal	21,393	—	9,604	565	399	1,420	—	1,508	7,548	—	—
Uttar Pradesh Agricultural	843	394	—	—	—	158	—	—	—	291	71
Varanaseya Sanskrit Vishwavidyalaya [3]	691	—	600	—	20	—	—	—	—	—	—
Vikram	38,025	807	16,777	4,042	634	2,454	1,152	2,244	9,523	240	152
Visva Bharati	693	31	342	—	92	—	—	—	74	—	154

SOURCE OF DATA: University Grants Commission. *Basic Facts and Figures: 1963–64.* 1964. p. 36–38.

[1] Students in intermediate colleges are in their 11th and 12th years of study. See part II, chapter 3 for further information on intermediate colleges.

[2] Includes all State universities founded by 1963 (except Shivaji, founded in 1962) and the four central universities "declared of national importance."

[3] Statistics incomplete.

Table 14.—*Number of higher education students, by field of study and by State or Territory, and percent that number represents of the total number of students in the State or Territory: 1964–65*

[----- indicates source did not show any figures]

Field of study

State or Territory [1]	Total	Agriculture		Arts		Commerce		Education		Engineering and technology		Law		Medicine		Science		Veterinary science		Other	
		Number	Per-cent	Number	Per-cent	Number	Per-cent	Number	Per-cent	Number	Per-cent	Number	Per-cent	Number	Per-cent	Number	Per-cent	Number	Per-cent	Number	Per-cent
1	2	3	4	5	6	7	8	9	10	11	12	13	14	15	16	17	18	19	20	21	22
Total [2]	1,528,227	44,228		641,186		147,789		29,528		78,114		32,000		61,742		478,702		5,711		9,227	
Andhra	78,691	1,181	1.5	18,181	23.1	5,526	7.0	1,487	1.9	6,169	7.8	1,291	1.6	6,915	8.8	37,003	47.1	626	0.8	312	0.4
Assam	48,197	391	0.8	32,667	67.9	2,367	4.9	391	0.8	967	2.0	527	1.1	1,177	2.4	9,464	19.6	246	0.5	-----	-----
Bihar	113,903	1,089	0.9	61,253	53.8	5,774	5.1	1,042	0.9	6,632	5.8	2,846	2.5	2,941	2.6	31,670	27.8	650	0.6	6	
Gujarat	83,787	1,241	1.5	30,966	37.0	12,329	14.7	1,148	1.4	6,019	7.2	3,319	3.9	3,686	4.4	24,289	29.0	100	0.1	690	0.8
Jammu and Kashmir	13,023	334	2.6	5,176	39.7	235	1.8	420	3.2	971	7.5	-----	-----	650	5.0	5,237	40.2	-----	-----	-----	-----
Kerala	83,452	284	0.3	28,632	34.3	3,590	4.3	2,450	2.9	4,008	4.8	524	0.6	2,734	3.3	40,978	49.1	252	0.3	-----	-----
Madhya Pradesh	89,264	1,856	2.1	36,696	41.1	10,833	12.1	2,326	2.6	6,062	6.8	3,152	3.5	4,202	4.7	23,225	26.0	492	0.6	420	0.5
Madras	88,278	988	1.1	23,002	26.1	5,697	6.4	1,828	2.1	6,580	7.5	1,161	1.3	6,013	6.8	41,673	47.2	705	0.8	631	0.7
Maharashtra	166,334	3,909	2.4	59,363	35.7	29,519	17.7	3,725	2.2	5,781	3.5	5,050	3.0	6,844	4.1	51,682	31.1	361	0.2	100	0.1
Mysore	71,676	967	1.3	16,703	23.3	6,058	8.5	1,371	1.9	8,340	11.6	1,905	2.7	6,040	8.4	29,855	41.7	437	0.6	-----	-----
Orissa	27,202	970	3.6	11,826	43.5	786	2.9	611	2.2	1,856	6.8	428	1.5	1,841	6.8	8,625	31.7	259	1.0	-----	-----
Punjab [3]	79,830	2,023	2.5	39,900	50.0	1,581	2.0	4,069	5.1	7,884	9.9	983	1.2	4,832	6.1	17,749	22.2	386	0.5	423	0.5
Rajasthan	40,591	1,372	3.4	16,614	40.9	6,656	16.5	1,425	3.5	1,434	3.5	1,101	2.7	1,911	4.7	9,898	24.4	180	0.4	-----	-----
Uttar Pradesh	334,122	27,029	8.1	151,335	45.3	24,332	7.3	4,710	1.4	7,560	2.3	5,230	1.5	5,596	1.7	101,219	30.3	864	0.3	6,247	1.8
West Bengal	179,446	594	0.3	88,309	49.2	30,017	16.8	2,284	1.3	6,843	3.8	3,778	2.1	4,199	2.3	42,906	23.9	153	0.1	363	0.2
Delhi	30,431	-----	-----	20,563	67.6	2,489	8.2	241	0.8	1,008	3.3	705	2.3	2,161	7.1	3,229	10.6	-----	-----	35	0.1

SOURCE OF DATA: Statistics by the University Grants Commission, published by Inter-University Board of India and Ceylon. *University News*, September 1965.

[1] Nagaland and all Territories except Delhi are omitted because they contain no universities.

[2] Of the total number of graduate students in India, the percent in agriculture is 2.9; in arts—42.0; in commerce—9.7; in education—1.9; in engineering and technology—5.1; in law—2.1; in medicine—4.0; in science—31.3; in veterinary science—0.4; in other fields—0.6.

[3] Divided in November 1966 into two States, Punjab and Haryana.

Table 15.—*Number of higher education students by field of study; and the percent that number represents of the year's total enrollment: Selected years, 1916–17—1967–68*

[—————— indicates source did not show any figures]

Year	Total	Agriculture		Arts		Commerce		Education		Engineering and technology		Law		Medicine		Science		Veterinary science		Other	
		Number	Percent	Number	Percent	Number	Percent	Number	Percent	Number	Percent	Number	Percent	Number	Percent	Number	Percent	Number	Percent	Number	Percent
1	2	3	4	5	6	7	8	9	10	11	12	13	14	15	16	17	18	19	20	21	22
1916-17	61,145	-----	-----	29,655	48.9	-----	-----	61	0.1	383	0.6	5,272	8.7	2,409	4.0	22,364	36.9	-----	-----	446	0.7
1926-27	92,262	537	0.6	44,747	48.5	832	0.9	796	0.9	1,506	1.6	9,220	10.0	4,485	4.0	28,611	31.0	-----	-----	1,528	1.6
1936-37	126,371	885	0.7	61,289	48.5	2,239	1.8	2,603	2.1	2,459	1.9	8,028	6.4	5,215	4.1	41,211	32.6	-----	-----	2,432	1.9
1946-47	265,844	4,302	1.6	124,667	46.9	20,322	7.6	2,006	0.8	5,348	2.0	9,774	3.7	8,847	3.3	85,735	32.2	-----	-----	4,843	1.8
1956-57	769,468	10,389	1.3	395,672	51.4	66,674	8.7	13,000	1.7	21,237	2.8	20,707	2.7	23,431	3.0	210,039	27.3	3,572	0.5	4,747	0.6
1964-65	1,528,227	44,228	2.9	641,186	42.0	147,789	9.7	29,528	1.9	78,114	5.1	32,000	2.1	61,742	4.0	478,702	31.3	5,711	0.4	9,227	0.4
1965-66	1,728,733	51,190	3.0	706,641	40.3	165,283	9.6	33,546	1.9	85,555	4.9	37,318	2.2	70,088	4.0	565,254	32.7	6,257	0.4	7,641	0.4
1966-67	1,949,012	52,935	2.7	786,124	40.3	184,452	9.5	38,241	2.0	95,422	4.9	44,970	2.3	77,286	4.0	664,899	33.6	6,553	0.3	8,130	0.4
1967-68	2,218,972	51,639	2.3	918,345	41.4	219,831	9.9	43,102	1.9	104,266	4.7	44,581	2.0	83,422	3.8	737,858	33.3	6,610	0.3	9,318	0.4

SOURCE OF DATA: Figures for 1916-17—1946-47 from University Grants Commission. *Report on Standards of University Education*. Delhi, 1965. p. 136. Figures for 1956-57 from Ministry of Education. *Education in Universities in India: 1956–57*. Figures for 1964-65—1967-68 from the annual reports of the University Grants Commission.

ment particularly in agriculture, education, health, and industry have probably influenced and will continue to influence more Indian students to study in those professional fields.

Degrees

Indian universities grant 150 degrees, 111 diplomas and certificates, and 58 oriental degrees and titles—a total of 319 academic awards (appendix C). There are 78 bachelor's degrees including 18 different ones of science, nine of arts, and nine of engineering; 57 master's degrees; and 15 doctor's degrees. The Bachelor of Arts, Bachelor of Commerce, and Bachelor of Science (one of which is confererd on a student after he passes examinations set by a university at the end of a 2- or 3-year college course) are the most common and "correspond in name and intent to similar degrees in the United States" [20] in the sense that they mark the completion of undergraduate education.

Postgraduate degrees require from 1 to 3 years beyond the B.A., B.Comm., and B.Sc. level (chart 1 and table 16). The first postgraduate programs almost invariably consist of certain prescribed courses and sometimes but not always a research paper.[21] The Master of Arts (M.A.) and Master of

Table 16.—*Admission requirements and duration of program for selected degrees: 1963*

Degree	Admission requirements		Years in degree program
	Certificate or degree	Years of schooling	
B.A. (Bachelor of Arts)	H.S.[1]	12	3
B.Comm. (Bachelor of Commerce)	do.	12	3
B.Sc. (Bachelor of Science)	do.	12	3
B.Arch. (Bachelor of Architecture)	P.U.[2] or H.S.[1]	12	5
B.E. (Bachelor of Engineering)	do.	12	5
B.P.E. (Bachelor of Physical Education)	do.	12	3
B.Pharm. (Bachelor of Pharmacy)	do.	12	4
B.Sc.(Nurs.) (Bachelor of Science in Nursing)	do.	12	4
B.Sc.(Ag.) (Bachelor of Science in Agriculture)	do.	12	4
B.V.Sc. (Bachelor of Veterinary Science)	do.	12	5
B.D.S. (Bachelor of Dental Surgery)	H.S.[1] or P.P.[3]	13	4
M.B.B.S. (Bachelor of Medicine and Bachelor of Surgery)	do.	13	5½
B.Ed. (Bachelor of Education)	Grad.[4]	15	1
B.Lib.Sc. (Bachelor of Library Science)	do.	15	1
B.T. (Bachelor of Teaching)	do.	15	1
L.L.B. (Bachelor of Law)	do.	15	2
M.A. (Master of Arts)	do.	15	2
M.Sc. (Master of Science)	do.	15	2
L.L.M. (Master of Law)	L.L.B.	17	2

SOURCE OF DATA: *Handbook of Indian Universities.* Compiled by U.S. Educational Foundation in India. Delhi: Allied Publishers, Private, Ltd., 1963. p. 17–18.

[1] Higher Secondary Certificate.
[2] Pre-university course.
[3] Preprofessional course.
[4] B.A., B.Comm., or B.Sc.

[20] *Handbook of Indian Universities.* Compiled by the United States Educational Foundation in India. Delhi: Allied Publishers Private, Ltd., 1963. p. 17.
[21] Ibid. p. 17–18.

Science (M.Sc.) are awarded after 2 years of study beyond the B.A. and B.Sc. respectively.

For professional degrees, the number of school years required for admission to each program may differ from one university to the other, but the length of the degree program itself is usually the same for a particular program at all universities. The Bachelor of Education (B.Ed.) and Bachelor of Teaching (B.T.), awarded 1 year after the B.A. or B.Sc., are typical of the professional degrees. The Bachelor of Medicine, Bachelor of Surgery (M.B.B.S.), usually the first degree in medicine, is generally conferred after 18½ years of schooling or at the end of a 1-year pre-professional course followed by 5½ years of professional preparation (including 1 year of internship).

Research degrees, which include the Ph.D., D.Litt., D.Phil., and D.Sc., generally require a master's degree for admission to the program, and are based on research alone, with no course work and sometimes not even residence at the university necessary. As earned rather than honorary degrees, the D.Litt. and D.Sc., considered the highest degrees offered by Indian universities, require for admission to the program at least the master's degree and frequently the Ph.D.; and usually a period of 2 to 5 years must elapse after the candidate has received the master's degree or Ph.D. before he may start work for the D.Litt. or D.Sc. degree. To earn one of these advanced research degrees, a candidate must complete "an acceptable piece of research which is examined by a committee of three experts, one of them usually from abroad." [22] This task usually requires several years, the length of time varying with the individual and the topic.[23]

Certificates, usually granted for 1 year of undergraduate work, frequently indicate proficiency in some skill subject such as a language.

Diplomas, usually conferred for postgraduate work of 1 to 3 years, are sometimes considered the equivalent of a master's degree. A diploma may be granted by a college or institution not related to a university and therefore unable to offer programs leading to a degree.

Oriental degrees and titles are granted to students passing examinations in oriental languages (such as Arabic, Hindi, Sanskrit, or Urdu), or in Indian medicine, music, or theology. Commonly used titles are Shastri (approximately equivalent to Bachelor of Arts) and Acharya (approximately equivalent to Master of Arts). Most oriental degrees and titles are written in Sanskrit or in modern Indian languages and are not readily translatable into the standard degrees of India or of other countries. However, there are some equivalents: for instance, Chakravarti, Nrityacharya, Sangeetacharya, and Vidyavaridhi are the equivalent of the Ph.D.; Desikottama and Vachaspati of the D.Litt.; and Shastri sometimes of a bachelor's and sometimes of a master's degree.

[22] Ibid.
[23] University Grants Commission. *Report on Standards of University Education.* Delhi, 1965. p. 172–76.

2. University Organization and Regulations

Internal Organization

The internal organization of the first three and many subsequent Indian universities was patterned after that of the University of London. In both England and India, however, the organizational pattern has varied at times, although essentially it remains the same.

The officers and governing bodies of Indian universities usually have the same names, titles, and responsibilities in each university (table 17). Typical officers are the following:

1. *Chancellor*
   The Governor of the State in which the university is located has usually held this honorary and ceremonial office. The Committee on "Model Act for Universities" recommended that the Court of the university elect as chancellor a person of renown such as a Chief Justice of the High Court. In addition to performing ceremonial duties, the chancellor may assist in "settling conflicts and smoothing generally the relationship between various authorities of the universities." [1]

2. *Pro-chancellor*
   An honorary officer substituting as necessary for the chancellor, the pro-chancellor is usually a local dignitary.)

3. *Vice-chancellor*
   As the chief administrative and academic officer, the vice-chancellor usually serves a term of a few years and is eligible for reelection or reappointment for one or two terms. The method of selecting a vice-chancellor differs from one university to another. The Committee on "Model Act" recommended that this officer either should be designated by the visitor (see below) or responsible government, or should be elected by the university court from three persons recommended by a majority of the executive council.

4. *Rector*
   In Bombay and Jadavpur Universities, the rector is the chief administrator; in a few other universities, he serves only in an honorary capacity.

5. *Pro-vice-chancellor*
   The pro-vice-chancellor assists the vice-chancellor.

6. *Registrar*
   Having relatively long tenure, the registrar has wide-ranging responsibility for the daily and detailed academic administration, thus providing the continuity necessary for efficient operation of the university.

---

[1] Ministry of Education. *Report of the Committee on "Model Act for Universities."* 1964. p. 11.

Table 17.—Governing bodies and officers, by university: 1963

[Key: x = presence in university of governing body or officer; G = highest governing body; F = highest full-time officer; H = honorary officer]

Institution	Governing body									Officer							
	Court	Senate	Executive Council	Syndicate	Academic Council	Finance Committee	Faculties	Boards of Studies		Chancellor	Pro-Chancellor	Vice-Chancellor	Pro-Vice-Chancellor	Rector	Registrar	Visitor	
1	2	3	4	5	6	7	8	9	10	11	12	13	14	15	16	17	18
State University																	
Agra	G	G	x		x	x	x	x		x		F			x		
Aligarh Muslim	G		x		x	x	x	x		x	x	F	x	x	x	x	
Allahabad		G	x		x	x	x			x		F			x		
Andhra	G	G		x	x		x	x		x	x	F			x		
Annamalai		G		x	x	x	x			x	x	F		x	x	x	
Banaras Hindu	G	G	x	x	x	x	x	x		x	x	x	x	x	x		
Baroda	G	G		x	x		x	x		x	x	H			x		
Bhagalpur	G	G		x			x			x	x	F			x		
Bihar	G	G		x	x	x	x	x		x	x	F			x		
Bombay		G		x	x		x		G- The University	x		x		F	x		
Burdwan		G	x	x	x	x	x	x		x		F	x		x		
Calcutta	x		x	x	x	x	x	x		x	x	F			x		
Delhi	x	G	x	x	x		x	x		x		F		x	x	x	
Gauhati	G		x	x	x	x	x	x		x		F			x		
Gorakhpur					x		x			x		F			x		
Gujarat				x	x	x	x		G- Council	x			x		x		
Indira Kala Sangeet Vishwavidyalaya	G	G	x	x	x	x	x	x		x	x	F			x		
Jabalpur			x		x		x			x		F			x		
Jadavpur			x		x	x	x	x	G- Special Board	x	x	F		F	x		
Jammu and Kashmir		G			x		x			x		F	x		x	x	
Jodhpur		G		x	x	x	x	x		x	x	F	x		x		
Kalyani	G				x		x			x		F			x		
Kameshwara Singh Darbhanga Sanskrit		G			x		x			x		F			x		
Karnatak		G		x	x		x	x		x	x	F			x		
Kerala	G	G	x	x	x		x			x		F			x		
Kurukshetra	G	G	x		x	x	x			x		F			x		
Lucknow			x	x	x	x	x	x		x		F			x		

83

Table 17.—Governing bodies and officers, by university: 1963 (continued)

Institution	Court	Senate	Executive Council	Syndicate	Academic Council	Finance Committee	Faculties	Boards of Studies	(10)	Chancellor	Pro-Chancellor	Vice-Chancellor	Pro-Vice-Chancellor	Rector	Registrar	Visitor	(18)
	2	3	4	5	6	7	8	9	10	11	12	13	14	15	16	17	18
Madras		G		x	x	x	x	x		x	x	F			x		
Magadh		x				x	x	x		x		F			x		
Marathwada	G	G	x		x	x	x	x		x		F			x		
Mysore	G	G		x	x	x	x	x		x	x	F			x		
Nagpur	G	G	x	x	x	x		x		x		H			x		
North Bengal					x	x	x			x		F			x		
Orissa University of Agriculture and Technology									G- Board of Management						x		F- President
Osmania		G		x	x	x	x	x		x		F			x		
Panjabi		G			x		x	x		x	x	F			x		
Patna	G	G		x	x		x	x		x		F			x		
Poona			x		x	x	x	x		x		F			x		
Punjab		G			x	x	x	x		x		F			x		
Punjab Agricultural				x	x				G- Board of Management			F			x		
Rabindra Bharati				x	x				G- The University			F			x		
Rajasthan				x	x		x	x		x		F			x		
Ranchi				x	x	x	x	x		x		F			x		
Roorkee				x	x		x	x		x		x			x		
Sardar Vallabhbhai Vidyapeeth	G	G	x		x		x			x		F			x		
Saugar					x		x	x		x	x	F			x		
Shivaji		G			x		x	x		x		F			x		
Shreemati Nathibai Damodar Thackersey Women's		G		x			x			x					x		
Sri Venkateswara		G		x	x		x	x		x		H			x		
Utkal		G		x	x		x	x		x		F			x		
Uttar Pradesh Agricultural			x		x	x			G- Board of Management			F			x		
Varanaseya Sanskrit Vishwavidyalaya	G	G			x				G- Shistra Parishad [1]		x	F		x	x	x	
Vikram				x	x		x	x		x	x	F			x		
Visva Bharati	G	G	x		x		x	x		x		F			x		

Institution "deemed to be a university"

Institution									Supreme/general body	Executive head(s)
Gujarat Vidyapeeth	G	x				x		x	H	G– Mandal [1]	Acharya
Gurukul Kangri Vishwavidyalaya		x	x	x	x		x	x			F– Director
Indian Agricultural Research Institute	x	x					x	x		G– Postgraduate Council	F– Director
Indian Institute of Science	G	x	x	x	x			x		G– Governing Body	Chairman–Director
Indian School of International Studies		x	x	x	x			x	F		
Jamia Millia	G	x	x	x	x			x	H		
Kashi Vidyapeeth		x	x	x	x			x		G– Nirishak Sabha [1]	

Institution "declared to be of national importance"

Institution									Supreme/general body	Executive head(s)
All-India Institute of Medical Sciences			x	x			x			G– Institute	President, Director
Hindi Sahitya Sammelan										Ad hoc body appointed by Federal Government	Chairman
Indian Institute of Technology (Delhi)	x			x	x		x	x		G– Board of Governors	F– Director, Deputy Director
Indian Institute of Technology (Madras)	x			x	x		x	x		G– Board of Governors	F– Director, Deputy Director
Indian Institute of Technology (Maharashtra)	x			x	x		x	x		G– Board of Governors	F– Director, Deputy Director
Indian Institute of Technology (Uttar Pradesh)	x			x	x		x	x		G– Board of Governors	F– Director, Deputy Director
Indian Institute of Technology (West Bengal)	x			x	x		x	x		G– Board of Governors	F– Director, Deputy Director
Indian Statistical Institute										G– Institute	President, Chairman, Director, Secretary

SOURCE OF DATA: University Grants Commission. *Handbook of Universities in India: 1963.* 1964.

[1] Refers to a house, chamber, or general body of persons representing the institutions; may be composed of administrators, alumni, officers, teachers, and others.

7. *Visitor*

In the Indian Institutes of Technology, the Indian Institute of Science, and in the four central universities—Aligarh Muslim, Banaras Hindu, Delhi, and Visva Bharati—the President of India holds the title of visitor in an ex-officio capacity. The Committee on "Model Act" recommended that each State Governor should be the ex-officio visitor for State universities within his own State; and that the visitor of any university should have authority to inspect that university and inquire into any of its affairs.[2]

In addition to the officers just described, most universities also have deans of faculties and department heads (usually chosen from the teaching staff), treasurers or finance officers, engineers, librarians, and proctors, and—in at least one university—a dean of students. Some of the newer institutions are headed by a director (the title used for the chief administrator of the Indian Institutes of Technology), president, and chairman of the board of governors.

The usual governing bodies of Indian universities are the following:

1. *Court (or Senate)*

Composed of 100 or more representatives of both academic and lay interests, the court may have among its members not only university officers and teachers, but also alumni, community leaders, government officials, principals of related colleges, representatives of industry and trade, and persons helping to support the university. The Committee on "Model Act" states that lay representatives "can render great service to the university by their greater knowledge of the world and their ability to represent the general desires and aspirations of society."[3] The court deals with major policy matters including budget policy and acts as a consultative body on any major problem. Its chairman is almost always the vice-chancellor. In some institutions, the court must approve the policies and decisions of the executive and academic councils, but the Committee on "Model Act" is of the opinion that the court should not be considered a superior body, and that all three governing bodies should independently exercise the powers given them by the legislative act establishing the university.

2. *Executive Council (or Syndicate)*

Although composed of only 15 to 20 members, the executive council may include the same groups of persons, academic and lay, included in the much larger court and also persons nominated by the vice-chancellor. The executive council, almost always presided over by the vice-chancellor, administers examinations, appoints members of the teaching staff, determines fees, and raises funds. In some institutions, the university court must approve its policies and decisions.

3. *Academic Council*

Varying in size with the number of academic departments and with the size and complexity of the academic staff, the academic council includes deans, department heads, college principals, teachers chosen by election or seniority, and sometimes persons with expert knowledge from outside the university. Almost always presided over by the vice-chancellor, the academic council has responsibility for the entire educational program, determining admission requirements, curriculums, courses of study, examinations, and degrees; and therefore also has responsibility for the university's academic standards.

[2] Ibid. p. 32.
[3] Ibid. p. 19.

4. *Finance Committee*

Appointed by the executive council from its own members, the finance committee usually consists of approximately five persons, several of whom must be persons from outside the university. The finance committee advises the executive council on matters relating to the administration of university property and funds.

5. *Faculties*

The number of faculties in each university is prescribed by its statutes. Headed by a dean, each faculty usually consists of several teachers from each department within its field of study and sometimes a few persons with expert knowledge from outside the university. Of the members from the university in each faculty, some must be department heads and not more than one may come from each related college. Subject to the control of the academic council, each faculty has charge of the courses of study and directs the research work in its respective departments.

6. *Boards of Studies*

Operating within each department of the university, the boards each are usually composed of the university teachers, senior teachers from related colleges, and often teachers from other universities. The head of the department is usually ex-officio chairman of its board. Generally subject to the approval of the academic council and sometimes of the executive council, the boards prepare courses of study, recommend textbooks, and suggest persons to act as examiners.

7. *Selection Committees*

Existing in many universities and strongly recommended by the Committee on "Model Act," [4] the selection committee for each subject evaluates the qualifications of candidates for teaching positions and makes recommendations for teacher appointments to the executive council. Selection committees at present include a variety of persons; the Committee on the "Model Act" recommends that they include the university vice-chancellor ,the department head involved, and experts from outside the university—as many as three to select a professor and perhaps fewer to select lecturers.

8. *Board of Postgraduate Studies and/or Research*

Some universities have established boards of postgraduate studies and/or research to encourage and evaluate the expanding programs at upper university levels.

9. *Board of Inspection*

Affiliating universities each establish a board of inspecction to visit and evaluate their respective affiliated colleges.

10. *Board of University Teaching*

Several universities have recently established a board of university teaching to coordinate undergraduate and postgraduate teaching in both university departments and related colleges.

Other governing bodies in universities include the departments within each field of study and boards dealing with matters of student welfare such as discipline, extramural activities, health, recreation, residence conditions, sports, and student counseling. The agricultural universities have boards of management, and the institutes of technology have boards of governors. A few institutions have bodies known simply as "the university" or "the institute."

Internal and external politics in Indian universities have been a continuing subject of concern to those interested in higher education.

---

[4] Ibid. p. 23.

Traditionally, departments in Indian universities each have only one professor, two or more readers, and several lecturers. The restriction of each department to a single professor greatly limits a teacher's opportunity for promotion, thereby creating a situation conducive to political maneuvering, which in turn lessens a university's academic standards.

The selection of a vice-chancellor has also been occasion for political maneuvering. In 1950, the University Education Commission (under the chairmanship of Dr. Sarvepalli Radhakrishnan, a former university vice-chancellor) wrote of "the many forms of pressure to relax standards of all sorts which are being applied to universities today," and referring to the selection of a vice-chancellor mentioned the "deplorable effects on a university when the appointment of its chief officer becomes a prolonged intrigue for power." [5] The report further stated:

> Open canvassing and voting for rival candidates may have been tolerable while the post was not much more than a compliment which the university could bestow, though even so it was undignified and led to the formation of factions. But as a means of securing a man of character and reputation for an arduous and highly skilled service it is, to put it bluntly, disastrous folly. [6]

Fifteen years later the Committee on Standards of the University Grants Commission stated:

> It is not a secret that in several states the vice-chancellorship of a university has become a matter of patronage or reward for services rendered or anticipated. [7]

Internal politics involving staff and students has sometimes gone so far that a university has ceased operations at least temporarily. For example, in 1957, after the federally controlled Banaras Hindu University experienced many incidents of student unrest and a rapid change of eminent vice-chancellors, the Federal Government set up an Enquiry Committee to examine the general state of affairs and consider the many complaints concerning all aspects of the university's work. After a detailed examination of the entire problem, the Enquiry Committee concluded:

> . . . we have had very clear indication that indiscipline prevails among students because of indiscipline among teachers as well . . . and we note with a great deal of regret that the present state of indiscipline in the University is due as much to some of the teachers in the University as to the students thereof. [8]

The report further pointed out that— [9]

- A high degree of nepotism and favoritism existed in the selection of teachers.

- Cliques among the teachers from a particular geographic area had wrested most of the authority from the university, thus preventing its proper functioning and to a large extent destroying its all-India character.

- Feeding and sanitation conditions were not satisfactory.

---

[5] Ministry of Education. *Report of the University Education Commission* (Reprint of 1950 edition). Delhi: Manager of Publications, 1962. I: 422.
[6] Ibid.
p. 93.
[7] University Grants Commission. *Report on Standards of University Education.* Delhi, 1965.
[8] Ministry of Education. *Report of the Banaras Hindu University Enquiry Committee.* 1958.
p. 7.
[9] Ibid.

88

When in 1966 the longstanding problem at Banaras reached another crisis, the university closed its doors. The occurrence at Banaras Hindu University is certainly not typical of all or even of many Indian universities, but it does indicate that internal policies and student undiscipline rightly concern Indian educators.

External interference has also caused difficulties. The University Grants Commission pointed out an incident in which a State government issued to two universities orders defining the qualifications of persons who could be appointed to teaching positions in each university.[10] Reference has already been made to another incident of external interference in which a State government affiliated a college to a university without the university's knowledge that such an affiliation was even contemplated.[11]

Determination of Courses of Study

Affiliating, unitary, or federal, a university decides the content and maintains control of the course taught by its related colleges. The procedure by which it determines the courses is similar from one type of university to another.

Agra University (Affiliating)

The statutes of Agra University require "a Board of Studies in each subject prescribed for a degree."[12] Constituted by the subject's controlling faculty, the board must consist of:[13]

- The member or members representing its department on the faculty.
- Two experts elected by the faculty (presumably non-university persons).
- Two teachers of the subject in affiliated colleges.

Board members hold office for 3 years.

The board of studies has the power "to initiate proposals regarding new courses of study and regarding changes in the existing courses."[14] It must meet once a year, in or around March, to draw up "courses of study for the various examinations with which it is concerned."[15] It then circulates its draft courses—

> . . . among the members of the Faculty concerned and, if in the opinion of the Convener the criticism received from any member of the Faculty justify reconsideration of the courses, another meeting of the Board may, with the special permission of the Vice-Chancellor, be called for this purpose in November.[16]

---

[10] University Grants Commission. *Report on Standards of University Education.* Delhi, 1965. p. 93.

[11] Ministry of Education (*and* University Grants Commission). *Proceedings of the Vice-Chancellors' Conference held on October 28–29, 1961.* 1962. p. 45.

[12] *Agra University Handbook: 1963–64.* Agra: The University, 1963. p. 65. The same board may deal with two or more allied subjects upon approval by the executive and academic councils.

[13] Ibid. p. 66.

[14] Ibid.

[15] Ibid. p. 114.

[16] Ibid.

After approving the course proposals, the faculty passes them on to the academic council, which consists of: [17]

- All deans of faculties.
- All teachers of the university that hold the rank of professor.
- Three teachers of affiliated colleges.
- Five experts from outside the university.
- The vice-chancellor.

The academic council also scrutinizes and makes "its recommendations on the proposals submitted by the Boards of Studies through the Faculties . . . ." [18]

The proposals for courses or course changes next go to the executive council which has the power "to prescribe the courses of study for the examination, certificates and degrees of the University." [19]

Thus at Agra University four duly constituted bodies in turn consider its courses of study:

1. Board of studies
2. Faculty
3. Academic council
4. Executive council

The senate as the supreme governing body of the university can review the executive council's acts only if the latter has not acted in accordance with the Agra University Act, and thus in the usual determination of courses is not involved in the process.[20]

Bombay University (Federal)

For every subject (or group of subjects) Bombay University has a board of studies consisting of: [21]

- The head of every concerned university department.
- Each university professor in the subject.
- The head of every corresponding college department in the subject.
- Two co-opted teachers who are not heads of departments.
- Three co-opted persons who are not teachers.

The board recommends textbooks and courses of study, submits course proposals to the appropriate faculty, and advises on all matters relating to the departments in the subject.[22]

---

[17] Ibid. p. 61–62.
[18] Ibid. p. 60.
[19] Ibid. p. 17.
[20] Ibid. p. 15.
[21] *Handbook of the University of Bombay.* Bombay: The University, 1963. II:I:23,88.
[22] Ibid. p. 89.

The 1953 Bombay University Act states that the academic council shall make

> . . . regulations, in consultation with the Boards of Studies, concerned [with] laying down courses of study . . . , [and have] control and general regulation of and be responsible for, the maintenance of the standard of teaching, research, and examinations within the university.[23]

This consultative status given to the academic council at Bombay University suggests a more important role in the determination of courses of study than has the academic council at Agra University.

On the syndicate (the university's executive authority), the 1953 Bombay University Act does not explicitly confer the power to prescribe courses that the corresponding authority (the executive council) has at Agra University; this power is explicitly given to the senate, which on recommendation of the syndicate, shall

> . . . make provision for instruction, teaching and training in such branches of learning and courses of study as it may think fit, for research and for the advancement and dissemination of knowledge.[24]

However, the statutes do require reports to the syndicate concerning curricular matters by the provision that:

> Every authority of the University except the Senate shall report on any subject that may be referred to it by the Syndicate.[25]

Bombay University is one of the few universities that provide boards of university teaching.[26] In Bombay such boards have power to make recommendations to the syndicate concerning all university post-graduate activities and to coordinate the university's postintermediate and postgraduate instructional facilities,[27] thus playing a part in curricular construction.

Thus, in the order indicated above, at Bombay University several of the following duly constituted bodies may be involved in determining the curriculum:

1. Board of studies
2. Faculty
3. Academic council
4. Syndicate
5. Senate
6. Board of university teaching (when appropriate)

Baroda University (Unitary)

The procedures for curriculum development at Baroda University are similar to those at Bombay University; the main difference is that at

---

[23] Ibid. p. 21.
[24] Ibid. p. 16.
[25] Ibid. p. 60.
[26] S. R. Dongerkerry, "University Education." *Administration of Education in India*. Baroda, 1962. p. 227.
[27] *Handbook of the University of Bombay*. Bombay: The University, 1963. II:I:24.

Baroda there is no academic council for consultation. Each of the 42 boards of study recommends courses of study to the appropriate faculty, which considers them and in turn makes recommendations. The syndicate has authority "to arrange for coordination of studies and teaching in University and affiliated colleges and in recognized institutions." The senate makes "provision for prescribing courses of study, training, and research." The bodies determining the curriculum are therefore:

1. Board of studies
2. Faculty
3. Syndicate
4. Senate

Recommendations

The University Grants Commission, after studying the curriculums in Indian universities, reported that—

> Both undergraduate and postgraduate courses generally remain unchanged for a long time with the result that teaching in the different subjects tends to become out-of-date. Even in universities where attempts are made to revise syllabuses radical alterations are difficult to make. Except in a few universities no serious attempt has yet been made to evaluate syllabuses in the light of modern developments.[28]

To modernize the curriculums, the Commission recommended that—

1. *The aims of each course be clarified.*

The first exercise that we recommend in any attempt to formulate courses is that of defining what we expect to achieve at a particular level. Unless this is done, syllabuses are likely to lack purposiveness and clarity of content. A statement of objectives will help both teachers and students to realise what the aims of teaching and learning are in a particular subject and at a particular level. It will then be possible also to have a clear idea of the way in which examinations could be made to measure the intellectual attainment of students instead of their ability to reproduce information as is the case at present.[29]

2. *The procedures for revising curriculums be simplified.*

One reason why our courses of study have not kept pace with developments in different fields is that the procedure for revising them is very rigid and laborious. In most universities decisions of the Boards of Studies are not final till they are approved by other bodies like the Faculty, Academic Council and the Syndicate . . . . As a result of such protracted procedures, including consideration by non-academic bodies, reform of courses gets delayed and quite often many of the valuable suggestions originally made by the boards are modified or dropped. We therefore think that it is necessary to make the Boards of Studies themselves responsible for the formulation and modification of syllabi and to assign to other bodies only a nominal role, if necessary.[30]

3. *Teachers trained in newer educational developments be employed and included in boards of study.*

---

[28] University Grants Commission. *Report on Standards of University Education*. Delhi, 1965. p. 25.
[29] Ibid. p. 25–26.
[30] Ibid. p. 26.

Necessary reforms are very often held in abeyance on the ground that there is a paucity of teachers who can deal with the new topics competently. We are thus caught in a vicious circle in which universities continue to instruct along the old lines and the students turned out by them, when "fed back" into the teaching profession, bring about further deterioration. Not seldom senior teachers in some of the universities are responsible for this state of affairs. These are the people who qualified some thirty years ago and are either unacquainted with or are incapable of learning the new theories. They will neither do the job of modernisation themselves nor give a chance to younger people. Sometimes the universities do not have the required equipment and physical amenities for carrying out reforms of a far-reaching nature. As in the case of any other reform, once it is delayed, it becomes more and more difficult to bring it about. Teachers are trained on certain lines, equipment is built up according to certain norms, and certain teaching techniques are adopted, all of which result in a rigid set-up. It requires courage and wisdom to alter a situation of this kind . . . .[31]

. . . It is also of the utmost importance to include in the Boards of Study a number of younger teachers who are better acquainted with the latest development in the different subjects. Indian universities must check the tendency to treat membership of such bodies as a preserve of "senior" teachers. Until merit becomes the over-riding criterion of selection of personnel for such bodies, the process of modernization of courses is bound to suffer.[32]

In addition to making recommendations for improving the university curriculums, the University Grants Commission has set up review committees in different subjects to examine existing syllabuses, course outlines, and reading materials, and then to suggest to teachers and to boards of studies possible improvements in the light of modern developments in the various fields. The first such committees published reports on biochemistry, botany, chemistry, education, English, library science, and mathematics.

Contributing to the same effort to improve courses of study, the All-India Council for Technical Education established boards of technical studies to prepare materials for technical education courses leading to a diploma or certificate (part IV, chapter 5).[33]

Admissions

The very rapid increase in college and university enrollments, particularly since Indian Independence (chart 4), has created serious overcrowding—high student-staff ratios and thus excessively large classes in many colleges. As the quantity increased, the quality of incoming students decreased, endangering high academic standards. Even as early as 1935 or 1940, the mounting pressure for admission was bringing into universities students unable to profit from college education.[34]

---

[31] Ibid. p. 26–27.
[32] Ibid. p. 26. For courses recommended by the Education Commission, see appendix C, section II.
[33] Ministry of Education. *Higher Education in India.* Delhi, 1953. p. 7, 8.
[34] Ministry of Education. *Report of the University Education Commission* (Reprint of 1950 edition). Delhi: Manager of Publications, 1962. I:100.

The need to limit the quantity and control the quality of students was pointed out both by the University Education Commission and the University Grants Commission:

> Every college in an affiliating university and every teaching university should deliberately fix a maximum limit to the number of students it admits every year.[35]
>
> . . . the selection of students is central in any discussion on educational reform . . . [and] the most relevant question for a consideration of standards in a university is the quality of those admitted.[36]

Some Indian educators think higher education should not be restricted to the "intellectually elite" because "a good deal of useful work" can be done by people of lower intellectual levels "for whom a college education would be useful";[37] others think higher education should be restricted to the relatively small proportion of the college-age population having the intellectual capacity to benefit from it.

There is much evidence that the admissions system in Indian colleges and universities is in need of study and reform. The high degree of wastage—the percentage of students who start but do not complete a college course successfully—might have many causes, but the primary one, according to the University Grants Commission, has been an insufficiently selective admissions policy:

> While a number of factors such as ill-equipped libraries and laboratories, defective teaching techniques, inefficient teachers, difficulties regarding the medium of instruction, etc., have some relation to the high failure rate, the "open door" admission policy followed by universities and colleges is, in our opinion, the most important cause.[38]

Wastage is measured inversely by the percent of students who pass degree examinations. During the 12 years from 1949–50 to 1961–62 (table 18), over 50 percent of the candidates passed their degree examinations for the B.A. or the B.Comm. in only 2 of those years (1949–50 and 1951–52); and for the B.Sc. in none of the years. For the B.A.Hons. and B.Sc.Hons., with students expected to be superior in ability and motivation, the percentages of students passing in the same years ranged from only 57.7 to 77.2.

For professional degrees, the percentages passing were higher than for the undergraduate degrees. The trends, however, were mixed: in agriculture, the percent passing decreasd, from 88.8 to 69.4; in engineering, it increased from 71.4 to 75.0; in medicine, it increased steadily from 45.9 to 57.9; and in veterinary science, it varied with no significant trend.

For postgraduate arts and science degrees, the percentages passing were somewhat higher, ranging from 70.0 (for the M.A. in 1956–57) to 83.13 (for the M.A. in 1962–63).

[35] Ibid. p. 101.
[36] University Grants Commission. *Report on Standards of University Education.* Delhi, 1965. p. 18.
[37] K. G. Saiyidain and H. C. Gupta. *Access to Higher Education in India.* Delhi, 1962. p. 50.
[38] University Grants Commission. *Report on Standards of University Education.* Delhi, 1965. p. 19.

Table 18.—*Percent of students who passed selected degree examinations: 1949–50—1962–63*

[----- indicates source did not show any figures]

Degree	Year														
	1949–50	1950–51	1951–52	1952–53	1953–54	1954–55	1955–56	1956–57	1957–58	1958–59	1959–60	1960–61	1961–62	1962–63
1	2	3	4	5	6	7	8	9	10	11	12	13	14	15
B.A. [Bachelor of Arts]	50.8	47.5	51.7	45.5	44.9	48.5	45.6	47.9	47.8	44.3	44.2	43.2	46.1	46.1
B.A.(Hons.) [Bachelor of Arts with honors]	77.2	65.0	67.8	64.3	71.6	68.6	71.0	67.6	67.3	71.0	71.1	63.4	60.1	57.7
B.Com. [Bachelor of Commerce]	50.3	47.5	50.7	45.6	45.5	47.2	46.1	49.5	46.0	47.6	48.1	45.3	46.7	48.2
B.E. [Bachelor of Engineering]	71.4	71.5	67.0	-----	74.8	70.7	72.3	73.5	72.5	75.1	74.4	75.7	72.4	75.0
B.Sc. [Bachelor of Science]	44.4	48.9	45.9	44.2	46.1	45.9	47.1	46.2	48.6	48.7	48.4	44.1	45.2	45.6
B.Sc.(Hons.) [Bachelor of Science with honors]	64.7	70.1	71.3	73.2	70.1	70.5	69.0	66.3	65.7	70.6	70.8	63.3	58.8	60.3
B.Sc.(Ag.) [Bachelor of Science in Agriculture]	88.8	83.5	73.8	77.0	80.3	84.4	78.6	80.3	82.2	85.0	83.0	78.2	78.8	69.4
M.B.B.S. [Bachelor of Medicine and Bachelor of Surgery]	45.9	41.5	45.7	46.3	49.4	48.9	49.3	50.3	50.7	53.0	52.1	56.8	56.8	57.9
B.V.Sc. [Bachelor of Veterinary Science]	71.1	64.5	56.4	61.1	60.8	63.5	63.1	74.1	70.4	-----	69.3	65.6	66.0	64.5
M.A. [Master of Arts]	78.0	74.6	73.5	77.0	76.0	75.2	75.6	70.0	80.6	81.3	80.2	82.2	81.7	83.3
M.Sc. [Master of Science]	74.4	77.7	81.1	78.7	79.7	77.4	75.6	77.5	80.3	79.0	80.2	79.6	79.9	77.2

SOURCE OF DATA: Figures for 1949–50 through 1958–59 from K.G. Saiyidain *and* H.C. Gupta. *Access to Higher Education in India.* Delhi, 1962. p. 29.   Figures for 1959–60 through 1962–63 from University Grants Commission. *Basic Facts and Figures: 1963–64.* 1964. p. 81–87.

A University Grants Commission study [39] showed that Indian institutions of higher education usually require that a student, to be admitted to the first degree course, must have completed the next lower level of education—which might be the pre-university course, the higher secondary school, or the intermediate course—or have attained his Secondary School Learning Certificate (S.S.L.C.).[40] To be admitted to the M.A. or M.Sc., the student must have earned a bachelor's degree (table 16). A few institutions have established a minimum age for entrance to the pre-university course or the first year of college—usually 15 for the former and 16 for the latter. Most institutions, however, have no minimum age for admission, so that the immaturity of those students who finish precollege work before age 16 may cause them to fail in completing their degree programs.

To solve the mounting admission pressures in higher education institutions, the Education Commission has recommended that— [41]

1. The numbers and interests of students admitted should be carefully related to the nation's manpower needs.

2. Every college and university should institute a selective admissions program based on its actual and effective capacity and on an effort to "relate selection more directly to innate talent" and less to examination marks.

3. Correspondence courses and evening colleges should be substantially expanded.

No easy solution to the problem is foreseen. All developing nations emphasize education in general, and scientific and technological education in particular; and their peoples demand opportunities to acquire such education. If a much larger proportion of the human race is to be educated for a longer period of time—an aim in most regions of the world including India and the United States—new approaches to the problems of quantity and quality, and of citizens' desires and national needs will have to be found. Both India and the United States are approaching these problems in an educational context free of barriers from race, creed, and social or economic status.

Examinations and Evaluation

Because the first three Indian universities were strictly affiliating institutions like the University of London, the acts establishing them limited their functions to the holding of external examinations and to the granting of degrees; they had no teaching function.

Whatever the merits of this external examination system in 1857, it fell into disrepute as time went on. In 1950 the University Education Commission stated:

> For nearly half a century, examinations, as they have been functioning, have been recognized as one of the worst features of Indian education . . . . We only note that while the magnitude of the problem has been growing at an

---

[39] Ibid. p. 137–52.

[40] From 1949 to 1959, less than half of the candidates for the S.S.L.C. attained it. Thus at the secondary stage a high degree of wastage occurs; and in regard to higher education a highly selective process.

[41] Ministry of Education. *Report of the Education Commission: 1964–66.* 1966. p. 305–09.

alarming rate nothing constructive in the way of reform has happened. . . . In our visits to the universities we heard, from teachers and students alike, the endless tale of how examinations have become the aim and the end of education, how all instruction is subordinated to them, how they kill all initiative in the teacher and the student, how capricious, invalid, unreliable and inadequate they are, and how they tend to corrupt the moral standards of university life.[42]

The University Education Commission made a series of both general and specific recommendations for correcting the "Evils now Existing in the Examination System." [43] Twelve years later (in 1962) the University Grants Commission recognized that the examination system had been "under criticism for a long time" and needed reform; noted that despite much discussion little had been done to improve the system; and offered the following explanation:

Psychological resistance to changing the old system, inadequate financial resources to meet the cost of improvements, shortage of trained personnel for carrying out the measures of reform in a scientific way, and the pressures to which the universities are subjected in favour of continuing the existing arrangements have all contributed.[44]

The many committees and commissions that have studied the examination system throughout the years have agreed in general on what should be done; alternative methods have been investigated; meetings and seminars have been held; experts from and in other countries have been consulted; and the inevitable relationships between teaching and learning and examining have been pointed out. Yet relatively little change has been effected.

The major recommendations to improve the examination system have been the following:

1. Supplement or supplant the traditional external examining system by a method for internal assessment with the teachers themselves responsible for constructing and marking examinations.

2. Provide continuous assessment throughout a course instead of a sole examination at the end of it.

3. Test not only acquisition of memorized knowledge but also comprehension and the ability to apply principles, to analyze, to synthesize, and to evaluate.

4. Use several types of objective tests and examinations instead of essay questions only.

5. Use oral examinations for appropriate purposes.

6. Apply reliable statistical techniques to marking systems.

7. Eliminate the evils inherent in the present system of paid examiners.

8. Institute tutorials and seminars including discussion groups in addition to the usual lectures.

9. Establish additional seminars and workshops to enable large numbers of teachers to become skilled in using newer examination practices and techniques.

---

[42] Ministry of Education. *Report of the University Education Commission* (Reprint of the 1950 edition). Delhi: Manager of Publications, 1962. p. 327–28.
[43] Ibid. p. 240.
[44] University Grants Commission. *Report on Examination Reform*. Delhi, 1962. p. 1.

10. Establish national and regional research centers for the study and evaluation of test and examination problems; and provide quick and widespread dissemination of their solutions.

The Education Commission specifically recommended that— [45]

- All teaching universities and major universities should replace syllabuses and the external examinations based upon them with internally organized courses and continuous evaluation by teachers.

- Affiliated colleges should combine internal assessment with external examinations by the parent university.

- Payment of examiners should be abolished.

---

[45] Ministry of Education. *Report of the Education Commission: 1964-66.* 1966. p. 290.

3. Special Aspects of University Education

The Language Problem

According to the 1961 census, 826 languages are spoken by Indians. The variations and dialects of these languages, called mother-tongues, total 1,652.[1] Indigenous to the Indian people, these languages existed for years, centuries, and millenia before the Constituent Assembly tackled the problem of languages in independent India. As a result of its deliberations, 14 of these languages acquired a degree of official status by being listed in the Eighth Schedule of the Constitution of 1950, and a 15th (Sindhi) was added by an amendment in 1967 (part I, chapter 3 under section Cultural Diversity). About 90 percent of the Indian people speak one of these languages as their native tongue (table 19).

Table 19.—*Estimated number of persons speaking major Indian languages:*[1] *1951 and 1961*

Language	1951 [2]	1961
Total [3]	323,970,435	382,334,647
Assamese	4,988,226	6,803,465
Bengali	25,121,645	33,888,939
Gujarati	16,310,771	20,304,464
Hindi, Urdu, and Punjabi [4]	149,942,171	167,709,704
Kannada	14,471,764	17,415,827
Kashmiri	[5] 5,086	1,956,915
Malayalam	13,380,109	17,015,782
Marathi	27,049,520	33,286,771
Oriya	13,153,909	15,719,398
Sanskrit	555	2,544
Tamil	26,546,764	30,562,706
Telugu	32,999,915	37,668,132

SOURCE OF DATA: Figures for 1951 from Ministry of Information and Broadcasting. *India: 1964.* Government of India, 1964. p. 20.

Figures for 1961 from Ministry of Education. *India 1967.* Government of India, 1967. p. 14.

[1] Figures are given for the 14 major Indian languages listed in the 1950 Constitution (Eighth schedule); a 15th language—Sindhi—was added in the Constitution as modified in 1967; the number speaking Sindhi in 1961 was 1,371,932.

[2] There are no 1951 census figures for Jammu and Kashmir, Part B Tribal area of Assam, Goa, Daman and Diu, Dadra and Nagar Haveli, and Pondicherry.

[3] The total population of India in 1951 is listed as 360,950,365; for 1961 as 439,072,582.

[4] No separate figures are available for 1951. In 1961, the number speaking Hindi was 133,435,360; Punjabi, 10,950,826; and Urdu, 23,323,518.

[5] This number in particular reflects the lack of census figures for Jammu and Kashmir.

[1] Ministry of Information and Broadcasting. *India—A Reference Annual.* 1967. p. 13.

Although Hindi is the most common language of India and although the Constitution has proclaimed it the national language, opposition has arisen to efforts to insist on its use throughout the nation. The strongest opposition came from more than 100 million adherents of four language groups in southern India—those speaking Kannada, Malayalam, Tamil, and Telugu (the major Dravidian languages). In 1965 when the Prime Minister of India referred to English as an "associate" language and strongly urged further extension of the use of Hindi, violent demonstrations against Hindi took place; more than 60 persons were killed in South India; two southern Federal ministers resigned but later withdrew their resignations; and students agitated for more than a month.[2]

For many years, language has been officially recognized in India as a serious problem for education. In the first three decades of the 19th century, a debate took place as to whether the East India Company should financially support indigenous learning and literature or European learning and literature in the English language (part III, chapter 1 under section Macaulay's Minute of 1835).

As its spheres of influence increased, the company needed "a class of persons qualified by their intelligence and morality for high employment in the civil administration of India."[3] Since these persons were to be largely Indians educated for civil administration, the question of language of instruction became crucial. Macaulay's Minute of 1835 was decisive; a government resolution was passed, and from 1835 English was adopted as a medium of instruction in all schools and at all educational levels expecting financial support from the Company.

By 1882, however, because it was difficult to maintain English as a medium at the primary stage, the regional language became the medium of instruction at that level. From 1921 to 1947, English at the secondary level was also gradually abandoned:

> At first, modern Indian languages were adopted as alternative media of examination; then they were used as media of instruction in a few easier subjects; and finally their use as media of instruction was extended to all subjects, inclusive of science and mathematics. In the post-independence period, therefore, the problem of the medium of instruction had to be tackled at the university stage only.[4]

Many commissions and groups have considered language problems in education—most importantly as the medium of instruction and of examination. Among such commissions and groups are the following:

1. The Wardha, or Zakir Hussain Committee (1937).

2. The Committee on Medium of Instruction set up by the Education Ministry under Dr. Tara Chand (1948).

3. The University Education Commission (1949).

4. The Secondary Education Commission (1952–53).

---

[2] Reported in *The New York Times*. February 24, 1965.

[3] Ministry of Education. *Report of the University Education Commission* (Reprint of 1950 edition). Delhi, 1962. I:11.

[4] National Council of Research and Training, Ministry of Education. *Review of Education in India: 1947–61.* Delhi, 1962. p. 29.

5. The Language Commission (1956).

6. The University Grants Commission (Kunzru Committee). (1957).

7. The Working Group appointed by the University Grants Commission (1959).

8. The Chief Ministers Conference (1961).

9. The National Integration Conference (1961).

10. The National Integration Council (1962).

11. The Vice-Chancellors' Conference (1962).

12. The Education Commission (1964–66).

The teaching of languages is a related problem. In 1964, a total of 52 languages were taught by Indian universities (table 20).[5] Only English, Hindi, Sanskrit, German, Urdu, and French were taught by at least half of the institutions teaching languages. Only eight of the 56 universities teaching English listed it as a foreign language.

English has remained the major language of instruction and examination in Indian higher education, although the number of universities attempting to offer many courses in regional languages is increasing, with teachers

Table 20.—*Number of universities teaching selected languages: 1964*

Language	Number of universities	Language	Number of universities
Arabic	23	Malayam	9
Ardhamagadhi	4	Manipuri	1
Assamese	5	Marathi	22
Avesta (ancient Iranian)[2]	3	Modern Armenian	1
Bengali	24	Mongolian	1
Burmese	2	Nepali	7
Cambodian[3]	1	Old Javanese	1
Chinese	8	Oriya	9
English	56	Pali	11
French	35	Persian	30
German	37	Portuguese	2
Greek	6	Prakit	5
Gujarati	14	Punjabi	9
Gurmukhi[4]	2	Russian	14
Hausa	1	Sanskrit	46
Hebrew	6	Sindhi	4
Hindi	49	Singhalese	2
Indonesian	2	Spanish	5
Italian	8	Swahili	1
Japanese	3	Syriac	3
Kanarese[5]	1	Tamil	19
Kannada	14	Telugu	17
Kashmiri	1	Thai	1
Khasi	1	Tibetan	9
Latin	12	Turkish	1
Maithili	5	Urdu	36

SOURCE OF DATA: Inter-University Board of India and Ceylon. *Universities Handbook, India and Ceylon: 1964.* Delhi, 1965.

[1] The languages listed as taught in Indian universities total 52. The number of universities reporting was 70; the number not reporting was 13. Many universities teach several languages.

[2] Also called Pahlavi.

[3] Also called Kher.   [4] A version of the Punjabi language.   [5] A version of the Kannada language.

[5] The Indian Institute of Technology at Bombay was planning to offer courses in the Russian language by correspondence. Inter-University Board of India and Ceylon. *University News.* January 1966. p. 14.

able to instruct in several languages in great demand. In 1962, only 2,216 students attended the four universities not using English. At the postgraduate level, English is even more exclusively used: as of 1964, it was the only medium in 32 of the 42 universities reporting; in nine institutions it was used with Hindi as an alternate; in one institution (Gurukul Kangri Vishwavidyalaya) for science teaching; and in one institution (S.N.D.T. Women's University) as an alternate.[6]

In almost all discussions about language in education, the following points recur:

1. In primary education, children should be taught in their mother-tongue (often the regional language), because they learn better in early school years when taught in their home language.

2. In secondary education, regional languages will continue to be used, because adherence to them is strong and basic to other aspects of local culture.

3. A national language is needed for interstate and interuniversity communication, for the business of the Federal Government and of national organizations, and for all those persons whose commitments take them personally or through correspondence to many parts of India.

4. An international language is needed for intergovernmental negotiations, for intellectual intercourse with students, teachers, and scholars of other countries, and for combating the isolationism produced by lack of international intellectual communication.

5. If one language can serve as both national and international language, it would probably be English. If not, Hindi (if accepted in all regions) might become the national language with English an alternate, and English would become the international language.

The advantages of using English both nationally and internationally were pointed out by the University Education Commission:

> Now it is true that the English language has been one of the potent factors in the development of unity in the country. In fact the concept of nationality and the sentiment of nationalism are largely the gift of the English language and literature to India. This debt alone is so considerable and the fear that in the absence of the binding force of English, reversion to old differences and divisions is so great, that many advocate the retention of English as an instrument for the continuance and fostering of the unity which it helped to create, but in addition English has supplied us with the key to the fundamental ideas of modern civilization, to modern science and philosophy and, what is even more important, for all practical purposes English will continue to be our principal means of maintaining contact with the outside world. Besides, English is an international language and if catastrophic events do not alter the present posture of world forces it will soon be the world language.[7]

Nevertheless, a national change away from English was favored by the University Education Commission:

> We have paid a heavy price for learning through English in the past. Instead of laying stress upon thinking and reasoning we emphasized memorizing, in place of acquiring knowledge of things and realities we acquired a sort of mastery over words. It affected originality of thought and development of

---

[6] University Grants Commission. *Report on Standards of University Education*. Delhi, 1965. p. 230–33.

[7] Ministry of Education. *Report of the University Education Commission* (Reprint of 1950 edition). Delhi: Manager of Publications, 1962. I:316.

Table 21.—Number of universities using certain languages[1] for instruction and examination, by State or Territory:[2] 1963

[_ _ _ _ _ _ _ _ indicates source did not show any figures]

State or Territory [3]	Bengali	English	Gujarati	Hindi	Kannada	Marathi	Punjabi	Sanskrit	Tamil	Telugu	Urdu
Total	5	65	4	30	1	4	2	3	2	1	5
Andhra		2									
Assam		1									
Bihar	1	5		5							1
Gujarat		3	3	3							
Jammu and Kashmir		1									
Kerala		1									
Madhya Pradesh		6		6		1				1	1
Madras		3							2		
Maharashtra		7	1	1		3					
Mysore		4			1						
Orissa		2									
Punjab [4]		4		1			2				1
Rajasthan		4		3							
Uttar Pradesh		10		9				3			1
West Bengal	4	8		1							
Delhi		4		1							1

SOURCE OF DATA: University Grants Commission. *Handbook of Universities in India: 1963.* 1964.
[1] Of the 69 universities represented in this table, 38 use a combination of languages, as shown in table 22. All courses do not have instruction and examination in every language used by a university.
[2] The number of States using each language in the table was as follows: Bengali—2; English—16; Gujarati—2; Hindi—9; Kannada—1; Marathi—2; Punjabi—1; Sanskrit—1; Tamil—1; Telugu—1 Urdu—5.
[3] Nagaland and all Territories except Delhi are omitted because they contain no university.
[4] Divided in November 1966 into two States, Punjab and Haryana.

Table 22.—Number of universities using a particular language or combination of languages:[1] 1963

Language or combination of languages	Number
Total [2]	69
English only	29
Hindu only	1
Urdu only	1
English and Bengali	3
English and Hindi	16
English and Kannada	1
English and Marathi	2
English and Punjabi	1
English and Tamil	2
Hindi and Gujarati	1
Hindi and Sanskrit	1
English, Hindi, and Bengali	1
English, Hindi, and Gujarati	2
English, Hindi, and Marathi	1
English, Hindi, and Sanskrit	2
English, Hindi, and Urdu	1
English, Hindi, Gujarati, and Marathi	1
English, Hindi, Urdu, and Bengali	1
English, Hindi, Urdu, and Punjabi	1
English, Hindi, Urdu, and Telugu	1

SOURCE OF DATA: University Grants Commission. *Handbook of Universities in India: 1963.* 1964
[1] All courses do not have instruction and examination in every language used by a university.
[2] Information was available for only 69 of the 83 universities existing in 1963.

literature in the mother tongue. We have impoverished ourselves without being able to enrich the language which we so assiduously studied. It is a rare phenomenon to find the speaker of one tongue contributing to great literature in a different language. The paucity of great literature which is the inevitable consequence of devotion by the educated to a language other than their own is a double loss—intellectual and social for great literature is a powerful factor in fostering culture, refinement, and true fellowship. Whatever the advantages of English and the immediate risks in a change over to the new, the balance of advantage on a long view of the matter lies in the change." [8]

In higher education, the Education Commission considered that regional languages and particularly English should be used:

> . . . all teachers in higher education should be essentially bilingual in the sense that they would be able to teach in the regional language and in English, and all students . . . should be able to follow lectures and use reading materials in the regional language, as well as in English. . . . In major universities it will be necessary, as a rule, to adopt English as the medium of education because their students and teachers will be drawn on an all-India basis. This is the only feasible approach if their all-India character is to be maintained. [9]

A clear-cut language pattern for all institutions, all regions, and all people in India may not be the ultimate solution. All Indian children, however, will need to be bilingual and a great many trilingual.

Higher Education of Women

Historically, the education of Indian girls has been neglected in that the percentages of them attending school or college have been low. Since Independence, the situation has been improving fairly rapidly partially because of special efforts and financial grants. From 1960–61 to 1965–66, the percentages of girls of different age groups attending school increased markedly.

Age group	Total [10] 1960–61	[11] 1965–66	Girls [10] 1960–61	[11] 1965–66	Boys [10] 1960–61	[11] 1965–66
6–11	61.1	76.4	40.4	61.6	80.5	90.4
11–14	22.8	28.6	10.8	16.5	34.3	39.9
14–17	11.5	15.6	4.2	6.9	18.4	23.7

From these figures it can be seen both that education of girls lags well behind that of boys at all age levels, and also that substantial percent increases are taking place in all groups. Further steady improvement in the percentages of girls attending school at all levels was forecast by the Ministry of Education.

In higher education, fewer than 20 percent of the total enrollment are women (table 23). In agriculture, commerce, engineering, law, and veterinary medicine, women account for fewer than 10 percent of the students. In education, women constitute over 35 percent of the enrollment, and in medicine not quite 25 percent. Almost 90 percent of the women in college are enrolled in arts or in science.

---

[8] Ibid. p. 317.

[9] Ministry of Education. *Report of the Education Commission: 1964–66.* 1966. p. 292–93. For further recommendations on language by this Commission, see appendix C, section VI.

[10] Ministry of Education. *Review of Education in India: 1947–61.* 1961. p. 147–58.

[11] Ministry of Education. *Annual Report: 1965–66.* 1967. p. 3–4.

Table 23.—*Number of higher education students, by field of study and by sex; and percent of women students in each field: 1963–64*

Field of study	Total	Men	Women	
			Number	Percent of total in col. 2
1	2	3	4	5
Total_____	1,384,697	1,126,184	[1] 258,513	
Agriculture_____	41,116	41,045	71	0.2
Arts [2]_____	579,049	412,963	166,086	28.7
Commerce_____	130,578	128,695	1,883	1.4
Education_____	26,727	17,195	9,532	35.7
Engineering and technology_____	73,015	72,501	514	0.7
Law_____	29,571	28,519	1,052	3.6
Medicine_____	54,708	41,939	12,769	23.3
Science_____	435,925	373,042	62,883	14.4
Veterinary science_____	5,624	5,581	43	0.8
Other_____	8,384	4,704	3,680	43.9

SOURCE OF DATA: University Grants Commission. *Basic Facts and Figures: 1963–64.* 1964. p. 34.
[1] This number represents 18.7 percent of the number in col. 2.
[2] Includes oriental learning.

Of the four Institutes of Technology responding to an inquiry of the University Grants Commission, two (at Kharagpur and Madras) indicated they had women enrolled and two (at Delhi and Kanpur) indicated that they did not. Three of the agricultural universities (Orissa, Punjab, and Uttar Pradesh) indicated no women students and one (Rajasthan) a few women. S.N.D.T. Women's University reported no men and Gurukul Kangri Vishwavidyalaya reported no women. All other institutions reported both men and women students.

The percent of women students of the total enrollment in each institution varies from less than one percent to more than 20 percent in 17 universities, and over 30 percent in six universities, with Visva Bharati leading with 45.4 percent women.[12] Several new colleges are established each year for women only. Twenty-four such women's colleges were started in 1962–63 bringing the total number to 235 as of that date.[13] The Education Commission reporting that women students represented 13 percent of the total university enrollment in 1965–66, recommended that

> the proportion of women students to the total enrolment at this stage should be increased to 33 per cent during the next ten years to meet the requirements for educated women in different fields.[14]

The practice concerning segregated colleges varies from State to State, with Maharashtra, for example, preferring mixed colleges while Madras prefers separate colleges. The Education Commission points out that there does not appear to be any special justification for segregated colleges for women at the postgraduate level since: "Here men and women students should work together under the best guidance that is available." [15] The

[12] *Handbook of Indian Universities.* Compiled by the United States Education Foundation in India. Delhi: Allied Publishers, 1963. p. 6–9.
[13] University Grants Commission. *Annual Report: 1962–63.* 1964. p. 20.
[14] Ministry of Education. *Report of the Education Commission: 1964–66.* 1966. p. 313. For further comment on women's education by the Education Commission, see appendix C, sections X (under Scholarships) and XII.
[15] Ibid.

primary occupations for which women are preparing in college are the same as anywhere else: teaching, social work, nursing, home science, dietetics, and institutional management.

Indian women have contributed not only to family life but to cultural, educational, and political leadership through the ages. The University Education Commission said that there could not be "an educated people without educated women . . . . and that if education had to be limited to men or women, that opportunity should be given to women, for then it would most surely be passed on to the next generation." [16] The deity of the Hindu Pantheon chosen for knowledge, the creative arts, and the intellectual life was the goddess Sarasvati.

Education of the Disadvantaged

Mahatma Gandhi repeatedly called on the Indian people to cease' the inhuman treatment of "untouchables" and other backward people. When the Constituent Assembly unaminously approved the outlawing of "untouchability" there was an immediate ovation to Gandhi. The Assembly included among the Constitution's Directive Principles of State Policy the specific injunction:

> The State shall promote with special care the educational and economic interests of the weaker sections of the people, and, in particular, of the Scheduled Castes and the Scheduled Tribes, and shall protect them from social injustice and all forms of exploitation.[17]

The Ministry of Education has developed procedures for selecting the most eligible young men and women for financial aid. The amount of such scholarship aid has risen from $108,000 in 1947 to $2,989,000 in 1966–67; of this latter figure, $40,000 was set aside for overseas scholarships.[18] The Education Commission has recommended overall program increases and administrative decentralization to the States and universities.

Financing Higher Education

India has already demonstrated its commitment to financial support for educational development. During the period of the first three Five-Year Plans (1950–51—1965–66), expenditures for education increased at the rate of 11.7 percent annually—more than twice the 5.4 percent annual growth in the national income during the same period.

Within total educational expenditures, the place of higher education has inproved. The expenditure for higher education constituted 24.5 percent of all educational expenditures in 1950–51 and 32.6 percent in 1965–66.[19]

While it is difficult to find comparable statistics on educational expenditures over the years, the following figures give some idea of the large

---

[16] Ministry of Education. *Report of the University Education Commission* (Reprint of 1950 edition). Delhi: Manager of Publications, 1962. I:393.

[17] *The Constitution of India.* Part IV, article 46.

[18] Figure for 1947 from Ministry of Education. *Scholarships for Castes and Tribes and other Backward Classes.* 1952. p. 14.

Figures for 1966–67 from Ministry of Education. *Annual Report: 1965–66.* 1967. p. 103.

[19] Ministry of Education. *Report of the Education Commission: 1964–66.* 1966. p. 466, 468.

increases in funds allocated for higher education since 1950, and also the financial goals which the Education Commission envisioned: [20]

Year	Annual expenditures for higher education (in equivalent dollars) *
1950–51	$56,100,400
1957–58	72,646,789
1958–59	83,651,894
1959–60	95,401,246
1960–61	108,938,718
1961–62	122,448,649
1962–63	135,600,000
1965–66	390,798,200
1975–76	562,936,100
1985–86	449,606,500

* Figures for years through 1965–66 have been converted from rupees to dollars on a 5-to-1 basis; for years after 1965–66 on a 7.5-to-1 basis, with rounded figures.

The great increase in projected expenditures reflects an anticipated increase in the number of college students and in costs per student. Total enrollments in colleges and universities are expected to reach 2,202,000 by 1975–76 and 4,160,000 by 1985–86. At the same time, average annual costs per student to the university will probably rise as follows: [21]

Field of study	1965–66	1975–76	1985–86*
Undergraduate			
Arts or commerce	$65	$97	$122
Science	233	200	267
Postgraduate			
Arts or commerce	-----	-----	480
Science	-----	-----	800

* Figures for years through 1965–66 have been converted from rupees to dollars on a 5-to-1 basis; for years after 1965–66 on a 7.5-to-1 basis, with rounded figures.

In 1960–61, the percent of expenditures coming from student fees was 37.4 for internal university teaching departments, 48.5 for colleges of arts and sciences, and 22.2 for professional colleges. [22]

Accurate information on college costs is not easily available for most institutions of higher education. The Education Commission published a summary table giving average fees paid per student at different stages and in different fields. Students attending colleges of arts and sciences pay an average annual fee of about $38; students in professional institutions pay an average annual fee of about $48. [23] Board and room charges for engineering and technical colleges indicate a national average of approximately $16 to $20 per year for lodging and about $75 for board. [24] Including costs for books and incidentals and excluding clothing, entertainment, and travel, total college costs for a student amount to an average of $130 to $175 per year. Fees for final degree examinations may add as much as $20 more. Even at these rates, low in comparison with United States rates, many young men and women with small family incomes experience real economic

---

[20] Figures for 1950–51, 1965–66, 1975–76, and 1985–86 from Ibid p. 467–68, 482.

Figures for 1957–62 through 1961–62 from Ministry of Education. *Report off the Committee of Members of Parliament on Higher Education.* 1964. p. 7.

Figures for 1962–63 from Ministry of Information and Broadcasting. *India—A Reference Annual.* 1965. p. 72.

For further comment by the Education Commission, see appendix C, section V.

[21] Ministry of Education. *Report of the Education Commission: 1964–66.* 1966. Enrollments and costs, p. 509 and p. 304 respectively.

[22] Ibid. p. 110.

[23] Ibid.

[24] Ministry of Education. *Facilities for Technical Education in India.* 1965. Vol. II.

difficulty in attending college. A recent estimate of income level in India indicates that "more than 60 percent of the people in India have an income of less than $4 per month."[25]

The Education Commission thinks that fees should not be regarded as a source of revenue for education. In fact, income from fees droppd to 15.3 percent of the total income for education. Breaking the figures down into percentages by levels of education, upper primary schools derived more than seven percent from fees, secondary schools almost 40 percent, and at the level of higher education 37.3 percent. The Commission gave priority to the abolition of fees at the primary and secondary stages because the Indian Constitution calls for free as well as compulsory education for every child to the age of 14. It is doubtful that fees can be eliminated as a dependable source of income for higher education institutions in the near future. The Commission however recommended free college studentships for 30 percent of the total enrollment and for members of backward classes;[26] and expressed the hope that by 1975–76 at least 15 percent of all undergraduate and 25 percent of all postgraduate students would be receiving scholarships, and that by 1985–86 the proportions would be 25 percent for undergraduate students and 50 percent for graduate students.[27]

Student Life

The declared goal of much of the unrest and protest on Indian university campuses during the last few decades has been improvement of living conditions for both men and women students, especially for the latter. In 1950, having discovered deplorable conditions in both boarding and lodging facilities, the University Education Commission recommended that universities require their related colleges to meet definite minimum standards of sanitation, space, and furnishing for a certain proportion of their student bodies. By 1963–64, less than one in five college students in India lived in a dormitory (table 24). The Commission pointed out that living facilities should provide educational opportunities for social growth and for student-faculty association, and that—

> No single factor has a more vital effect upon the atmosphere and morale of a college or a university than the prevalent conditions under which students live.[28]

In respect to other subjects of student welfare, the University Education Commission found that the type of student government "used effectively in some universities and colleges in the United States" [29] was operating in a few Indian colleges with excellent results. Having described the functions of the dean of students in the United States, the Commission recommended that each college and university in India establish such an office. It also suggested an Advisory Board of Student Welfare to be of "real assistance in solving student problems and promoting student welfare." [30] Including the

---

[25] Inter-University Board of India and Ceylon. *University News.* April 1966. p. 5.
[26] Ministry of Education. *Report of the Education Commission: 1964–66.* 1966. p. 112.
[27] Ibid. p. 116.
[28] Ministry of Education. *Report of the University Education Commission* (Reprint of 1950 edition). Delhi: Manager of Publications, 1962. I:373.
[29] Ibid. p. 382.
[30] Ibid. p. 388.

Table 24.—*Selected data on the staff-student ratio and the residential facilities of students, by university: 1963–64; and on teachers, by university: 1964–65*

[- - - - - - indicates source did not show any figures]

University [1]	1963–64					1964–65		
	Number of students	Number of teachers [2]	Number of students per teacher [3]	Number of students in dormitories	Percent of students in dormitories [4]	Number of teachers	Number of staff quarters	Percent of teachers in staff quarters [5]
	2	3	4	5	6	7	8	9
Total	1,184,697	60,031		219,263		76,615	10,174	
Agra	58,189	3,458	16.8	7,418	12.7	3,881	357	9.2
Aligarh Muslim	5,148	413	12.5	2,693	52.3	478	114	23.8
Allahabad	9,662	504	19.2	3,703	38.3	557	147	26.4
Andhra	34,065	2,108	16.2	7,290	21.4	2,583	190	7.4
Andhra Pradesh Agricultural						284	1	0.4
Annamalai	3,522	288	12.2	2,405	68.3	364	113	31.4
Banaras Hindu	8,732	713	12.2	3,439	39.4	789	339	43.0
Bangalore						1,084	9	0.8
Baroda	11,191	428	26.1	2,305	20.6	676	158	23.4
Bhagalpur	20,286	972	20.9	2,622	12.9	1,148	1,088	9.4
Bihar	30,694	1,206	25.5	3,030	9.9	1,425	166	11.6
Bombay	55,669	1,895	29.4	3,829	6.9	3,214	126	3.9
Burdwan	24,083	1,066	22.6	4,332	18.0	1,271	266	20.9
Calcutta	120,829	5,745	21.0	10,727	8.9	6,600	432	6.5
Delhi	26,932	1,608	16.7	2,751	10.2	1,897	292	15.4
Gauhati	46,239	1,975	23.4	6,877	14.9	2,636	361	13.7
Gorakhpur	16,800	900	18.7	1,414	8.4	1,087	125	11.5
Gujarat	54,744	1,845	29.7	7,623	13.9	3,070	272	8.9
Indira Kala Sangeet Vishwavidyalaya	91	4	22.8	[6] 16	[5] 17.6	7	N.A.	N.A.
Indore						536	21	3.9
Jabalpur	11,628	639	18.2	2,771	23.8	627	166	26.5
Jadavpur	3,956	302	13.1	746	18.9	345	30	8.7
Jammu and Kashmir	11,407	654	17.4	1,581	13.9	813	22	2.7
Jawaharlal Nehru Krishi Vishwavidyalaya						263	96	36.5
Jiwaji						642	49	7.6
Jodhpur	5,384	307	17.5	1,311	24.3	394	9	2.3
Kalayani	662	86	7.7	662	100.0	121	73	60.3

See footnotes at end of table.

Table 24.—Selected data on the staff-student ratio and the residential facilities of students, by university: 1963–64; and on teachers, by university: 1964–65 (continued)

University [1]	1963–64					1964–65		
	Number of students	Number of teachers [2]	Number of students per teacher [3]	Number of students in dormitories	Percent of students in dormitories [4]	Number of teachers	Number of staff quarters	Percent of teachers in staff quarters [5]
1	2	3	4	5	6	7	8	9
Kameshwara Singh Darbhanga Sanskrit	5,216	652	8.0	---	---	1,457	250	17.2
Karnatak	21,606	1,117	19.3	3,694	17.1	4,254	318	7.5
Kerala	66,323	3,065	21.6	18,299	27.6			
Kurukshetra	1,301	119	10.9	352	27.1	168	101	60.1
Lucknow	15,767	882	17.9	2,732	17.3	1,116	118	10.6
Madras	70,671	4,084	17.3	28,505	40.3	5,989	805	13.4
Magadh	24,021	865	27.8	944	3.9	1,017	49	4.8
Marathwada	10,912	517	21.1	2,170	19.9	684	63	9.2
Mysore	46,476	2,192	21.2	6,628	14.3	1,787	163	9.1
Nagpur	34,805	1,556	22.4	4,157	11.9	1,929	98	5.1
North Bengal	8,035	421	19.1	1,525	19.0	498	105	21.1
Orissa University of Agriculture and Technology	986	97	10.2			106	150	141.5
Osmania	27,536	1,575	17.5	2,881	10.6	2,083	121	5.8
Panjabi	4,124	300	13.7	1,366	33.1	409	45	11.0
Patna	10,946	549	19.9	3,349	30.6	645	73	11.3
Poona	27,808	1,112	25.0	5,443	19.6	1,791	130	7.3
Punjab	61,634	3,256	18.9	14,286	23.2	4,000	713	17.8
Punjab Agricultural	1,399	135	10.4	810	57.9	534	172	32.2
Rabindra Bharati	182	22	8.3			54	N.A.	N.A.
Rajasthan	31,309	2,099	14.9	6,915	22.1	1,945	254	13.1
Ranchi	22,788	1,075	21.2	7,817	34.3	1,285	415	32.3
Ravi Shankar						1,733	141	19.2
Roorkee	2,333	163	14.3	2,333	100.0	218	138	63.3
Sardar Vallabhbhai Vidyapeeth	7,381	314	23.5	2,889	39.1	503	163	32.4
Saugar	25,080	1,531	16.4	3,201	12.8	1,142	245	21.5
Shivaji	17,389	695	25.0	3,001	17.3	1,043	63	6.0
S.N.D.T. Women's	4,624	249	18.6	325	7.0	313	5	1.6
Sri Venkateswara	11,471	864	13.1	4,447	38.8	1,212	178	11.4
Udaipur	1,116	102	10.9	627	56.2	352	27	7.7
Utkal	21,393	1,166	18.3	5,499	25.7	1,698	512	30.2

Uttar Pradesh Agricultural	843	82	10.3	843	100.0	103	82	7.96
Varanaseya Sanskrit Vishwavidyalaya	[6]691	[6]38	[6]18.2	[6]244	[6]35.3	75	1	1.3
Vikram	38,025	1,863	20.4	3,795	10.0	986	84	8.5
Visva Bharati	693	158	4.4	641	92.5	199	140	70.4

given were founded in 1964.
[2] Tutors and demonstrators not included.
[3] The average number of students for each teacher in all universities is 19.7.
[4] The average percent of students in dormitories for all universities is 18.5.
[5] The average percent of teachers in staff quarters in all universities is 13.3.
[6] Information incomplete.

SOURCE OF DATA: Figures for 1963–64 from University Grants Commission. *Basic Facts and Figures: 1963–64.* 1964. p. 45–46, 69. Figures for 1964–65 from University Grants Commission. *Report on Standards of University Education.* Delhi, 1965. p. 244–45.

[1] Includes all State universities founded by 1964 and the four central universities "declared of national importance." The six universities for which no 1963–64 data are

vice-chancellor as chairman, other academic and student personnel administrators, faculty representatives, and prominent citizens,[31] the Advisory Board would give greater attention to the personal and social welfare of students (including counselling, guidance, health, and placement services) and would also help local and national student organizations make positive contributions to campus life.

In 1966, the Education Commission strongly supported the earlier report and made similar recommendations, including greater emphasis on new student orientation and on financial aid for needy students (appendix C, sections IX and X).

Regarding the general student unrest in Indian colleges and universities, the Education Commission reviewed the situation and suggested some causes:

> Briefly, there have been many ugly strikes and demonstrations—often without any justification—leading to violence, walk-outs from classrooms and examination halls, ticketless travel, clashes with the police, burning of buses and cinema houses and, sometimes, even manhandling of teachers and university officers. There is a variety of causes which has brought about these ugly expressions of uncivilized behavior, e.g., the uncertain future facing educated young men leading to a sense of frustration which breeds irresponsibility; the mechanical and unsatisfactory nature of many curricular programmes; the totally inadequate facilities for teaching and learning in the large bulk of institutions, the poor student-teacher contact—many a student goes through the entire undergraduate course without exchanging a word with his teachers; the inefficiency and lack of scholarship on the part of many teachers and their failure to interest themselves in the students' problems; the absence of imagination and tact combined with firmness on the part of heads of institutions; the prevalence of what has come to be known as teacher politics in some colleges and universities, the attempt by political parties to interfere in their work, and by no means the least, the impact of the conditions of public life in the country, the falling standards of discipline among the adults and a weakening of their civic consciousness and integrity.[32]

Both the Education Commission and the University Grants Commission found a widespread belief that the various manifestations of student unrest reflect a common "transitional situation in the world as a whole following the war [and are the] result of new democratic and socialistic urges that have disturbed old cultural patterns without having brought into being new widely accepted modes of behaviour." [33]

Whether there is a common cause or not, the evidence of protest and unrest is world-wide.

Teachers

Recruitment

In no area of employment, public or private, is the effective recruitment of persons of high quality more important than in the teaching staffs of

---

[31] Ibid.
[32] Ibid. p. 296–97.
[33] University Grants Commission. *Report on the Problem of Student Indiscipline in Indian Universities.* Delhi, 1960. p. 4.

colleges and universities. High quality performance as a college or university teacher affects generations of college students who in turn provide the leaders of a nation. In India recognition of the importance of the teaching staffs is shown in the high qualifications universities establish for persons appointed to the three common grades of lecturer, reader, and professor. A lecturer must have acquired a master's degree. A reader must also have spent 5 to 10 years in either teaching, research, writing, or some combination of these. A professor (usually only one to a department) is expected to have high academic qualifications, 5 to 10 years of experience, scholarly reputation, and the ability to guide research.

Hiring qualified teachers is made difficult by the following problems:

1. *Competition from the Indian Government and industries.*
   (The rapidly expanding development programs have made both the Government and industry keen competitors for the most able scholars and research workers.)

2. *Competition from foreign universities and industries.*
   (A sizable proportion of Indian scholars and teachers who go abroad stay for indefinite periods, accept positions in industry, universities, or other institutions, and some even seek foreign citizenship, remaining away permanently).

3. *Cumbersome university hiring procedures.*
   (Hiring often involves formal and informal contacts with both university officers and governing bodies and also sometimes with the Public Service Commission of the State concerned. For example, the hiring process for one college involves advertisement for candidates in various newspapers by the Public Service Commission, assistance by an education officer of the State government, and almost no involvement by the principal of the college.)

4. *Lack of teacher mobility within the country.*
   (Language, other regional factors, or procedural problems make transferral of a teacher from one institution to another difficult. A college teacher must apply for transfer to another institution both through his own department head or principal and also through his employer (the State or university); a university teacher applies usually only within the university, but is subject at times to nepotism or political pressure. Increased mobility not only would make recruitment easier but would also provide a healthy cross-fertilization of ideas in various fields of knowledge.)

Because of generally lower salary scales in affiliated colleges than in university departments and constituent colleges, the former have an extra disadvantage in securing able teachers. It has been recommended that staff members throughout a university and its related colleges be paid on the same scale for the same grade and level of teaching.

Salaries

Responsible Indian leaders recognize the importance of teachers' salaries. The 1965 pay scale recommended by the University Grants Commission is from 20 to 60 percent higher than its 1956 recommendations (table 25); it has been accepted and put into effect by 42 universities, and is being seriously considered by others.[34]

---

[34] University Grants Commission. *Annual Report: 1964–65.* 1966. p. 25.

The Education Commission has recently set goals even higher than those of the University Grants Commission (table 25), and has also suggested that teachers be allowed to keep additional earnings from consultant or research work up to 50 percent of their annual salaries.[35] The Ministry of Agriculture has agreed to the University Grants Commission salary scales for the agricultural universities.

Teaching Load

Of major importance to many teachers is their teaching load, often measured by the number of hours per week devoted to lecture, tutorial, or seminar work. Universities vary widely in their practice on this factor, with loads ranging from 4 to 6 hours to 20 hours per week for lecturers. Another measure of the load is the student-teacher ratio, where again there is much variation among universities (table 24).

Staff Housing

Most universities make some effort to furnish staff housing (table 24). In 1964–65, a total of 19 had provided quarters for at least 20 percent of their staffs, and one institution (Orissa Agricultural University) reported facilities for 100 percent of its staff. The Education Commission suggested that the target for the next 20 years should be to provide residential accommodation for about 50 percent of the teachers in university departments and constituent colleges and for 20 percent of the teachers in affiliated colleges.[36]

Other Benefits

The University Grants Commission has taken the following steps to provide other teacher benefits:

1. Inaugurated a plan to encourage foreign travel by teachers, if universities pay 50 percent of the cost.

2. Contributed regularly to retirement funds for university teachers.

3. Influenced universities to raise their retirement age to 60, with possible extension to age 63 and in special cases to age 65.

4. Contributed regularly to enable universities and colleges to pay an honorarium to retired teachers for continued teaching and research. (More than 200 retired teachers had been included in this plan by the end of the school year 1965–66.) [37]

A growing interest in teachers' associations of all kinds has produced several strong professional groups, some publishing professional journals and holding stimulating conferences, and others concerned more with teacher

---

[35] Ministry of Education. *Report of the Education Commission: 1964–66.* 1966. p. 62. For further recommendations by the Education Commission, see appendix C, section XI.
[36] Ibid.
[37] University Grants Commission. *Annual Report: 1965–66.* 1967. p. 27.

Table 25.—*Range of salary per month for university and college teaching staff adopted or recommended by various commissions and organizations: Selected years, 1956–66*

[———— indicates source did not show any figures. Amounts in equivalent U.S. dollars]

Commission or organization (year, and whether recommended or adopted)	University department or constituent college				College principal or other chief administrators	Affiliated college			
	Professor	Reader	Lecturer	Instructor		Head of department	Reader	Senior lecturer	Junior lecturer
1	2	3	4	5	6	7	8	9	10
University Grants Commission (1956—recommended)	$160–250	$100–160	$50–100	$30 and up	$120–160				
Ministry of Scientific Research and Cultural Affairs (1963—adopted)					(1) (2)	(3) (2)	2 $120–230	2 $60–$170	2 $60–$112
Indian Institutes of Technology (1964—adopted)	5 260– 320 / 320– 380	6 220– 260	6 140– 250	6 80– 190 / 75– 130	4 160– 250 / 400– 500 / 120– 160	4 $120–$200			
University Grants Commission (1965—recommended)	200– 300	140– 220	80– 160		120– 160			4 70–170	4 70– 170
Education Commission (1966—recommended)	5 220– 320 / 320– 360	140– 250	80– 190		7 140– 220 / 160– 250 / 200– 300				

SOURCE OF DATA: Figures for University Grants Commission (1956) from University Grants Commission. *Report of the University Grants Commission: 1953–1957.* 1958. p. 23.

Figures for Ministry of Scientific Research and Cultural Affairs (1963) from Ministry of Education. *Technical Education in India Today.* 1963. p. 49.

Figures for Indian Institutes of Technology (1964) from University Grants Commission. *Handbook of Universities in India: 1963.* 1964.

Figures for University Grants Commission (1965) from University Grants Commission. *Annual Report: 1964–65.* 1966. p. 26, 27.

Figures for Education Commission (1966) from Ministry of Education. *Report of the Education Commission: 1964–66.* 1966. p. 27.

1 Same as chief engineer in a State's Public Works Department.

2 Adopted only in technical institutions granting the first degree, excluding the Indian Institutes of Technology. The term used here for approximate equivalent of head of department is professor; of reader, assistant professor; of senior lecturer, lecturer; and of junior lecturer, associate lecturer.

3 Same as superintendent of engineering in a State's Public Works Department.

4 Adopted only in polytechnical institutions. The term used here for approximate equivalent of senior lecturer is lecturer; of junior lecturer, instructor, senior scale.

5 Source did not indicate the applicability of each of the two ranges.

6 The term used here for approximate equivalent of reader is associate professor; of lecturer, assistant professor; of instructor, lecturer and associate lecturer.

7 The first range is for principal I, the second for principal II, the third for principal III.

115

salaries and welfare items. The Education Commission urged the growth and expansion of teachers' associations.[38]

Beginning in 1964, the University Grants Commission sponsored a series of Summer Institutes for College Teachers, mainly on scientific or mathematical subjects. For these Institutes, the United States Agency for International Development (U.S.AID) has provided not only considerable equipment and educational materials, but also United States scientists to serve as teachers. The number of schools, Indian teachers in attendance, and United States scientists teaching during the years 1964 to 1967 were as follows: [39]

Year	Schools	Indian teachers	U.S. scientists
1964	16	659	16
1965	29	1,052	37
1966	34	1,235	79
1967	49	1,867	55

International Exchange

India participates widely in international cultural exchange activities, both sending and receiving. In 1961–62, more than 3,500 students from more than 60 countries attended Indian universities (table 26).

Indians also go abroad to study in increasing numbers: [40]

Year	Number of Indians studying abroad
1947–48	800
1952–53	1,200
1955–56	3,400
1958–59	3,800
1963–64	13,000

[38] Ministry of Education. *Report of the Education Commission: 1964–66*. 1966. p. 65.

[39] University Grants Commission. Annual Reports for 1965–66, 1966–67, and 1967–68. p. 18, 16, and 14, respectively.

[40] Ministry of Education. *Educational Activities of the Government of India: 1963*. 1963. p. 124.

Table 26.—*Number of foreign students in general and professional courses at Indian universities, by students' home country*: 1961–62

[_____ indicates source did not show any figures]

Country	University courses		
	Total	General [1]	Professional [2]
Total_____	**3,571**	**2,494**	**1,077**
Aden_____	9	4	5
Afghanistan_____	6	3	3
Australia_____	1	1	_____
Austria_____	1	_____	1
Belgium_____	1	1	_____
Bhutan_____	14	8	6
Brazil_____	7	7	_____
British Guiana_____	9	1	8
Burma_____	58	28	30
Cambodia_____	8	8	_____
Canada_____	1	1	_____
Ceylon_____	633	543	90
China_____	9	6	3
East Africa_____	374	206	168
Ethiopia_____	9	4	5
Fiji (Island)_____	33	20	13
France_____	3	3	_____
Ghana_____	6	5	1
Guinea_____	2	2	_____
Holland_____	1	_____	1
Hong Kong_____	1	1	_____
Indonesia_____	16	9	7
Iran_____	15	10	5
Iraq_____	9	5	4
Ireland_____	1	1	_____
Italy_____	1	1	_____
Japan_____	12	9	3
Jordan_____	4	3	1
Korea_____	3	_____	3
Lebanon_____	1	_____	1
Malaya_____	353	228	125
Maldive (Island)_____	1	1	_____
Malta_____	1	1	_____
Mauritius (Island)_____	55	27	28
Nepal_____	589	297	292
Nigeria_____	11	1	10
North Borneo_____	2	_____	2
Nyasaland_____	3	1	2
Pakistan_____	590	564	26
Persian Gulf_____	1	1	_____
Philippines_____	4	2	2
Poland_____	3	3	_____
Rhodesia_____	9	5	4
Rumania_____	2	2	_____
Saudi Arabia_____	3	2	_____
Seychelles_____	1	_____	1
Sikkim_____	39	22	17
Singapore_____	4	3	1
Sudan_____	8	3	5
South Africa_____	33	16	17
Thailand_____	95	73	22
Tibet_____	24	24	_____
Trinidad_____	11	4	7
Turkey_____	2	2	_____
U.A.R._____	2	1	1
U.K._____	3	2	1
U.S.A._____	26	24	2
Vietnam_____	1	_____	1
West Germany_____	1	1	_____
West Indies_____	15	10	5
Yugoslavia_____	3	2	1
Zanzibar_____	18	8	10
Others_____	410	274	136

SOURCE OF DATA: University Grants Commission. *Basic Facts and Figures: 1963–64.* 1964. p. 95–96.
[1] Includes arts, oriental learning, and science.
[2] Includes agriculture, commerce, education, engineering and technology, law, medicine, and veterinary science.

117

4. Undergraduate Arts and Science Education

In 1967–68, the number of students working toward the B.A., the B.Comm., and the B.Sc. comprised 84.6 percent of the total number of higher education students (table 15). Those working only toward the B.A. and B.Sc. comprised 74.7 percent.

Indian students in arts and science pursue fewer subjects than do comparable students in the United States, but pursue those subjects quite thoroughly. In the external examination system usual in Indian universities, the examining university determines not only the number and variety of courses to be completed for a particular degree, but also their content. A student is examined at the end of a particular course on the content of that course as outlined in detail in its syllabus, rather than on its content as taught in the particular college class he may attend. Thus examinations are the same for every student in a particular university taking the same course, whether in a university department or in a related college, thereby providing a fairly objective evaluation.

In most universities, examinations for a degree are given at the end of the degree program. In others, the course requirements are spaced throughout the 3-year program with one or more examinations given each year and with the successful passing of one year's examination required for admission to the next year's examination.

The requirements for the B.A. and the B.Sc. in Madras and Bombay Universities provide examples of two different systems.

Madras University [1]

A candidate for the B.A. or B.Sc. degree at Madras University is generally required to take five examinations, one in each of the following subjects:

1. English

2. Second language

3. Main subject chosen by student

---

[1] Information about requirements for the bachelor's degrees at Madras University is taken from Inter-University Board of India and Ceylon. *Universities' Handbook, India and Ceylon, 1964.* Delhi, 1965. p. 333–34.

4. Related subject chosen by student

5. Another related subject chosen by student.

B.A. Degree

For the B.A. degree, in addition to English and a second language, a student chooses a main subject and two related subjects from one of the following 11 combinations:

Main subject (One is to be chosen)	plus	Related subjects (Two are to be chosen)
Drawing and painting		History of Indian art, and history of world art.
Economics		Commerce, history, politics, and statistics
Geography		Anthropology, commerce, economics, history, philosophy, politics, psychology, and statistics.
History		Economics, geography, history of fine arts, history of Indian music, musicology and history of Western music, philosophy, and politics.
History of fine arts		Drawing and painting, general musicology and history of Indian music, general musicology and history of Western music, and history.
Indian music		A language, history, history of fine arts, musicology and history of western music, philosophy, and psychology.
Oriental culture		Comparative religion, epigraphy, ethics, iconography, Indian logic, and South Indian history.
Philosophy		Economics, history, politics, psychology, and sociology.
Politics		Economics, history, philosophy, and psychology.
Psychology		Anthropology, history of fine arts, philosophy, sociology, and statistics.
Western music		Economics, general musicology and history of Indian music, history, history of world art, philosophy, and politics.

Or instead of one of the preceding combinations a student may select one subject from each of three subject groups:

1. History	2. Anthropology	3. Economics
Law	Psychology	Geography
Philosophy	Politics	Sociology

Or finally he may substitute for the three subjects one of the following 15 languages:

Arabic	Kannada	Sanskrit
English	Latin	Syriac
French	Malayalam	Tamil
Hebrew	Marathi	Telugu
Hindi	Persian	Urdu

B.Sc. Degree

For the B.Sc. degree, in addition to English and a second language, a student chooses a main subject and two related subjects from one of the following nine combinations:

Main subject *plus* (One is to be chosen)	Related subjects (Two are to be chosen)
Botany	Chemistry and either geography, physics, or zoology
Chemistry	Physics and either botany, mathematics, or zoology
Geography	Geology and either astronomy, mathematics, physics, or statistics
Geology	Chemistry and either geography, physics, or zoology.
Mathematics	Chemistry, numerical mathematics,* physics, and statistics
Physics	Chemistry and mathematics
Physiology	Botany, chemistry, physics, and zoology
Statistics	Economics, mathematics, numerical mathematics, and physics
Zoology	Chemistry and either botany, geography, geology, or physiology

* To be taken along with statistics only.

Bombay University [2]

At Bombay University the B.A. and B.Sc. degrees are based on a 2-year degree program taken after successful completion of a 2-year intermediate course in the arts (part II, chapter 3, under section The Educational Ladder).

B.A. Degree

Five subjects are required for the B.A. degree, and each subject includes two courses:

- English (One of the two courses must include composition.)

[2] *Handbook of the University of Bombay.* 1963. II:2:74–142.

- Four other subjects, selected from at least three of the following subject groups:[3]

1. *Ancient Indian culture:*
   Art and religion of ancient India, cultural history of India, literature and philosophy of ancient India.

2. *Anthropology:*
   Cultural anthropology, and physical anthropology.

3. *Economics:*[4]
   Economic history, political science, principles of economics, society and social evolution, and statistical methods.

4. *History:*
   Ancient and medieval India, ancient Europe, constitutional history, cultural history of India, English history, Islamic culture, modern Europe, modern India, Persian history, and political science.

5. *Languages:*[5]
   Classical Oriental and European: Arabic, Ardh-Magadhi, Avesta-Pahlavi, Greek, Hebrew, Latin, Pali, Persian, and Sanskrit.

   Modern European: English, French, German, Italian, Portuguese, and Spanish.

   Modern Indian: Gujarati, Hindi, Kannada, Marathi, Sindhi, and Urdu.

6. *Mathematics:*
   Pure mathematics, applied mathematics, algebra and geometry, calculus and differential equations, and statistics.

7. *Philosophy:*
   Education, experimental psychology, history of philosophy, moral and social philosophy, and psychology.

8. *Politics:*
   Constitutional history, political science, and public administration and local government.

9. *Psychology:*[6]
   Advanced psychology, and psychology.

10. *Science:*
    Botany, chemistry, general science, geography, geology, physics, and zoology.

11. *Sociology:*
    Society and social evolution.

Appendix D provides samples of syllabuses both for English and for one subject within each of three subject groups.

B.Sc. Degree

The pattern of requirements for the B.Sc. degree at Bombay University differs slightly from that for the B.A.. For the B.Sc., a student selects any two of a list of science subjects, designating one of them as the principal and the other as the subsidiary subject. The syllabus for any subject

---

[3] Identical subjects under two separate groups are not considered two separate subjects.
[4] Principles of economics and statistical methods must not both be chosen.
[5] Both courses in each of the three subjects must be based on modern texts of prose, poetry, and drama. In Modern Indian, one of the courses must be on poetry and the other on drama and prose.
[6] Those who choose the subject advanced psychology must also take the subject psychology.

designated principal is more detailed and covers more topics than the syllabus for the same subject when designated subsidiary. The 13 subjects listed are as follows:

1. Animal physiology

2. Botany

3. Chemistry [7]

4. Comparative anatomy and embryology

5. Economics (as a subsidiary subject only)

6. Experimental psychology

7. Geography

8. Geology

9. Mathematics

10. Microbiology

11. Physics [7]

12. Statistics (as a principal subject only) [8]

13. Zoology

---

[7] Any student choosing chemistry or physics as either a principal or subsidiary subject must take a college course in calculus if he has not chosen mathematics for one of his subjects for the intermediate examination in science.
[8] Economics must be taken as the subsidiary subject.

5. Professional and Technical Education

India's leaders recognize the national importance of professional and technical education. The goals of India's developmental plans are an adequate supply of food, health conditions equal to the best modern medicine can provide, and high technological and industrial production; their accomplishment requires professional and technical education of an advanced nature, particularly in the fields of agriculture, medicine, and technology.

Professional and technical education programs in India begin at different levels in the educational ladder and require varying lengths of time (chart 2). Although such programs begin at the end of the higher secondary course or preuniversity year, others— such as those in education, law, and library science—require a bachelor's degree for admission. Thus some professional courses are primarily undergraduate while others are postgraduate (as in the United States).

Agriculture and Veterinary Science

Over the years India has not raised enough food to provide her children and adults with an adequate diet. Crop failure caused by drought in 1965 and 1966 led to the "New Strategy for Agricultural Development" of 1967–68—a program for improved irrigation, increased use of fertilizers, and other modern measures—but importing and rationing have nevertheless been necessary. The increase in population has been about 90 million in 11 years [1]—enough to consume the increased agricultural production that has been attained during a similar period. With present farm practices and population growth, the relative situation may not improve. One of the answers to this basic problem lies in improved methods and materials, which in turn depend on better professional and technical education.

Agriculture

The Indian Government has been encouraging the States to establish new agricultural universities with programs patterned after those of the

---

[1] From figures in part I, chapter 3, under "Population."

land-grant colleges of the United States, combining education, research, and extension services. The first such institution was established in Uttar Pradesh in 1960; the next three in the States of Orissa, Punjab, and Rajasthan in 1962; and the final two so far in Andhra Pradesh and Mysore in 1964.[2] Others are planned for Madhya Pradesh and Madras, and several recommendations have been made that each State should establish at least one such institution.

Agricultural education and research began to develop in India during the first decade of the 20th century. During those years, the Pusa Research Institute (now the Indian Agricultural Research Institute at Delhi) was founded, the Federal and Provincial Governments reorganized their agricultural departments, and the Indian Agricultural Service was started. In 1929, the Indian Council on Agricultural Research was established to promote, guide, and coordinate agriculture and animal husbandry. In 1952, the Indian Council of Agricultural Education was established, having been recommended by the Central Advisory Board of Education. An advisory body, this council coordinates and provides uniform standards for agricultural education both at the college level and below, advises State governments, and prepares model syllabuses for teaching agriculture, animal husbandry, and dairying.

By 1966, there were six agricultural universities of the land-grant pattern and others were being organized. In addition, there were approximately 60 agricultural colleges. The 1967–68 agricultural enrollment of 51,639 represents a very rapid increase—of almost 400 percent—since the 1956–57 enrollment of 10,389 (table 15). More than half the agriculture students in 1964–65 were in the State of Punjab (table 14).

At the postgraduate and research levels, the 1964–65 agricultural enrollment was only 2264 (table 27). In 1966 the Education Commission estimated that during the next 20 years India would need 100,000 additional persons (an annual average of 5,000) with postgraduate degrees in agriculture for teaching, research, and development.[3] To expand the postgraduate enrollment sufficiently to meet this need would be very difficult; to maintain and even raise the quality of postgraduate work at the same time would increase the difficulty.

An important agency guiding the development of agricultural universities is the Committee on Agricultural Universities, established by the Department of Agriculture of the Ministry of Food and Agriculture. Working closely with State agricultural officials, the Committee has helped to work out details of the legislative acts establishing agricultural universities.

Three significant recommendations have been made for the development of agricultural universities. The first was made by the Committee on Agricultural Universities, and the others by agencies including the Education Commission and the University Grants Commission:

1. *Extension services should be brought under the agricultural universities.* (Previously under State agricultural departments, extension services could

---

[2] These institutions are: Uttar Pradesh Agricultural University, Orissa University of Agriculture and Technology, Punjab Agricultural University, Udaipur University (renamed in 1963 from Rajasthan Agricultural University), Andhra Pradesh Agricultural University, and the University of Agricultural Sciences.

[3] Ministry of Education. *Report of the Education Commission: 1964–66.* 1966. p. 352.

better serve the nation's farmers by being brought into the university, so that the tested ideas of the university's research department might be passed on to the extension worker and from him to the farmer.)

2. *All colleges of agriculture, animal husbandry, and veterinary science should become constituent colleges of a university.*
   (Becoming constituent colleges, under the same board of management, colleges would have departments fully integrated with the university and curriculums and internal assessment could replace the external examinations of the affiliated college.)

3. *A commission similar to the University Grants Commission should be designated for agricultural education.*
   (Since agricultural institutions are the responsibility not of the Ministry of Education but of the Ministry of Food and Agriculture, they are not related to the University Grants Commission in the same way as are other education institutions. The Education Commission has recommended an Indian Council on Agricultural Research to coordinate agricultural institutions, and suggested some overlapping of membership with the University Grants Commission.)[4]

Veterinary Science

In 1964–65, veterinary science was taught in 18 professional colleges affiliated to universities in 14 States. Six such colleges were founded before Independence, the earliest in 1886 and 1893. Four have each become, and others will become, part of an agricultural university. Enrollment in veterinary colleges in 1964–65 was 5711, only a 30 percent increase over the 1956–57 enrollment (table 15). The one postgraduate veterinary institution, the Post Graduate College of Animal Sciences at Izatnagar in Uttar Pradesh (home of the Indian Veterinary Research Institute), had an enrollment in 1963–64 of 296 and of 372 in 1964–65 (table 27).

Engineering and Technology

In 1847, 10 years before the first Indian universities, Thomson Engineering College was established at Roorkee to train civil engineers. Although never affiliated with a university, it granted diplomas considered equivalent to degrees. In 1856, the Calcutta College of Civil Engineering was opened in Calcutta; and 2 years later a school renamed the Poona College of Engineering became affiliated with Bombay University, and a school in Madras renamed the Guindy College of Engineering became affiliated with Madras University. Mechanical and chemical engineering were first offered at Jadavpur University in 1908 and 1921 respectively; and electrical engineering at the Indian Institute of Science at Bangalore in 1915.[5]

By Independence in 1947, a total of 17 engineering colleges [6] with 5,348 students had been established (table 15). By 1964–65, a total of 133 such colleges [7] were teaching almost 78,114 students (table 15), of which 1,719 were at the postgraduate and research levels (table 27). In 1967–68, en-

[4] Ibid. p. 367.
[5] Ministry of Education. *Report of the University Education Commission* (Reprint of 1950 edition). Delhi: Manager of Publications, 1962. I :224–225.
[6] Ibid. p. 230.
[7] Inter-University Board of India and Ceylon. *University News.* May 1966. p. 14.

rollment in engineering and technology had reached 104,266, an increase of almost 400 percent over the 1956–57 enrollment of 21,237 (table 15).

Such an increase is necessary to meet India's rising demand for skilled graduates in engineering and technology, particularly in view of the high percent of students not completing their courses (20 percent in engineering and as high as 40 percent in some other courses).[8]

Engineering colleges have had difficulty in securing enough teachers and in providing them with sufficient practical experience to make them fully effective in terms of the professional and vocational objectives of their students. In 1963, as high as 38.9 percent of the teaching positions in 83 engineering colleges were unfilled.[9]

The All-India Council for Technical Education

The main advisory body for both the Federal and State Governments regarding engineering and technical education is the All-India Council for Technical Education. With approximately 80 members, it has established

> . . . seven Boards of Technical Studies in specified fields; four Regional Committees, one each for North, South, East, and West zones into which the country is divided for this purpose, and a Coordinating Committee that coordinates the work of the various Committees and Boards and has the power to take decisions on behalf of the Council when it cannot meet.[10]

The boards of studies develop standards and courses in various subjects to guide the engineering institutions. Each regional committee surveys facilities in its region in order to determine need. Special committees advise the Council concerning needs at the postgraduate level.

After surveying the past work of the Council, the Education Commission in 1966 concluded that while it "performs a useful function as a high level policy formulating agency" [11] it would be desirable to place the "responsibility for stimulation and organization" on the universities themselves. As in the field of agricultural education, the Commission recommended that an organization resembling the University Grants Commission be established for engineering education, overlapping membership with the University Grants Commission. The Council would still coordinate activities of engineering institutions with Federal industrial agencies.[12]

The Indian Institutes of Technology

In 1945 the Federal Government appointed the Sarkar Committee to consider whether India should have several regional technical institutions or one central all-India technological institution with affiliated colleges. The

---

[8] Institute of Applied Manpower Research. *Fact Book on Manpower.* Delhi, 1963.

[9] Ministry of Education. *Report of the Education Commission: 1964–66.* 1966. p. 379.

[10] G. K. Chandiramani. *Technological Education in India* (Ministry of Education Publication No. 239). Delhi: Manager of Publications, 1957. p. 3.

[11] Ministry of Education. *Report of the Education Commission: 1964–66.* 1966. p. 386.

[12] Ibid.

Sarkar Committee recommended that at least four regional institutions should be established—one each in the North, East, South, and West. The Government accepted the establishment of two, one each in the East and the West.

In 1950 the first regional technological institution, the Indian Institute of Technology at Kharagpur, was founded; and in 1956 Parliament declared it a degree-granting institution "of national importance." Soon afterwards came the Indian Institutes of Technology at Bombay in 1958, at Kanpur and at Madras in 1959, and at Delhi in 1961. All five Institutes were incorporated as institutions "of national importance" under the Institutes of Technology Act of 1961.

Each Institute is expected to provide residence and courses of study for 1,600 undegraduate and 400 postgraduate and research students.[13] The education offered is not only theoretical but practical, because Indian industry does not provide practical training programs such as are given by industries in the United States and Britain. As the Institutes, working in close collaboration with industry, develop engineering and technical courses based on the most modern technologies, they are helping to lay the basis for an industrial economy.

Each of the five Institutes receives some international aid: the one at Bombay from the Soviet Union,[14] the one at Kanpur from the United States,[15] the one at Kharagpur from several international agencies, the one at Madras from West Germany, and the one at Delhi from Britain.

The Institutes are set apart from the typical Indian university by the following common features:

1. A unitary form of organization, which allows for fast changes of curriculum and methods.

2. Freedom to experiment and change.

3. Aid from different foreign countries and international agencies.

4. A board of governors and a director (table 17).

5. Conferences of all five directors several times a year on each other's campuses.

6. The IIT Council, set up by the Institutes of Technology Act of 1961, which approves admission standards, budgets, 5-year development plans, scales of pay, various conditions of service, and common policies concerning degrees, duration of courses, fees, scholarships, and other matters of common interest.

Numbers of students and degrees awarded in each Institute in 1965–66 were as follows:

[13] L. S. Chandrakant. *Technical Education in India Today.* Delhi: Ministry of Scientific Research and Cultural Affairs, January 1963. p. 20–21.

[14] Both directly and through the United Nations Economic, Social and Cultural Organization (UNESCO).

[15] In 1968–69, the Indian Institute of Technology at Kanpur had approximately 1,300 undergraduate students, 600 postgraduate students, and 220 teachers. The largest United States Agency for International Development (U.S. Aid) educational assistance project in the world, the Institute receives technical assistance from a consortium of nine U.S. universities: California Institute of Technology, Carnegie-Mellon University, Case Western Reserve University, Massachusetts Institute of Technology, Ohio State University, Princeton University, Purdue University, University of California, and University of Michigan. (Indian Institute of Technology, Kanpur. *Bulletin: Courses of Study, 1968–69.* Kanpur: The Institute, 1968. p. 1.)

Institute at—	Number of students	Degrees awarded Bachelor's	Master's	Ph.D
Total _____	7,984	162	270	18
Bombay _____	1,897	185	101	4
Delhi _____	1,184	---	---	--
Kanpur _____	1,100	66	---	--
Kharagpur _____	2,363	395	169	14
Madras _____	1,440	116	---	--

Enrollment at all the Institutes in 1965–66 was almost 10 percent of the total engineering and technology enrollment (85,555) for the same year (table 15).

Although not patterned after the Indian Institutes of Technology, the Indian Institute of Science (in Bangalore) was designated after Independence by the Federal Government for major development grants for advanced study and research in technology. In 1963 this institute taught over 600 postgraduate students, more than a third of the total postgraduate and research enrollment in the country (table 27). A 2-year postgraduate course leading to the master's degree, recommended for various technical fields by a special Committee on Postgraduate Engineering Education and Research, has been introduced in 10 universities.[18]

The Medical Fields

Because the health of the Indian people was among the poorest in the world at the time of Independence, health programs have had top priority in each Five-Year and Annual Plan. From 1941 to 1961, life expectancy increased from age 32 to 42.[19] Almost all indexes for measuring health improvement and control and eradication of communicable disease showed improvement during the first three plans, 1951–1966. Sanitary conditions have improved. A highly successful mosquito eradication program has drastically reduced malaria, which had accounted for more than 75 million cases of disease and a million deaths a year. Cancer, cholera, filariasis, leprosy, smallpox, trachoma, tuberculosis, and venereal disease are all subject to active governmental control programs. Much still remains to be done, however.

There is a shortage of professionally trained persons in the medical field. In 1960 the estimated ratios of doctors to population ranged from 1 to 2,000 (in Delhi) to 1 to 29,000 (in Jammu and Kashmir). Although the ratio for the nation was 1 to 6,175, the rural area ratios were not as good, reaching 1 to 430,000 for areas in the States of Gujarat and Maharashtra. A doctor for a quarter- or a half-million persons means in effect no doctor at all for large proportions of the population.[20] Leaders in medical education are trying hard to improve its quality and output to meet the nation's need.

---

[16] Government of India. *Institutes of Technology Act: 1961*. Delhi: Manager of Publications, 1961. p. 14.
[17] Ministry of Education. *Annual Report: 1965–66*. 1967. p. 65–66.
[18] University Grants Commission. *Annual Report: 1963–64*. 1965. p. 5, 49–50.
[19] Planning Commission. *Third Five-Year Plan: 1961–66*. 1961. p. 652.
[20] Institute of Applied Manpower Research. *Fact Book on Manpower*. 1963. III:38–39.

The need for all kinds of professionally trained workers in the medical sciences is summarized dramatically by 1965 statistics showing the number of persons in India for one of each of various medical workers.[21]

One medical worker	Number of persons
Doctor	6,175
	[1] 1,238
	[2] 45,327
Nurse	11,019
Dentist	92,597
Pharmacist	6,607

[1] In urban areas.
[2] In rural areas.

Medicine

Institutions.—Modern medical education in India began early in the 19th century. The first institution for medical education was established in Calcutta in 1922;[22] later two medical colleges—one in Calcutta and one in Madras—were started in 1835, and one in Bombay in 1845.[23] The first medical schools trained assistants who had no individual responsibility for treatment of major complaints.[24] Gradually such medical schools closed or were converted to medical colleges. By 1936–37 there were 10 medical colleges including one exclusively for women. Later, medical colleges (which originally had granted their own diplomas) became affiliated with universities.

By 1965, a total of 81 medical colleges were affiliated with 32 universities, Nagaland being the only State with no medical students. In 1964–65, medical college enrollment had reached a total of 61,742, including 3,176 postgraduate and research students (tables 15 and 27).

The All-India Institute of Medical Sciences, established and "declared of national importance" by Parliament in 1956, is an autonomous institution responsible for developing a model medical education program. For training top-level administrative officers in the medical field, the Ministry of Health established in 1964 the National Institute of Health Administration and Education.

Internationally, Indian leaders of medical education take an active part in groups such as the Colombo Plan, the World Health Organization, and the World Medical Association (which held its 1966 Third World Conference on Medical Education in India).

Indigenous systems of medicine.—Indian medicine includes both the modern Western system and also the indigenous systems practiced widely

[21] Ministry of Information and Broadcasting. *India—A Reference Annual.* 1965. p. 101.
[22] T. Lakshminarayana. *A Report on Medical Education in India: 1959.* Delhi, 1959. p. 8.
[23] C. S. Patel. "A History of the Medical Council in India." *Silver Jubilee Souvenir: 1934–59.* Delhi: Medical Council of India, 1959. p. 17.
[24] Ministry of Education. *Report of the University Education Commission* (Reprint of 1950 edition). Delhi: Manager of Publications, 1962. I:263.

Bombay University, founded in 1857

in India for many centuries. Of one of these indigenous systems, P. Thomas has written:

> The one branch of science in which Hindus have done exceptionally well is medicine. The indigenous Ayurvedic system is as old as the race and still competes successfuly with the Allopathic (western) system.[25]

The approach of the indigenous systems is "to treat, not just the specific disease, but the whole personality in its entire make-up and in the total environment." [26] Ayurvedic medicine is based on Hindu religion and philosophy; Unani medicine, of Greek and Arabic origin, was introduced into India by the Muslims and is taught in colleges termed "Tibbia colleges." Official Government encouragement is given to both systems (and also to Homeopathy).

Ayurvedic drugs, made mostly from plants, are produced in large quantities and used extensively in India. Reserpine, a common ingredient in drugs for treatment of hypertension by Western medicine today, was used by Hindu practitioners of Ayurvedic medicine in India centuries ago, as was belladona also.[27]

[25] P. Thomas. *Hindu Religion, Customs, and Manners.* Bombay: D. B. Taraporevala Sons and Co., Ltd. p. 108.
[26] Ministry of Education. *Report of the University Education Commission* (Reprint of 1950 edition). Delhi: Manager of Publications, 1962. I:272–3.
[27] L. S. Goodman *and* Alfred Gilman. *The Pharmacological Basis of Therapeutics,* 3d edition. New York: The Macmillan Co., 1965. p. 178, 522.

In 1950 the University Education Commission called attention to the possibility of discovering other valuable drugs through Ayurvedic research.[28] In 1959 the Government asked a committee to make recommendations on the "training, research and pharmaceutical products and status of practice in Ayurveda." [29] As a result of the committee's recommendations, an Institute for Ayurvedic Studies and Research was established to allocate grants, develop policies, stimulate research, and otherwise aid the development of Ayurvedic research. At least 10 universities have recognized indigenous medicine to the extent of affiliating some Ayurvedic and Tibbia colleges (also some Homeopathic ones).[30] Many unaffiliated colleges teaching solely one or more of the indigenous systems of medicine are gradually including courses of Western medicine so as to achieve university affiliation.

Organizations.—The first medical councils were established on a Provincial basis in 1912 at Bombay and in 1914 at Madras and Bengal to undertake

> . . . maintenance of a register of qualified medical practicioners, the supervision of medical education, inspection of examinations, exercise of disciplinary control over medical practitioners and . . . advising local governments in regard to the recognition of the various medical qualifications.[31]

All-India Institute of Medical Sciences, founded in 1956

[28] Ministry of Education. *Report of the University Education Commission* (Reprint of 1950 edition). Delhi: Manager of Publications, 1962. I:272–73.
[29] Ministry of Information and Broadcasting. *India—A Reference Annual: 1957.* 1957. p. 96.
[30] These include Agra, Aligarh, Banaras, Gujarat, Kerala, Lucknow, Madras, Nagpur, Poona, and Saugar Universities and Gurukul Kangri Vishwavidyalaya.
[31] T. Lakshminarayana. op. cit. p. 10.

Before 1931, Indian medical colleges were inspected periodically by the General Medical Council, which maintained a register listing those doctors holding degrees enabling them to practice anywhere in the British Commonwealth. Disputes between this Council and Indian universities led to an act in 1933 establishing the Indian Medical Council, with broad powers to set standards for courses of study, examinations, and recognition of foreign medical qualifications. The Indian Medical Council Act of 1956 provides the Council with greater powers and responsibilities. It has the duty to:[32]

1. Inspect medical colleges (in cooperation with State Medical Councils).
2. Maintain an Indian Medical Register.
3. Prescribe standards for postgraduate medical education.
4. Suggest methods of improving the professional education program.

The affiliating universities may also set requirements regarding number and qualification of teaching staff and students, laboratory and hospital facilities, and many other related matters.

The Council has also fixed minimum standards of college medical education and tried to stimulate high quality postgraduate medical education. In 1967–68 postgraduate studies were offered by 90 medical colleges.[33]

As for agricultural and engineering education, so for medical education the Education Commission suggested a coordinating, fund-granting, and standard-setting organization similar to the University Grants Commission and with membership overlapping with it. Membership in the professional organizations should overlap with that of the University Grants Commission because

> . . . all higher education should be regarded as an integrated whole. . . . professional education cannot be divorced from general education, and . . . it is essential to bring all higher education, including agriculture, engineering and medicine, within the purview of the University Grants Commission.[34]

Nursing

The general nursing course is a 3-year program requiring for admission successful completion of secondary education. Although more advanced nursing programs, such as those for psychiatric or pediatric nurses, require for admission a bachelor's or a postgraduate degree, the great majority of nursing schools and colleges are not related to a university and thus cannot grant degrees. Only eight universities have constituent or affiliated nursing colleges.[35] Delhi University offers an advanced 2-year nursing course leading to a master's degree, which requires for admission both a B.Sc. in Nursing and 3 years of nursing experience.

In 1908 the Trained Nurses Association, affiliated with the International Council of Nurses, was founded in India to upgrade nursing education standards and to improve nursing practice and working conditions. Its membership is restricted to nurses with recognized training.[36] To

[32] Ibid. p. 11.
[33] Ministry of Information and Broadcasting. *India—A Reference Annual: 1967.* 1967. p. 98.
[34] Ministry of Education. *Report of the Education Commission: 1964–66.* 1966. p. 343.
[35] These are Calcutta, Delhi, Kerala, Madras, Osmania, Poona, and Rajasthan,, and S.N.D.T. Women's Universities.
[36] Planning Commission. *Social Welfare in India.* Delhi, 1960. p. 192–93.

"bring about a uniform standard of training throughout the country," [37] Parliament in 1949 established the Indian Nursing Council and also a Nurses Registration Council to maintain a register of nurses with recognized training.

Pharmacy

The bachelor's degree in pharmacy is granted 3 years after completion of an intermediate course in science or 4 years after completion of the pre-university course; 1 or 2 additional years are required for the master's degree. Courses toward the bachelor's degree are offered by 11 universities,[38] toward the master's by seven universities [39] and the All-India Institute of Medical Sciences.[40] Diplomas may be earned at five universities,[41] and certificates at three.[42]

In 1948, Parliament established a Pharmacy Council of India to maintain minimum standards for pharmaceutical education.

Dentistry

The Bachelor of Dental Surgery degree is usually awarded 4 years after completion of the pre-professional course or 5 years after completion of the pre-university course, and the Master of Dental Surgery 2 years after the B.D.S. degree. Ten universities confer bachelor's degrees in dentistry, and two confer master's degrees.[43] In 1948 the Dental Act established the Dental Council of India to provide uniform standards for dental education.

Other Professional Fields [44]

Architecture

The profession of architecture in India has a very small number of registered practitioners. During the period 1952–1961, only 536 were graduated in architecture from degree-level institutions. As of January 1963, India had only 659 registered architects and of those 18 were reported to be abroad. Ten universities grant the bachelor's degree—Bombay, Calcutta, Kerala, Lucknow, Madras, Mysore, Osmania, Panjabi, Punjab, and Vikram Universities. Calcutta University grants the master's degree, and Nagpur University grants a diploma in architecture. In addition, the Indian Insti-

---

[37] Ibid.
[38] These are Agra, Andhra, Banaras, Bombay, Gujurat, Madras, Mysore, Nagpur, Punjab, Rajasthan, and Saugar Universities.
[39] These are Andhra, Banaras, Bombay, Gujurat, Punjab, Rajasthan, and aSugar Universities.
[40] Ministry of Information and Broadcasting. *India—A Reference Annual*. 1965. p. 101.
[41] These are Bombay, Gujarat, Panjabi, Rajasthan, and Saugar Universities.
[42] These are Andhra, Panjabi, and Punjab Universities.
[43] Bombay, Calcutta, Kerala, Lucknow, Madras, Mysore, Osmania, Panjabi, Punjab, and Vikram Universities confer the bachelor's degree; Bombay and Punjab Universities confer the master's degree. University Grants Commission. *Handbook of Universities in India: 1963.* 1964. p. 265–75.
[44] Except as indicated, the source of information for this section is University Grants Commission. *Handbook of Universities in India: 1963.* 1964. p. 265–75.

tute of Technology at Bombay offers a bachelor's program in naval architecture, the Institute at Kharagpur the master's and diploma courses in architecture, and the University of Calcutta a diploma in town and regional planning.

Business Administration and Commerce

Although in 1964–65 almost 150,000 students were enrolled in commerce departments at the undergraduate level and more than 8,000 at the postgraduate and research levels (table 12), commerce courses are not considered truly professional in the sense that they prepare students for a high level of leadership in the business world. As the University Education Commission indicated, "much of our courses in Commerce have been on the Craftsman's level." [45] Business management and administration are being taught to a slight degree—a Master of Business Administration has been established by Andhra University and diplomas are offered at Aligarh, Bombay, Calcutta, Delhi, and Madras Universities. National standards have not as yet been adopted in this professional field.

Forestry

Although there is no indication of professional degrees being offered by the three colleges of forestry,[46] the Ministry of Agriculture does offer appropriate certificates for its postgraduate programs at Dehra Dun in the North and Coimbatore in the South. For admission to the course preparing government forestry officers,[47] a B.Sc. in a science subject or mathematics is required.

Home Science

Seventy-nine colleges affiliated to 27 universities in 14 States (including Delhi) offer collegiate work in home science. Of these 27 universities, five offer courses at the master's level [48] and the University of Baroda offers work at the Ph.D. level.[49] Leaders in the field of home science have been trying to improve courses and establish standards in home science education, evaluating and adapting the experience of other countries to the needs and conditions of Indian family life. Home science courses have been introduced into more than 700 secondary schools.

---

[45] Ministry of Education. *Report of the University Education Commission* (Reprint of 1950 edition). Delhi: Manager of Publications, 1962. I:277.

[46] Ministry of Education. *Review of Education in India (1947–61)*. 1961. p. 171.

[47] Ministry of Food and Agriculture. *The Forest Research Institute and Colleges.* 1949. p. 19.

[48] These are Baroda, Delhi, Kerala, Madras, and Mysore Universities.

[49] Information supplied by Dr. Rajammal P. Devadas, president of the Home Science Association of India and principal of the Sri Avinashilingam Home Science College, Coimbatore.

Journalism

Few universities offer professional work in journalism. One university (Osmania) offers a degree; six offer diplomas,[50] and Nagpur University offers a certificate. For admission to the diploma course,[51] a bachelor's degree is generally required.

Law

This is the only major profession in India in which there is not a severe shortage of graduates. Many students (70 percent at Bombay University) who complete a university law course do not even take the bar examination given by the State Bar Council, but use their legal training for careers in business, banking, or other similar occupations.

Admission to the law course requires the bachelor's degree in either arts or science. Enrollment in the law course in colleges and universities was estimated at 32,000 for 1964–65, including a postgraduate enrollment of 1,036 (table 12).

Within the 33 universities offering law degrees, 75 colleges and 5 university departments offer law courses to the bachelor's degree; 14 colleges and four university departments to the master's degree; and nine universities offer the doctorate in law, five through affiliated colleges and four through university departments.[52]

In 1950, the University Education Commission found "conditions in law colleges generally at a low ebb" and recommended that "our law colleges be thoroughly reorganized",[53] giving more attention to: (1) course length; (2) course purpose—to train scholars, lawyers, or both; (3) development of specialized and technical aspects of law; and (4) quality of teaching staff.

Under the Advocates' Act of 1961, the Federal Government created the All-India Bar Council, to: (1) visit law colleges, (2) develop syllabuses, (3) suggest uniform minimum requirements for admission and graduation, and (4) help upgrade all aspects of legal education. Through the Bar Council Examinations, the State Bar Councils control rights both to be enrolled as an ordinary pleader and also to practice law in the High Courts.

The Indian Law Institute, established in 1958 in Delhi for carrying on legal research, has had a working committee on the problems of legal education.

Library Science

For admission to the 1-year Bachelor of Library Science program, a bachelor's degree in arts or science is required; for admission to a diploma program, completion of an intermediate course or in some cases a Bachelor

---

[50] These are Calcutta, Gujarat, Madras, Nagpur, Osmania, and Punjab Universities.

[51] Ministry of Education. *Guide to Education in India—Facilities for Professional Studies in Education, Law, and Journalism.* 1961. p. 73–74.

[52] These are Agra, Aligarh, Allahabad, Andhra, Bombay, Delhi, Lucknow, Poona, and Rajasthan Universities.

[53] Ministry of Education. *Report of the University Education Commission* (Reprint of 1950 edition). Delhi: Manager of Publications, 1962. p. 258, 262.

of Arts or Science degree. Six universities offer courses for bachelor's degrees in library science—Aligarh, Banaras, Delhi, Kerala, Madras, and Rajasthan Universities; Delhi and Madras Universities offer the master's degree; and 19 universities offer diplomas and certificates.

Physical Education

The Central Advsory Board of Physical Education and Recreation, established in 1950 by the Government of India, issued "A National Plan of Physical Education and Recreation," [54] closely linked to such national plans as those for physical fitness, scouting, and National Cadet Corps. In 1957, the Government of India established in Gwalior the first degree college in physical education—Lakshmibai College of Physical Education, named for a heroine of the 1857 Indian Revolution. First affiliated with Vikram University and later with Jiwaji University (founded in Gwalior in 1964), this coeducational college offers a variety of physical education courses, including 'yogic' exercises and indigenous physical cultural activities leading to the B.P.E. degree.[55] In 1963, Laksmibai established a 2-year postgraduate course leading to the M.P.E. degree.[56] During 1965–66 there were 85 students admitted to the 3-year course for the B.P.E. and 14 admitted to the 2-year postgraduate M.P.E. course.

In addition to Lakshmibai College, two other institutions—the Government College of Physical Education of Panjabi University and the Department of Physical Education of Punjab University—offer the bachelor's degree; the latter institution also offers the master's; [57] and 19 institutions grant a diploma after a 1-year course requiring for admission a bachelor's degree. Most colleges offering diploma courses are not affiliated with universities.

Public Administration

After the British Government assumed responsibility from the East India Company for Indian affairs, the Indian Civil Service expanded into a vast national system for internal administration. The East India College at Haileybury provided 2-year training courses for candidates to examinations for the higher posts, held in England. The Indian Civil Service had greatly expanded in order to control an extensive area and population.

Leaders of independent India, renaming the civil service the Indian Administrative Service, directed it toward goals of independence, self-reliance, self-sufficiency, and national and international leadership. The University Education Commission cogently pointed out that efficient use of vast sums of public money is "a matter of great public moment".[58] In a

[54] Ministry of Education. *Education in Eighteen Years of Freedom.* 1965. p. 41.
[55] Shri Prem Kirpal. "Inaugural address." *All-India Seminar on Physical Education for Principals of Physical Education Institutions.* 1959. p. 47.
[56] Ministry of Education. *Education in Eighteen Years of Freedom.* 1965. p. 41.
[57] University Grants Commission. *Handbook of Universities in India: 1963.* 1964.
[58] Mnistry of Education. *Report of the University Education Commission* (Reprint of 1950 edition). Delhi: Manager of Publications, 1962. I:279.

survey of public administration in India, Paul Appleby rated "the government of India among the dozen or so most advanced governments of the world".[59]

Postgraduate courses in public administration leading to the M.A. and Ph.D. degrees are offered by Nagpur University; diploma courses by Karnatak, Lucknow, Madras, Osmania, and Patna Universities; and a Diploma in Local Self Government (L.S.G.D.) is offered by Allahabad and Nagpur Universities.

Social Work

In 1965, five departments and seven colleges or institutes, affiliated to 10 universities, offered postgraduate courses in social work. Such courses lead to the M.A. degree in social work in Andhra, Delhi, Madras, and Patna Universities; to the Master of Social Work (M.S.W.) in the Agra, Baroda, Kerala, and Lucknow Universities; to the Master of Applied Sociology (M.A.S.) in Kashi Vidyapeeth; and to a Diploma in Social Work (D.S.W.) in Andhra and Calcutta Universities, and the Tata Institute of Social Sciences.[60] In addition, four institutions not affiliated with universities [61] grant diplomas or certificates in social work.

The Tata Institute, begun in 1936 as the Sir Dorabji Tata Graduate School of Social Work, has the largest program of any school of social work, taking 60 students each year.[62] Other schools are the Delhi School (1947–48), the Kashi Vidyapeeth (1947), the Institute at Lucknow (1949), the Faculty of Social Work at Baroda (1950), and the Madras School of Social Work (1952).

The Ministry of Education in 1950 established an Advisory Board on Social Welfare to prepare a uniform syllabus for a 2-year postgraduate social welfare program.[63] At a conference of Heads of Schools of Social Work called by the Board in 1957, the syllabus was revised to include: (1) correctional services, (2) family and child welfare, (3) industrial relations and personnel management, (4) institutional and aftercare services, (5) medical social work, (6) psychiatric social work, (7) rural welfare and community development, and (8) tribal welfare.[64]

The Association of Schools of Social Work in India was established in 1959, to:[65]

1. Arrange seminars and refresher courses.

2. Encourage publication of literature.

3. Exchange ideas and experience.

4. Maintain standards for social work education.

---

[59] Paul H. Appleby. *Public Administration in India.* Delhi: Manager of Publications, 1953. p. 8.
[60] University Grants Commission. *Handbook of Universities in India: 1963.* 1964. passim.
[61] These institutions are the Madras School of Social Work, the National Institute of Social Science at Bangalore, the Bombay Labour Institute, and the Nirmala Niketan in Bombay.
[62] University Grants Commission. *Social Work Education in Indian Universities.* 1965. p. 13.
[63] Ibid. p. 19.
[64] Ibid. p. 19–20.
[65] Ibid. p. 21.

5. Promote and coordinate research.

6. Provide for conferences.

As yet no national organization has authority to establish standards for social work education, or to serve as a channel for Government grants to improve professional programs. The University Grants Commission has been recommended for the latter purpose.[66] The Association of the Alumni of Schools of Social Work has recommended a definite set of standards for social work education programs,[67] dealing with: (1) admissions requirements and procedures, (2) course organization, (3) evaluation and examination procedures, (4) length of program, (5) qualification of teachers, and (6) teacher-student ratios. Baroda University and The Tata Institute rely entirely on internal evaluation of student performance (by the subject teachers) rather than on external examinations.[68]

---

[66] Ibid. p. 63.
[67] Ibid. p. 73–79.
[68] Ibid. p. 18.

6. Postgraduate and Research Education

The number of students enrolled in postgraduate and research courses shows a steady advance, from less than 20,000 in 1950–51 to more than six times that many (128,729) in 1967–68 (table 27). In spite of the very great need for highly trained persons in such fields as agriculture, engineering and technology, the medical professions, and veterinary science, the entire enrollment in 1964–65 in these fields, combined with those of education and law, was only 12 percent of the total postgraduate and research enrollment; the courses in arts, science, and commerce still attracted 88 percent of the most advanced students in India (from table 27).

The number of doctorates granted by Indian universities is relatively small, but increasing. In science and technology, 100 doctorates were granted in 1950, and 540 in 1963.[1] The first postgraduate degrees in the basic sciences, however, showed a much larger increase during the same period—from 896 to 5,380.[2]

The number of universities offering postgraduate courses is also increasing. In 1964–65, a total of 26 more universities offered postgraduate courses than in 1956–57, and 21 more than in 1960–61 (table 28). Of the 66 universities reporting in 1964–65, a total of 60 had postgraduate enrollments (ranging from 5 to 5,000), but only 41 had research enrollments (ranging from 1 to 890). In recent years, the number of postgraduate students has been more than ten times that of research students:[3]

Year	Total	Postgraduate	Research
1965–66 _____	100,463	91,830	8,633
1966–67 _____	111,466	101,798	9,668
1967–68 _____	128,729	117,250	11,479

Postgraduate and research students are enrolled in both affiliated and constituent colleges within the universities. As of 1963–64, a total of 386 postgraduate colleges were affiliated with 36 universities, the greatest number of colleges being affiliated with Agra, Bombay, Gujarat, Kerala, Madras, Punjab, and Vikram Universities (table 29).

[1] Ministry of Education. *Report of the Education Commission: 1964–66.* 1966. p. 398.
[2] Ibid. p. 399.
[3] Figures for 1965-66, 1966-67 from University Grants Commission. *Annual Report: 1966-67.* 1968. p. 59.
Figures for 1967–68 from University Grants Commission. *Annual Report: 1967–68.* 1969. p. 41.

Table 27.—*Number of postgraduate and research students, by field of study: 1950-51—1967-68*

[------- indicates source did not show any figures]

Year	Total	Field of study								
		Agriculture	Arts	Commerce	Education	Engineering and technology	Law	Medicine	Science	Veterinary science
1	2	3	4	5	6	7	8	9	10	11
1950-51	21,444	397	13,153	2,052	375	203	211	340	4,713	-------
1951-52	23,672	402	14,014	2,452	525	322	219	440	5,298	-------
1952-53	25,476	425	15,421	2,515	558	367	242	442	5,506	-------
1953-54	28,262	400	17,094	2,444	684	426	293	590	6,331	-------
1954-55	31,065	364	18,167	2,485	770	480	344	667	6,988	-------
1955-56	33,551	487	20,364	2,713	757	513	355	914	7,448	-------
1956-57	35,508	582	21,706	3,058	864	617	408	1,168	8,095	10
1957-58	38,385	416	25,245	3,758	865	643	414	1,387	8,630	27
1958-59	49,338	827	29,836	4,851	843	698	584	1,637	9,992	70
1959-60	57,566	1,094	34,024	5,558	1,140	761	637	1,923	12,007	122
1960-61	60,624	-------	-------	-------	-------	-------	-------	-------	-------	-------
1961-62	72,859	1,452	43,199	6,764	1,313	707	933	1,887	16,387	191
1962-63	76,594	1,755	44,665	6,684	1,035	1,618	720	2,498	17,317	253
1963-64	82,580	2,264	46,770	7,256	1,496	1,564	1,278	2,335	19,251	296
1964-65	91,305	3,029	50,639	8,142	1,833	1,719	1,036	3,176	21,242	372
1965-66	100,463	-------	-------	-------	-------	-------	-------	-------	-------	-------
1966-67	111,466	-------	-------	-------	-------	-------	-------	-------	-------	-------
1967-68	128,729	-------	-------	-------	-------	-------	-------	-------	-------	-------

SOURCE OF DATA: Figures for 1950-51—1959-60 from Institute of Applied Manpower Research. *Fact Book on Manpower.* 2:61, 62.

1960-61 from *Universities Statistical Digest.* September 1962. 1:1:7.

1961-62—1963-64 from University Grants Commission. *Annual Report: 1963-64.* 1965. p. 28.

1964-65 from Inter-University Board of India and Ceylon. *University News.* September 1965. p. 10.

1965-66, 1966-67 from University Grants Commission. *Annual Report: 1966-67.* 1968. p. 59.

1967-68 from University Grants Commission. *Annual Report: 1967-68.* 1969. p. 41.

Table 28—*Number of postgraduate and research students, by university: Selected year, 1956-57—1964-65*[1]

[_____ indicates source did not show any figures]

University [2]				Year		
	1956-57	1960-61	1963-64	1964-65		
				Total	Post graduate	Research
Total_____	36,492	60,624	82,580	91,305	84,201	7,104
Agra_____	6,169	10,930	13,615	14,850	14,154	696
Aligarh Muslim_____	919	911	907	972	702	270
Allahabad_____	2,195	3,084	2,499	2,467	2,235	232
Andhra_____	411	756	1,390	1,688	1,354	334
Andhra Pradesh Agricultural_____	_____	_____	_____	70	70	_____
Annamalai_____	53	435	522	548	504	44
Banaras Hindu_____	1,592	1,601	1,630	1,647	1,292	355
Bangalore_____	_____	_____	_____	699	699	_____
Baroda_____	445	702	988	1,161	1,004	157
Bhagalpur_____	_____	_____	1,111	1,097	1,097	_____
Bihar_____	966	384	1,956	2,369	2,255	114
Bombay_____	3,128	4,119	3,227	3,872	3,459	413
Burdwan_____	_____	_____	600	837	837	_____
Calcutta_____	3,755	4,200	5,263	5,394	5,095	299
Delhi_____	1,469	2,592	3,773	3,760	2,870	890
Gauhati_____	510	717	1,734	1,695	1,688	7
Gorakhpur_____	_____	989	1,767	1,555	1,261	294
Gujarat_____	1,071	2,561	3,192	4,150	4,089	61
Indira Kala Sangeet Vishwavidyalaya_____	_____	_____	8	14	5	9
Indore_____	_____	_____	_____	1,489	1,437	52
Jabalpur_____	_____	703	1,847	1,996	1,803	193
Jadavpur_____	150	632	769	936	887	49
Jammu and Kashmir_____	78	205	440	572	532	40
Jawaharlal Nehru Krishi Vishwavidyalaya__	_____	_____	_____	269	268	1
Jiwaji_____	_____	_____	_____	1,143	1,143	_____
Jodhpur_____	_____	_____	491	573	470	103
Kalyani_____	_____	_____	148	185	155	30
Kameshwara Singh Darbhanga Sanskrit____	_____	_____	_____	_____	_____	_____
Karnatak_____	450	785	1,135	1,214	1,052	162
Kerala_____	362	959	1,726	2,309	2,236	73

Table 28.—*Number of postgraduate and research students, by university: Selected years, 1956-57—1964-65* (continued)

University	Year					
	1956–57	1960–61	1963–64	1964–65		
				Total	Post graduate	Research
Kurukshetra		8	366	467	384	83
Lucknow	2,014	2,805	2,783	2,686	2,287	399
Madras	940	1,996	2,841	2,866	2,638	228
Magadh			613	769	750	19
Marathwada		185	639	703	633	70
Mysore	195	450	1,307	647	622	25
Nagpur	938	2,077	2,067	2,073	2,043	30
North Bengal			223	331	329	2
Orissa University of Agriculture and Technology			23	105	105	
Osmania	525	1,017	1,204	1,332	1,102	230
Panjabi			272	320	320	
Patna	2,218	2,321	2,250	2,659	2,513	146
Poona	762	1,199	1,523	1,624	1,576	48
Punjab	2,374	2,381	2,369	2,617	2,461	156
Punjab Agricultural			170	434	404	30
Rabindra Bharati			7	25	25	
Rajasthan	1,414	2,793	2,212	1,719	1,571	148
Ranchi			758	908	815	93
Ravi Shankar				924	924	
Roorkee		93	226	221	221	
Sardar Vallabhbhai Vidyapeeth	131	317	526	563	537	26
Saugar	812	1,090	2,393	2,157	1,886	271
Shivaji			467	774	774	
S.N.D.T. Women's	80	198	174	192	177	15
Sri Venkateswara	65	210	398	401	360	41
Udaipur			42	392	358	34
Utkal	248	679	1,071	1,334	1,298	36
Uttar Pradesh Agricultural			55	87	87	
Varanaseya Sanskrit Vishwavidyalaya		223	163	178	129	49
Vikram		3,203	4,307	2,069	2,041	28
Visva Bharati	53	114	166	197	178	19

SOURCE OF DATA: Figures for 1956–57 and 1960–61 from University Grants Commission. *Universities Statistical Digest.* September 1962. 1:1:6–7.

Figures for 1964–65 from Inter-University Board of India and Ceylon. *University News.* April 1966.

[1] A separate 1964–65 total is given for postgraduate and research students.

[2] Includes all State universities founded by 1964 and four institutions "declared of national importance."

Table 29.—*Number of postgraduate colleges, by university: 1963–64*

University	Number of colleges
Total	386
Agra	48
Andhra	5
Banaras Hindu	11
Baroda	2
Bhagalpur	1
Bihar	2
Bombay	35
Calcutta	5
Delhi	21
Gauhati	3
Gujarat	29
Jabalpur	13
Karnatak	2
Kerala	26
Lucknow	2
Madras	33
Marathwada	3
Mysore	6
Nagpur	12
North Bengal	1
Orissa University of Agriculture and Technology	1
Osmania	6
Panjabi	3
Poona	13
Punjab	23
Punjab Agricultural	1
Rajasthan	14
Ranchi	3
Sardar Vallabhbhai Vidyapeeth	1
Saugar	18
S.N.D.T. Women's	4
Shivaji	9
Sri Venkateswara	2
Utkal	5
Vikram	21
Visva Bharati	2

SOURCE OF DATA: University Grants Commission. *Report on Standards of University Education.* Delhi, 1965. p. 253.

Because affiliated colleges frequently lack a well-trained staff and adequate libraries and laboratories, the Education Commission recommended that

> . . . the bulk of postgraduate and research work should be organized in the universities or in university "centers" where good programmes can be developed cooperatively by 3 or 4 local colleges under the guidance of the university.[4]

The Education Commission also stated that 80 percent of graduate and research work should be done at constituent colleges and teaching departments of universities, but that to reach this quota during the 20-year period from 1965–66 to 1985–86, the departments and constituent colleges would have to increase their enrollment of gifted undergraduates from 155,000 to 320,000; and of postgraduate and research students from 45,000 to 750,000; or a total enrollment increase from 200,000 to 1.1 million.[5] Calcutta University, conforming more than most universities to the Commission's recommendations, has only five affiliated colleges with postgraduate students, although it has the largest postgraduate enrollment and the highest number of affiliated colleges.

[4] Ministry of Education. *Report of the Education Commission: 1964–66.* p. 310–12. For further recommendations on postgraduate and research education, see appendix C, section VII.
[5] Ibid. p. 312.

In the area of curriculum at the postgraduate level, the Education Commission has made strong recommendations that the present "rigidity and uniformity" of one-subject courses be broken by permitting students to select a combination of subjects related to the central area of interest. Such a system would involve interdisciplinary studies within the social sciences, within the humanities, and within the physical sciences and mathematics; or even an arrangement overlapping these broad divisions. The system would also include programs of area studies at suitable centers to meet "a pressing need for a large number of Indian scholars with specialized knowledge of the life, institutions, culture, and languages of specific regions of the world".[6]

The University Grants Commission has established a "limited number of university departments for advance training and research in certain selected fields"—called Centers for Advanced Study. Twenty-six centers now operate at 12 universities; 15 are Science Centers and 11 are Humanities and Social Sciences Centers (appendix E). A standing committee advises the Commission on all matters relating to the Centers, and an expert committee reviews the progress of each Center.[7] Total allocations through 1965 are summarized in table 30.

Table 30.—*Amount of money allocated[1] to Centers of Advanced Study, by category: 1962–63—1965–66*

[Amounts in equivalent U.S. dollars]

Category	Center		
	Total	Science	Humanities and social science
Grand Total	**$4,122,000**	**$2,912,800**	**$1,209,200**
Non-recurring			
Total	*2,246,800*	*1,720,400*	*526,400*
Books	249,000	118,000	131,000
Buildings	1,088,600	778,000	310,600
Equipment	909,200	824,400	84,800
Recurring			
Total	*1,875,200*	*1,192,400*	*682,800*
Academic staff	1,160,850	721,780	439,070
Nonacademic staff	210,010	155,780	54,230
Miscellaneous	504,340	314,840	189,500

SOURCE OF DATA: University Grants Commission. *Annual Report: 1964–65.* 1965. p. 6.
[1] From the fund of the University Grants Commission (part III, chapter 3).

National and international recognition have come to this project of Centers for Advanced Study, considered a promising approach to the "pursuit of excellence" and the achievement of "international standards." [8] The United Nations Economic and Social Council (UNESCO) and the Colombo plan have already provided funds for the Centers, and both the British Council and the Asia Foundation of the United States have indicated probable participation.[9]

It is hoped that participation in the Centers by staff members of uni-

[6] Ibid. p. 318–21.
[7] University Grants Commission. *Annual Report: 1964–65.* 1966. p. 6.
[8] University Grants Commission. *Centers of Advanced Study in Indian Universities.* Delhi, 1964. p. 1.
[9] Ibid. p. 3–4.

versity departments and affiliated colleges will substantially improve the quality of teaching and research in their own departments and colleges.

As for library facilities, both the University Education Commission in 1950 and the Education Commission in 1966 called attention to the inadequacies of university library service—small collections, difficult access to books, short library hours, and insufficiently trained staff. In 1964 only 18 out of 55 universities reporting had as many as 100,000 books, and of these only 2 had as many as 300,000.[10]

The University Grants Commission has inaugurated a program of grants to colleges and universities for library buildings, new books, small textbook libraries, journals, and other necessities. In 1963–64, a total of 46 universities received grants averaging more than $12,600 each for science books; 40 universities received grants averaging more than $9,600 each for purchasing books in the humanities and social sciences; and 22 universities received grants averaging more than $22,300 each for library buildings.[11] The Commission has also established a Library Committee which made comprehensive and useful recommendations on the major library problems.[12]

[10] From data in Inter-University Board of India and Ceylon. *Universities' Handbook, India and Ceylon: 1964.* 1965. passim.

[11] University Grants Commission. *Annual Report: 1964–65.* 1966. p. 52–56.

[12] University Grants Commission. *University and College Libraries.* Delhi, 1965.

7. Summary

The importance of education to the people of India was recognized in its ancient system of *gurus* and in its earliest universities, the latter well known by scholars from China and other parts of Asia. India's medieval universities attached the same importance to education as did the institutions that operated up to and through the early part of the British rule. With the British came Western influence, especially at the higher education level, and in 1857 they established India's first three modern universities—one each in Bombay, Calcutta, and Madras.

In 1947, following the country's independence, education received renewed emphasis. Committees and commissions that originated during the British period and others after that date issued countless reports on Indian education. Beginning with the report made in 1950 by the University Education Commission and continuing with the one made in 1966 by the Education Commission, the Federal and State Governments of India have subjected higher and professional education to a continual series of investigations and studies. The basic purpose of the entire series was to develop guidance and growth policies for all types of postsecondary education throughout the country. The reports emanating from the investigations and studies resulted in several major innovations:

1. A standard 3-year college program for the baccalaureate degree.

2. Examination reform, with internal assessment of a student's achievement by his teachers.

3. Increased number of tutorials and seminars and a greater amount of field work at the undergraduate level.

4. Interdisciplinary courses.

5. Extension and correspondence courses.

6. Six State agricultural universities having three functions: to provide extension services, do research, and teach.

7. Five Indian Institutes of Technology to provide modern engineering and technical education geared to India's major development programs.

8. Twenty-six Centers for Advanced Study to provide a high quality of advanced teaching and research.

9. Junior colleges (in the State of Kerala) to provide the 11th and 12th years of schooling.

146

Some of these nine innovations have not yet moved very far or spread very wide and others are needed to carry out unfulfilled recommendations of the 1950 and 1966 Commission reports.

The major questions now facing those responsible for higher and professional education in India may be summarized as follows:

1. Should the Federal Government, in view of its increasing financial support of higher education, be given more authority over it?

2. How can the Federal Government coordinate its efforts on behalf of higher education? (Responsibility is now divided among the Agriculture, Education, and Health Ministries.)

3. What should be the function of voluntary, nongovernmental groups (such as the Inter-University Board of India and Ceylon) in developing higher education?

4. How may a desirable degree of institutional autonomy for colleges and universities be preserved and unwarranted interference in their affairs eliminated?

5. How can postsecondary institutions be encouraged to innovate and experiment as the Commission reports recommended?

6. How should India solve problems of student unrest?

7. How can colleges and universities both provide higher educational opportunities for more students and also maintain and raise the quality of education offered? Will establishing more 2-year colleges for grades 11 and 12 help in this dual effort? (The Government of India has recommended that these grades be provided "in schools, colleges, or both, according to local conditions." [1])

Since Independence in 1947, India has been acutely aware of its many problems, not only in education but also in economic development, food, health, and population control. Moreover, it has made measureable progress in solving these problems. It has never slackened in its efforts to do so despite a traditional diversity of culture, language, and religion that at times resists modernization and national integration. While making these efforts it maintains a democratic form of society in the world's second most populous nation, which has the world's largest popular national electorate.

The following statement by the Government of India in 1968 shows its continuing awareness of the importance of educational progress to every aspect of the nation's development:

> The Government of India is convinced that a radical reconstruction of education on the broad lines recommended by the Education Commission is essential for economic and cultural development of the country, for national integration and for realising the ideal of a socialistic pattern of society. This will involve a transformation of the system to relate it more closely to the life of the people; a continuous effort to expand educational opportunity; a sustained and intensive effort to raise the quality of education at all stages; an emphasis on the development of science and technology; and the cultivation of moral and social values. . . . This is necessary if the country is to attain its rightful place in the comity of nations in conformity with its great cultural heritage and its unique potentialities.[2]

---

[1] Ministry of Education. *National Policy on Education: 1968.* Government of India Press, 1968. p. 9.
[2] Ibid. p. 2.

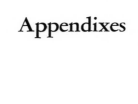

Appendixes

Appendix A. Summary of the Main Recommendations of the University Education Commission: 1950 [1]

I. *Administration*

1. University education should be placed on the Concurrent List of the Indian Constitution.

2. A Central University Grants Commission should be established.

3. No university should be purely affiliating.

4. Colleges controlled by a State government should become a constituent part of a university and be controlled by it.

5. The number of colleges affiliated with any university should be limited.

6. Universities should have a full-time vice-chancellor and other properly constituted authoritative bodies such as the senate, the executive council, and the academic council.

II. *Courses of Study*

1. The work for a bachelor's degree in any subject should be of 3 years' duration after the intermediate examination or its equivalent (instead of 2 years).

2. Students admitted to an honors program could be awarded a master's degree after 1 year of study beyond the bachelor's degree; others would need 2 years for a regular master's degree.

3. Courses in general education should be introduced in the ninth and tenth grades of secondary schools and continued in the intermediate and bachelor's programs, to enable the student to acquire a wholesome personality and to become a responsible citizen in addition to following a specific occupational interest.

III. *Educational Quality*

1. The minimum years of study required for university admission should be 12.

2. A large number of occupational institutes should be opened for students who would otherwise pursue a university education only for lack of more suitable opportunities.

3. A maximum student population should be set in each college and university.

[1] SOURCE OF DATA: Ministry of Education. *Report of the University Education Commission* (Reprint of 1950 edition). Delhi: Manager of Publications, 1962, Vol. I.

4. The minimum number of working days should be increased to 180.

5. Tutorials, library work, and written exercises should supplement lectures.

6. Library and laboratory services should be improved and expanded.

IV. *Examinations*

1. Objective examinations should be introduced to evaluate both students and candidates for admission.

2. The Ministry of Education and the universities should take full advantage of America's experience and knowledge in the creation of psychological and achievement tests.

3. One-third of the marks allotted to each subject in the existing examination system should reflect class work.

4. Examinations should be given at regular intervals throughout the proposed 3-year degree program, instead of solely at the end of it.

5. The government administrative services, instead of setting a degree as a minimum requirement for jobs, should give their own examinations. (It was hoped that this change would reduce the number of persons striving for a university degree solely as a necessary step toward employment.)

V. *Finance*

1. Private colleges should receive support from the State for building, equipment, and recurring expenditures.

2. Income tax laws should be amended to encourage donations for education.

3. Colleges and universities should receive additional grants for putting into effect the Commission's various recommendations.

4. The Federal Government should contribute an *extra* $20 million to develop university education in the succeeding 5 years.

5. The proposed University Grants Commission should allocate funds received from the Government.

VI. *Postgraduate Training and Research*

1. Regulations concerning M.A. degrees and M.Sc. degrees should be uniform.

2. The training period for a Ph.D. degree should be at least two years.[2]

3. Admission to a Ph.D. degree should be on an all-India basis.

4. Both teaching and affiliating universities should provide for more advanced research in all fields.

5. The Ministry of Education should offer a large number of scholarships to good students at the M.Sc. and Ph.D. level in order to combat the acute shortage of qualified scientific manpower.

6. Five marine biological stations should be set up in the coastal areas.

7. Interdisciplinary sciences like biochemistry and geophysics should be encouraged.

VII. *Religion*

1. All educational institutions should start work with a few minutes for silent meditation.

2. The lives of great religious leaders like Gautama the Buddha, Confucius, Jesus, Somkara, and Mohammad should be taught in the first year of the degree course.

---

[2] In India, a master's degree is usually a prerequisite for admission to a Ph.D. candidacy.

3. Selections of a universalist character from different scriptures should be studied in the second year.

4. Problems of the philosophy of religion should be considered in the third and final year.

VIII. *Student Activities and Welfare*

1. Students should be selected on the basis of merit alone.

2. Different academic streams should be offered.

3. Scholarships should be provided.

4. The universities should take some responsibility for students' health.

5. The National Cadet Corps should be started and extended in colleges.[3]

6. Residential units should be established and residential life made an integral part of college education.

7. University unions operated by and for students should be started.

8. An Office of Dean of Students and an Advisory Board of Student Welfare should be set up in each college.

IX. *Teachers*

1. The importance and responsibility of the university teacher should be recognized.

2. There should be four classes of teachers: professors, readers, lecturers, and instructors.

3. Every university should have some research fellows.

4. Salaries and payscales should be higher. (Specific recommendations were made on this subject.)

5. Promotions should be based entirely on merit.

6. Specific regulations should be drawn up concerning leave, hours of work, and the savings fund.

X. *Women's Education*

1. Colleges converted from men's colleges to coeducational colleges should provide "the ordinary amenities and decencies of life" for the women being admitted in increasing numbers.

2. Good guidance and counseling for women should be made available.

3. Educational opportunities for women should be increased.

4. Women teachers should be paid the same salaries as men teachers for equal work.

---

[3] Similar to the R.O.T.C. programs in American colleges and universities.

Appendix B. Excerpts from *The University Grants Commission Act, 1956*—Powers and Functions of the Commission.[1]

It shall be the general duty of the Commission to take, in consultation with the Universities or other bodies concerned, all such steps as it may think fit for the promotion and co-ordination of University education and for the determination and maintenance of standards of teaching, examination and research in Universities, and for the purpose of performing its functions under this Act, the Commission may—

(a) inquire into the financial needs of Universities;

(b) allocate and disburse, out of the Fund of the Commission, grants to Universities established or incorporated by or under a Central Act for the maintenance and development of such Universities or for any other general or specified purpose;

(c) allocate and disburse, out of the Fund of the Commission, such grants to other Universities as it may deem necessary for the development of such Universities or for any other general or specified purpose: Provided that in making any grant to any such University, the Commission shall give due consideration to the development of the University concerned, its financial needs, the standard attained by it, and the national purposes which it may serve;

(d) recommended to any University the measures necessary for the improvement of University education and advise the University upon the action to be taken for the purpose of implementing such recommendation;

(e) advise the Central Government or any State Government on the allocation of any grants to Universities for any general or specified purpose out of the Consolidated Fund of India or the Consolidated Fund of the State, as the case may be;

(f) advise any authority, if such advice is asked for, on the establishment of a new University or on proposals connected with the expansion of the activities of any University;

(g) advise the Central Government or any State Government or University on any question which may be referred to the Commission by the Central Government or the State Government or the University, as the case may be;

---

[1] University Grants Commission. *The University Grants Commission Act, 1956* (as modified up to January 1963). Delhi: Manager of Publications, 1963.

(h) collect information on all such matters relating to University education in India and other countries as it thinks fit and make the same available to any University;

(i) require a University to furnish it with such information as may be needed relating to the financial position of the University or the studies in the various branches of learning undertaken in that University together with all the rules and regulations relating to the standards of teaching and examination in that University respecting each of such branches of learning;

(j) perform such other functions as may be prescribed or as may be deemed necessary by the Commission for advancing the cause of higher education in India or as may be incidental or conducive to the discharge of the above functions.

13. (1) For the purpose of ascertaining the financial needs of a University or its standards of teaching, examination and research, the Commission may, after consultation with the University, cause an inspection of any department or departments thereof to be made in such manner as may be prescribed and by such person or persons as it may direct.

(2) The Commission shall communicate to the University the date on which any inspection under sub-section (1) is to be made and the University shall be entitled to be associated with the inspection in such manner as may be prescribed.

(3) The Commission shall communicate to the University its views in regard to the results of any such inspection and may, after ascertaining the opinion of the University, recommend to the University, the action to be taken as a result of such inspection.

(4) All communications to a University under this section shall be made to the executive authority thereof and the executive authority of the University shall report to the Commission the action, if any, which is proposed to be taken for the purpose of implementing any such recommendation as is referred to in sub-section (3).

14. If any University fails within a reasonable time to comply with any recommendation made by the Commission under section 12 or section 13, the Commission, after taking into consideration the cause, if any, shown by the University for its failure to comply with such recommendation, may withhold from the University the grants proposed to be made out of the Fund of the Commission.

15. The Central Government may, after due appropriation made by Parliament by law in this behalf, pay to the Commission in each financial year such sums as may be considered necessary for the performance of the functions of the Commission under this Act.

16. (1) The Commission shall have its own Fund; and all sums which may, from time to time, be paid to it by the Central Government and all the receipts of the Commission (including any sum which any State Government or any other authority or person may hand over to the Commission) shall be carried to the Fund and all payments by the Commission shall be made therefrom.

(2) All moneys belonging to the Fund shall be deposited in such banks or invested in such manner as may, subject to the approval of the Central Government, be decided by the Commission.

(3) The Commission may spend such sums as it thinks fit for performing its functions under this Act, and such sums shall be treated as expenditure payable out of the Fund of the Commission.[20]

Appendix C. Excerpts from *Report of the Education Commission: 1964-66* [1]

I. Administration [2]

Autonomy

Where there is an outstanding college (or a small cluster of very good colleges) within a large university which has shown the capacity to improve itself markedly, consideration should be given to granting it 'autonomous' status. . . . (XI, 132, (2))

The universities should give considerable autonomy to their departments. The principle that good ideas often originate at the lower levels must be recognized and respected in the governance of a university. . . . (XIII, 155, (2))

Inter-university Collaboration

The UGC may explore the possibility of bringing together all universities in a State in a 'consortium' to operate all the affiliated colleges in the State. (XII, 145, (5))

Inter-University Collaboration. Universities should join together, at the regional and national levels, in cooperative programmes and supplement mutually their available facilities, especially in research. . . . (XII, 147)

New Universities

The establishment of new universities is inescapable. The metropolitan cities of Bombay, Calcutta, Delhi and Madras should have, by the end of the fourth plan, two universities each which would supplement to some extent the work of each other. The demand from the States of Kerala and Orissa for additional universities is justifiable. The proposals for the establishment of a university for the hill areas of the North-Eastern Region should be supported as a major measure for spear-heading economic and social development in the area. (XII, 144)

The establishment of a new university can be justified only if it leads to a substantial improvement in standards and in the output and level of research. (XII, 145, (1))

No new university should be started unless the agreement of the UGC is obtained and adequate provision of funds is made. (XII, 145, (2))

Officers

The vice-chancellor should, as a rule, be a distinguished educationist or eminent scholar with adequate administrative experience. (XIII, 158, (3))

The term of office of the vice-chancellor should be five years and he should not be appointed for more than two terms in the same university. (XIII, 158, (4))

The Governors of the States should be the Visitors of all universities in the State and should have power to direct inspection or inquiry into the affairs of a unversity. (XIII, 159, (7))

II. Courses of Study

First Degree

The duration of the first degree should not be less than three years. The duration of the second degree may be 2 to 3 years. (II, 10, (1))

---

[1] Ministry of Education. *Report of the Education Commission: 1964-66.* 1966. p. 613-73.

[2] For purposes of this appendix, headings have been supplied and in some cases the original punctuation has been altered. Figures in parentheses are those of sections and paragraphs in the report.

Three-year special courses for the first degree which begin at the end of the first year of the present three-year degree courses should be started in selected subjects and in selected institutions. (II, 10, (3))

At the undergraduate stage, social service for 60 days in total (to be done in one or more stretches) should be obligatory for all students. (I, 3, (2), (3))

Nomenclature
A uniform system of nomenclature for the different stages and sub-stages of education should be evolved by the Government of India in consultation with State Governments. (II, 14)

Pre-university Course
The pre-university course should be transferred from the universities and affiliated colleges to secondary schools by 1975-76 and duration of the course should be lengthened to two years by 1985-86. (II, 78 (1))

Study Emphasis
The combination of subjects permissible for the first degree should also be more elastic than at present, both in the arts and in the sciences. . . . (XII, 149, (1))

Special efforts should be made to promote inter-disciplinary studies in universities which have adequately staffed departments in related subjects. . . . (XII, 148, (9))

Study of Humanities. The need for strengthening the humanities cannot be overstressed. In science education, we shall have to depend inevitably on developments in advanced countries with which we will not be able to catch up in the foreseeable future. To redress the balance, our scholars should strive to make significant contributions to the sum total of human knowledge and experience in the fields of the social and pedagogical sciences and humanistic studies, where our old traditions and the present challenges posed by social development present unique opportunities for creative work. (XII, 151)

III. Educational Quality

Admissions
Selective Admissions. Since the demand for higher education will be much larger than the provision that can be made for it or is needed on the basis of manpower needs, a system of selective admissions will have to be adopted. . . . (XII, 139)

The University Grants Commission should set up a Central Testing Organization for the development of appropriate selection procedures for different courses of higher education. (XII, 139, (3))

College Size
The general policy should be to encourage the establishment of bigger institutions which tend to be more efficient and economic. A college should normally have a minimum enrollment of 500 and it would be preferable to raise it to 1,000 or more in as many colleges as possible. . . . (XII, 141)

Independent Study
The number of formal classroom and laboratory hours should be somewhat reduced. The time thus saved should be devoted, under the guidance of instructors, to independent study, assigned reading, writing of essays, solving of problems and small research projects in which the student seeks out and learns to use independently the books and documents he needs. (XI, 133, (1))

It is most important to emphasize original thinking in the study of all subjects and to discourage memorizing. (XI, 133, (3))

Part-time Education
Opportunities for part-time education (correspondence courses, evening colleges) should be extended widely and should include courses in science and technology. By 1986, about a third of the total enrolment in higher education could be provided through a system of correspondence courses and evening colleges. (XII, 140)

IV. Examinations

Internal Assessment
In all teaching universities, external examinations should be replaced by a system of internal and continuous evaluation by the teachers themselves. (XI, 133, (10))

In universities with affiliated colleges, a system of internal assessment should supplement the external examination. (XI, 133, (11))

Reform
The University Grants Commission should set up a Central Examination Reform Unit to work in collaboration with the universities. Special units for examination reform should also be set up in some universities who can be persuaded to organize examination reform in a big way. (XI, 133, (12))

V. Finance

Source

Larger resources should be placed at the disposal of the UGC so as to increase the amount of Central assistance to all State universities on the basis of their performance and merit. (XII, 145, (7))

The State Governments should place adequate financial resources at the disposal of universities and simplify rules and procedures for operating them. (XIII, 157, (1))

There should be some reasonable sharing of developmental expenditure on universities between the UGC and State Governments. (XIII, 157, (3))

The finance of universities should be placed in a sound footing on the basis of advice given by the UGC to the State Governments and the universities after periodical review. (XIII, 157, (6))

University Autonomy

Universities should be immune from *direct* governmental intervention and also from *direct* public accountability. (XIII, 157, (7))

VI. Language

Media of Education

The regional languages should be adopted as media of education at the university stage in a phased programme spread over ten years. (XI, 134, (1))

In due course, all teachers in higher education should, as far as possible, be bilingual and postgraduate students should be able to follow lectures and use reading materials in the regional language as well as in English. (XI, 134, (8))

Study of Languages

The classical and modern Indian languages should be provided as elective subjects, no language being made a compulsory subject of study at the university stage. (XI, 134, (6))

Adequate facilities should be provided in universities and colleges for the study of English. Special units for teaching English should be established in universities to give a good working knowledge of it to new entrants by the adoption of modern teaching techniques. It would also be an advantage to teach some English as part of the elective subject course in the first year of the degree course. (XI, 134, (7))

VII. Postgraduate Training and Research

Postgraduate education and research work should ordinarily be organized in the universities or in university 'centres' where a good programme can be developed cooperatively by a group of local colleges. The increase in enrolments at the postgraduate stage should always be contingent on adequate increase in material and staff resources. A rigorous test of admission should be introduced and adequate scholarships should be available (to cover 50 percent of the students) and these should be supplemented by loan scholarships. The Government of India should be made almost exclusively responsible for postgraduate education and research. (XII, 142)

Students for the Ph.D. Courses should be carefully selected, a time-limit being set within which a student is expected to submit his thesis. There should also be a limit on the number of students to be guided by a teacher at any given time. (XII, 148, (5))

Course Requirements

A student should be expected to work from two to three years for a Ph.D. degree which should be regarded as the beginning and not the climax of the research career of the student. During the first year of the Ph.D. course, students should attend lectures and tutorials of an advanced nature to overcome inadequacy of preparation at the Master's Degree stage. (XII, 148, (4))

The procedure for evaluation of the Ph.D. degree should be improved, a defense of the thesis being considered an Essential requirement for the degree. (XII, 148, (6))

A study of a second world language should be obligatory for all Ph.D. students and compulsory for the Master's degree in certain subjects. (XII, 148, (7))

Educational Research

Urgent steps have to be taken to develop educational research and relate it effectively to the formulation of educational policies and improvement of education. . . . (XII, 152)

Major Universities

The most important reform in higher education is the development of some 'major universities' where first-class postgraduate work and research would be possible and whose standards would be comparable to the best institutions of their type in any part of the world. The UGC should select, as soon as possible, from amongst the existing universities, about six universities (including one of the IITs and one Agricultural University) for development as major universities. The programme should begin in 1966-67. (XI, 126)

It is necessary to establish 'clusters' of advanced centres in the major universities. They will add strength to, and enrich one another and be specially helpful in promoting inter-disciplinary research. About fifty such centres should be established, including some in modern Indian languages over the next five to ten years. At least one of them should concentrate on developing an inter-disciplinary approach to education. Other important areas to be covered are agriculture, engineering and medicine. (XI, 128)

The recurring and capital costs of the major universities should be met by the UGC. (XI. 130)

Improvement of Other Universities. The major universities should be utilized to provide teachers of quality to the other universities and to the affiliated colleges. . . . (XI, 131)

VIII. Religion

The Central and State Governments should adopt measures to introduce education in moral, social and spiritual values in all institutions under their (or local authority) control on the lines recommended by the University Education Commission and the Committee on Religious and Moral Instruction. (I, 5, (a))

The university departments in Comparative Religion should be specially concerned with the ways in which these values can be taught wisely and effectively and should undertake preparation of special literature for use by students and teachers. (I, 5, (b))

. . . A syllabus giving well chosen information about each of the major religions should be included as a part of the course in citizenship or as part of general education to be introduced in schools and colleges up to the first degree. It should highlight the fundamental similarities in the great religions of the world and the emphasis they place on the cultivation of certain broadly comparable and moral and spiritual values. (II, 6)

IX. Student Activities and Welfare

Accommodations
Hostel accommodation should be provided, as soon as possible, for about 25 per cent and 50 per cent of the enrolment at the undergraduate and postgraduate stages respectively. (X, 135, (3))

Activities
It is necessary to develop a rich and varied programme of co-curricular activities for students not only during term-time but also during vacations. (X, 135, (6))

Discipline
The responsibility for indiscipline taking place is multi-lateral and no effective solution is possible unless each agency—students, parents, teachers, State Governments and political parties—does its own duties. (XI, 137, (2))

Earnest efforts should be made to remove the educational deficiencies that contribute to student unrest and set up an adequate consultative and administrative machinery to prevent the occurrence of acts of indiscipline. (XI, 137, (3))

Services
Student Services. Student services are not merely a welfare activity but constitute an integral part of education. These should include orientation for new students, health services, residential facilities, guidance and counselling including vocational placement, student activities and financial aid. (X, 135)

There should be a full-time dean of student welfare for the administration of welfare services. (X, 135, (7))

X. Student Assistance

Free Education
Fees in Education. The country should work towards a stage when all education would be tuition free. . . . (VI, 53)

For the next ten years, the main effort with regard to fees in higher secondary and university education should be to extend provision of tuition free education to all needy and deserving students. As a first step, the proportion of free studentships should be increased to 30 per cent of the enrolment. (VI, 53, (3))

Grants for Books

Grants for the purchase of books, which need not necessarily be textbooks, should be made to talented students—the top 10 percent—in educational institutions. The scheme should begin in the universities and later on be extended to affiliated colleges and secondary schools. (VI, 54, (4))

Scholarships

University Stage. At the university stage the target for the provision for scholarships should be as follows:

(a) Scholarships should be available to at least 15 percent of the enrolment at the undergraduate stage by 1976 and to 25 per cent of such enrolment by 1986; and

(b) scholarships should be available to at least 25 percent of the enrolment at the postgraduate stage by 1976 and to 50 percent of such enrolment by 1986. (VI, 56, (4))

Scholarships for Study Abroad. There should be a national programme for the award of scholarships to the best talented students for study abroad. About 500 scholarships should be awarded each year. (VI, 61)

Loan Scholarships. It is necessary to institute a programme of loan scholarships to supplement the outright grant scholarships described above. . . . (VI, 62)

In all programmes of scholarships, preferential consideration should be given to the needs of girls. (VI, 64, (1))

The Government of India should assume the bulk of the responsibility for providing scholarships in higher education. . . . (VI, 54, (2))

XI. Teachers

Accommodations

In universities and colleges, the target should be to provide residential accommodation to about 50 percent of the teachers in the university and 20 per cent of them in affiliated colleges. (III, 24, (8), (d))

Additional Work

At the university stage, part-time consultancy or additional work, such as research by teachers in higher education should be permitted; and no payment should be required to be made to the institution if the earnings do not exceed 50 per cent of the salary. (III, 24, (10))

Advancement

Adequate facilities for professional advancement should be provided to all teachers. (III, 24, (3))

Qualifications

The introduction of these scales of pay should be linked with improvement in the qualifications of teachers and improvement in the selection procedures for their appointment. . . . (III, 17, (2))

The qualifications of teachers in affiliated colleges should be the same as those for teachers in the universities. The method of recruitment for them should also be similar. . . . (III, 17, (3))

Salaries

Intensive and continuous efforts are necessary to raise the economic, social and professional status of teachers and to feed back talented young persons into the professions. (III, 15)

Remuneration. The most urgent need is to upgrade the remuneration of teachers substantially, particularly at the school stage. (III, 16)

The scales proposed above for teachers in higher education have already been approved by Government. To facilitate their introduction, assistance from the Centre should be provided to meet additional expenditure on a sharing basis of 80 per cent from Central and 20 percent from State funds. In the case of private colleges, Central assistance may even be provided on a 100 per cent basis. (III, 17, (1))

XII. Women's Education

The education of women should be regarded as a major programme in education for some years to come and a bold and determined effort should be made to face the difficulties involved and to close the existing gap between the education of men and women in as short a time as possible. (VI, 71, (1))

Appendix D. Selected Degrees, Diplomas, and Certificates[1]

<table>
<tr><td colspan="2" align="center">DEGREES</td></tr>
<tr><td colspan="2">Bachelor of—</td></tr>
<tr><td>Agriculture</td><td>B.Ag.</td></tr>
<tr><td>Architecture</td><td>B.Arch.</td></tr>
<tr><td>Arts</td><td>B.A.</td></tr>
<tr><td>Arts in Education</td><td>B.A. (Ed.)</td></tr>
<tr><td>Arts in Fine Arts</td><td>B.A. (Fine)</td></tr>
<tr><td>Arts (General)</td><td>B.A. (Genl.)</td></tr>
<tr><td>Arts (Home Arts)</td><td>B.A. (Home Arts)</td></tr>
<tr><td>Arts with Honours</td><td>B.A. (Hons.)</td></tr>
<tr><td>Arts with Honours in Music</td><td>B.A. (Hons.) (Mus.)</td></tr>
<tr><td>Arts in Music</td><td>B.A. (Music)</td></tr>
<tr><td>Arts (Special)</td><td>B.A. (Spl.)</td></tr>
<tr><td>Ayurvedic Medicine</td><td>B.A.M.</td></tr>
<tr><td>Ayurvedic Medicine and Surgery</td><td>B.A.M.S.</td></tr>
<tr><td>Chemical Engineering</td><td>B.Ch.E. or B.Chemi. Engg.</td></tr>
<tr><td>Civil Engineering</td><td>B.C.E.</td></tr>
<tr><td>Civil Law</td><td>B.C.L.</td></tr>
<tr><td>Commerce</td><td>B.Com.</td></tr>
<tr><td>Dance</td><td>B.Dance</td></tr>
<tr><td>Dance with Honours</td><td>B.Dance (Hons.)</td></tr>
<tr><td>Dental Surgery</td><td>B.D.S.</td></tr>
<tr><td>Education</td><td>B.Ed.</td></tr>
<tr><td>Education (Basic)</td><td>B.Ed. (Basic)</td></tr>
<tr><td>Electrical Engineering</td><td>B.E.E.</td></tr>
<tr><td>Engineering</td><td>B.E.</td></tr>
<tr><td>Engineering (Chemical)</td><td>B.E. (Chemi.)</td></tr>
<tr><td>Engineering (Electrical)</td><td>B.E. (Electrical)</td></tr>
<tr><td>Engineering (Mechanical)</td><td>B.E. (Mechanical)</td></tr>
<tr><td>Engineering (Metallurgy)</td><td>B.E. (Metallurgy)</td></tr>
<tr><td>Engineering (Mining)</td><td>B.E. (Mining)</td></tr>
<tr><td>Engineering (Tele-Communication)</td><td>B.E. (Tele-Com.)</td></tr>
<tr><td>Indian Medicine</td><td>B.I.M.</td></tr>
<tr><td>Journalism</td><td>B.J.</td></tr>
<tr><td>Law</td><td>B.L. or L.L.B.</td></tr>
<tr><td>Library Science</td><td>B.Lib.Sc.</td></tr>
<tr><td>Mechanical Engineering</td><td>B.M.E.</td></tr>
</table>

---

[1] University Grants Commission. *Handbook of Universities in India: 1963.* 1964. p. v-x, and Part II.

Medicine and Bachelor of Surgery _____B.M.B.S. *or* M.B.B.S.
Medicine and Surgery (Ayurvedacharya) _____A.B.M.S.
Metallurgy _____B.Met.
Music _____B.Mus.
Music with Honours _____B.Mus. (Hons.)
Nursing _____B.Nursing
Oriental Learning _____B.O.L.
Pharmacy _____B.Pharm.
Physical Education _____B.P.E.
Sanitary Science _____B.S.Sc.
Science _____B.Sc.
Science with Honours _____B.Sc. (Hons.)
Science in Agriculture _____B.Sc. (Ag.)
Science in Agricultural Engineering _____B.Sc. (Ag. Engg.)
Science in Chemical Engineering _____B.Sc. (Chem. Engg.)
Science in Education _____B.Sc. (Ed.)
Science in Engineering _____B.Sc. (Engg.)
Science in Engineering (Chemical) _____B.Sc.Engg. (Chemi.)
Science (Home Arts) _____B.Sc. (Home Arts)
Science in Home Economics _____B.Sc. (Home Eco.)
Science in Home Science _____B.Sc. (Home Sc.) *or* B.Sc. (Home)
Science in Medicine _____B.Sc. (Med.)
Science in Mining _____B.Sc. (Min.)
Science in Mining Engineering _____B.Sc. (Min.Engg.)
Science in Nursing _____B.Sc. (Nursing)
Science in Technology _____B.Sc. (Tech.)
Science (Textiles) _____B.Sc. (Text.)
Science (Veterinary) _____B.Sc. (Vet.)
Teaching _____B.T.
Teaching (Basic) _____B.T.(Basic)
Technology _____B.Tech.
Tele-Communication Engineering _____B.Tel.E.
Textile Engineering _____B.Text. (Engg.)
Textile Technology _____B.Text.
Theology _____B.Th.
Unani Medicine and Surgery _____B.U.M.S.
Unani Tib and Surgery _____B.U.T.S.
Veterinary Medicine and Surgery _____B.V.M.S.
Veterinary Science _____B.V.Sc.
Veterinary Science and Animal Husbandry _____B.V.Sc.&A.H.

Master of—

Agriculture _____M.Ag.
Agricultural Engineering _____M.E. (Agl. Engg.)
Applied Sociology _____M.A.S.
Architecture _____M.A. (Arch.) *or* M.Arch.
Arts _____M.A.
Arts in Education _____M.A. (Ed.)
Arts in Fine Arts _____M.A. (Fine)
Arts in Social Work _____M.A. (Social Work)
Automobile Engineering _____M.E. (Auto.)
Business Administration _____M.B.A.
Chemical Engineering _____M.Ch.E.
Civil Engineering _____M.C.E.
Civil Law _____M.C.L.
Commerce _____M.Com.
Dance _____M.Dance
Dental Surgery _____M.D.S.
Education _____M.Ed.
Electrical Engineering _____M.E.E.

```
Engineering _____M.E.
Engineering (Chemical) _____M.E. (Chem.)
Engineering (Public Health) _____M.E. (Pub. Heal.)
Home Science _____M.H.Sc. or M.Sc. (Home)
Law _____M.L. or L.L.M.
Letters or Literature _____M.Litt.
Library Science _____M.Lib.Sc.
Mechanical Engineering _____M.M.E. or M.Mech.E.
Metallurgical Engineering _____M.Met.E.
Music _____M.Mus.
Obstetrics _____M.O.
Ophthalmic Surgery (Ophthalmology) _____M.S. (Ophthal.)
Oriental Learning _____M.O.L.
Pharmacy _____M.Pharm.
Physical Education _____M.P.E.
Planning _____M.P. or M.Planning
Science _____M.Sc.
Science in Agriculture _____M.Sc. (Ag.)
Science in Dairying _____M.Sc. (Dairying)
Science in Education _____M.Sc. (Ed.)
Science in Engineering _____M.Sc. (Engg.)
Science in Home Science _____M.Sc. (Home Sc.)
Science in Human Anatomy _____M.Sc. (Human Anatomy)
Science in Medicine _____M.Sc.(Med.)
Science in Nursing _____M.Sc.N. or M.Sc. (Nursing)
Science in Nutrition _____M.Sc. (Nut.)
Science (Technology) _____M.Sc. (Tech.)
Social Work _____M.S.W.
Surgery (Orthopaedic) _____M.S. (Orth.)
Surgery _____M.S.
Surgery (Plastic Surgery) _____M.Ch. (Plastic Surgery)
Technology _____M.Tech.
Tel-Communication Engineering _____M.Tel.E.
Theology _____M.Th.
Veterinary Science _____M.Sc. (Vet.) or M.V.Sc.
```

Doctor of—

```
Civil Law _____D.C.L.
Education _____D.Ed.
Engineering _____D.E. or D.Engg. or Dr.Engg.
Law _____D.L.
Letters or Literature _____D.Litt.
Medicine _____D.M. or M.D.
Music _____D.Mus.
Oriental Learning _____D.O.L.
Philosophy _____D.Phil. or Ph.D.
Science _____D.Sc.
Science (Engineering) _____D.Sc. (Engg.)
Theology _____D.Th.
Graduate in Homeopathic Medicine and Surgery_G.H.M.S.
```

DIPLOMAS

Diploma in—

```
Anaesthesia _____D.A.
Anatomy _____D.Anat.
Applied Linguistics _____Dip.A.Ling.
Ayurvedic Medicine _____D.A.M.
```

Basic Medical Science	Dip.B.M.S.
Business Administration	D.B.M.
Cardiology	Dip.Card.
Chemical Engineering	D.Ch.E.
Child Health	D.C.H.
Civil Engineering	D.C.E.
Clinical Laboratory Science	D.C.L.Sc.
Clinical Pathology *or* Psychology	D.C.P.
Cooperation	Dip.Coop.
Criminology and Forensic Medicine	D.C.F.M.
Dermatological Medicine	D.D.M.
Dermatology	D.D.
Dermatology and Venereology	D.D.V.
Diagnostic Radiology	D.D.R.
Dietetics	D.Diet.
Dramatics	D.Dram.
Early Childhood Education	Dip.E.C.Ed.
Education	Dip.Ed.
Educational Administration	Dip.Ed.Admn.
Educational Psychology	D.E.P.
Electrical Engineering	D.E.E.
Fine Arts	Dip.F.A.
Foreign Affairs	D.F.A.
Forensic Medicine	D.F.M.
Guidance and Counselling	D.G.C.
Gynaecology and Obstetrics	D.G.O.
History of Medicine	D.H.M.
Hygiene	D.Hy.
Indian Medicine	D.I.M.
Industrial Engineering	D.I.E.
Industrial Health	D.I.H.
Industrial Management	D.I.M.
Industrial Medicine	D.I.M.
International Affairs	D.I.A.
Journalism	Dip.J. *or* J.D.
Labour Welfare	D.L.W.
Languages	Dip.L.
Laryngology and Otology	D.L.O. *or* D.L.&O.
Library Science	Dip.Lib.Sc.
Maternity and Child Welfare	D.M.C.W.
Mechanical Engineering	D.M.E.
Medical Laboratory Technology	D.M.L.T.
Medical Pathology and Bacteriology	D.M.P.B.
Medical Psychology	D.M.P.
Medical Radiology	D.M.R.
Medical Radiology (Radio Diagonosis)	D.M.R.(D)
Medical Radiology (Radio Therapy)	D.M.R.(T)
Medical Radiology and Electricity	D.M.R.E.
Medical Radiology and Electrology	D.M.R.E.
Medical and Social Psychology	D.M.S.P.
Nusery School Education	Dip.N.Ed.
Nursing Education	D.N.E.
Nutrition	D.N.
Obstetrics and Gynaecology	D.O.G.
Ophthalmic Medicine and Surgery	D.O.M.S.
Ophthalmology	D.O.
Oriental Learning	D.O.L.
Orthopaedic Surgery	D.O.S. *or* D.Orth.S.
Oto-Rhino-Laryngology	D.O.R.L.
Paediatrics	D.Ped.

```
Pathology and Bacteriology _____D.P.B.
Pharmacy _____Dip.Pharm.
Physical Education _____D.P.E.
Physiology _____D.Physio.
Psychiatry _____D.P.
Psychological Medicine _____D.P.M.
Public Administration _____D.P.A.
Public Health _____D.P.H.
Public Health Nursing _____D.P.H.N.
Radiation Medicine _____D.R.M.
Sanitary Science _____D.S.Sc.
Social Science _____D.S.S. or Dip.S.S.
Social Work _____D.S.W.  or  Dip.S.W.
Statistics _____D.Stats.
Teaching _____Dip. T. or T.D.
Textile Chemistry _____D.T.C.
Therapeutic Radiology _____D.T.R.
Town and Regional Planning _____D.T.&R.P.
Tropical Medicine _____D.T.M.
Tropical Medicine and Hygiene _____D.T.M. & H.
Tuberculosis or Tuberculous Diseases _____D.T.D.
Tuberculosis and Chest Diseases _____D.T.C.D.
Venereology _____D.V.
Venereology and Dermatology _____D.V. & D.
(2)
```

CERTIFICATES

```
Certificate in Medical Laboratory Technology _____C.M.L.T.
```

Intermediate in—

```
Agriculture _____I.Ag.
Arts _____I.A.
Commerce _____I.Com.
Science _____I.Sc.
Science (Agriculture) _____I.Sc. (Ag.)
```

Licentiate in—

```
Civil Engineering _____L.C.E.
Medicine and Surgery _____L.M.S.
Public Health _____L.P.H.
Teaching _____L.T.
Tropical Medicine _____L.T.M.
Pre-Engineering Course _____Pre-Engg.
Pre-Medical Course _____Pre-Med.
Pre-Professional Course _____P.P.C. or Pre-Profl.
Pre-University Course _____P.U.C. or Pre-Univ.
Proficiency in Oriental Learning _____P.O.L.
```

[2] The Indian Institute of Science grants a diploma known simply as the Diploma in the Indian Institute of Science, or D.I.I.S.

Appendix E. Syllabuses for B.A. Degree Subjects:[1] English, Psychology, Moral and Social Philosophy, and Sociology and Social Evolution at Bombay University: 1963–64

English

Course 1

Two Shakespearean plays for detailed study, one a tragedy (on the recommendation of the Board of Studies, the Academic Council will change one each year).

Course 2

Two modern texts, one either a drama or dramas (1890 on), or a book of verse (1798 on); the other either a novel, a book of essays, or a book of selections from serious prose (1890 on). Candidates must write an essay carrying 40 marks.

Psychology

(Subject Group: Psychology)

Course 1—General Psychology

- Nature and scope of psychology—date and standpoint of psychology—relations to other sciences, especially biology, anthropology, sociology—branches of psychology—uses of psychology.

- Methods of psychology—analytical and comparative approach—nature and significance of introspection—value of observation of behaviour as a method—experiment in psychology (possibility and limits).

- General nature of the infra-human mind as revealed in animal behaviour—reflexist and purposivist interpretations of animal behaviour.

- Nature of instinct—instinct and intelligence—nature of human instincts and their place in human life—principal instincts and man.

- Nature of mental life—subject and object—cognition—affection and conation, consciousness—grades of consciousness (subconscious and unconscious).

- Presentative cognition—sensation as an aspect of perception—nature of physical stimuli and physiological basis of sensation—sense-organs and nervous systems (peripheral and central)—sensations (attributes and varieties)—phenomena and laws of special sensations—Weber-Fechner law.

Source of Information: *Handbook of the University of Bombay.* 1963. II:2:74-142.
[1] Each subject is part of a subject group and is composed of two courses.

- Perception as sensory organization and interpretation—laws of sensory organization—forms and patterns—figure and ground—perception of the world of real things and their qualities——perception of things in space and time—perception of the self—errors of perception (illusions and hallucinations).

- Nature of attention—attention and interest—conditions, effects, and uses of attention—types of attention—attention, inattention, distraction.

- Representative cognition (memory, imagination, and intellection, percept image and idea)—types of imagery—place of imagery in thought.

- Nature of memory, factors in memory, memorization or learning—retention, recall, recognition—laws of memory—laws of association—good and bad memory—improvement of memory—obliviscence.

- Memory and imagination—nature and types of imagination—limits of imagination—expectation—belief and doubt—invention—free imagination or fancy—dreams and daydreams.

- Intellection—conception—judgment, reasoning—role of language analysis and discrimination—synthesis and assimilation—abstraction.

- Self and the world as apprehended in representative thought.

- Nature of affective life—feelings of pleasure-pain—emotions, relations of emotions to instincts (McDougall's view, James-Lange theory of emotions)—emotional moods, disposition, temper, temperament—complexes and sentiments.

- Nature of conation—levels of conation (want, appetite, impulse, desire, wish, will)—nature and modes of non-voluntary and involuntary action—motives and intentions—conflict of motives—deliberation—decision—place of self in volition—self-control—self-determination as freedom—meaning of personality and character structure, factors of personality, nature and organization of character.

Course 2—Social Psychology

- Nature and scope of social psychology—data and methods—relations with allied studies, especially psychology, sociology, and politics.

- Individual basis of social life (unlearned and learned behaviour)—instincts and intelligence—feelings, emotions, sentiments—volition (reason and will)—personality and character—social character of the individual mind and personality—social factors in individual development—role of suggestion, sympathy, imitation.

- General nature of social life—forms of social stimulation and response—nature of social unity—theories of social mind—general will.

- Social grouping and organization—laws of social grouping—degrees of group organization—psychical nature of groups—classification and types of groups—hierarchy of groups.

- Mental life of groups—phenomena of group behaviour—laws of group behaviour—group spirit, group loyalty, group morale—role of leadership in group life.

- Social interaction—modes and laws of social interaction.

- Social heredity, tradition, language, customs, laws, morality, fashion, mythology, religion.

- Community, association, institutions—assembly and the public (their types and behaviour)—public opinion.

- Race and nationality, conditions of national life—mind and will of a nation—role of ideas in national life.

167

- Social change—conditions of social change—social conflicts and maladjustment —social order—social control—social progress.

Moral and Social Philosophy

(Subject Group: Philosophy)

Course 1—Ethics

- Problem, nature, and scope of ethics—relations to other studies, especially biology, psychology, politics, metaphysics, religion.

- Psychological basis of moral life—nature of conation—appetite, impulse, desire, wish, will, deliberation, volition—conduct, habit, character, character and self— motive and intention—moral judgment (its subject and object)—evolution of moral conduct and moral judgmnet.

- Theories of the moral ideal—hedonism, rationalism, perfectionism, evolutionism —value theory in ethics—the right and the good.

- Theories of the moral faculty—moral sense—reason—conscience.

- Nature and authority of the moral standard—bearing of ethical theory on moral practice—nature and limits of casuistry.

- Practical moral life—the individual and the society—the moral organism, egoism and altruism—origin and nature of rights and obligations of the individual— institutions of moral life—self-sacrifice and self-realization in moral life—nature and classification of virtue—pathology of moral life—nature of crime—vice and sin—theories of punishment.

- Philosophical implications of moral life—postulates of morality.

Course 2—Social Philosophy

- Problem, nature, and scope of social philosophy—its methods—relations to allied studies of sociology, social psychology, ethics, politics, philosophy of history, philosophy—value of social philosophy.

- Fundamental concepts of social life—society, group, community, association, institutions, customs, traditions.

- Society and the individual—psychological basis of social life (instinct, emotion, reason and will in the individual and society)—nature and significance of social life—personality and citizenship.

- Origin and nature of society—Greek and modern views, conflict and cooperation.

- Socal functions and institutions—marriage and family—neighbourhood—classes and castes—school and education—factory, work, labour—property—culture and civilization—religion.

- The state as a social institution—theories of the origin of the state—modern theories of the state (idealism, individualism, socialism, communism, anarchism, fascism, democracy)—social functions of the state (positive and negative)— nature and incidence of sovereignty—sovereignty of the state.

- The state and the individual—moral basis of obedience to the state—nature of political obligation—natural rights and liberty of the individual—limits of state action and coercion—duties and obligations of the individual—nature, sphere, and scope of law—right of disobedience.

- Form of states—nature and significance of the nation state—internationalism, idea of the world community and the world state.

168

Proceedings of the Conferences of the Indian National Commission for the Co-operation with UNESCO. Annually from 1954.

Proceedings of the First and Second Meetings of the All-India Board of Technical Studies in Architecture and Regional Planning. At Delhi, August 1946 and July 1947. 1949.

Proceedings of the State Education Ministers' Conferences. From the 1st conference in September 1957.

Proceedings of the Vice-Chancellors' Conference. Annually from 1961.

Report of the All-India Educational Survey. 1960.

Report of the Committee on Emotional Integration. 1962.

Report of the Committee on Ways and Means of Financing Educational Development in India (Kher Committee Report).

Report of the Education Commission: 1964–66. 1966. 673 p.

Reports of the Ministry of Education. Annually from 1949–50.

Report of the Second Commonwealth Education Conference. In January 1962. Delhi: 1962.

Report on Educational Developments in India: 1967–68. 1968.

Seven Years of Freedom. 1954.

Ten Years of Freedom. 1957.

General Publications

Central Expenditures on Education in India: 1948–49, 1950–51. 1951.

Education for International Understanding and Cooperation. 1959. 76 p.

Educational Activities of the Governments of India: 1963. 1963.

Educational Studies and Investigations, Vol. 1. National Council of Educational Research and Training, 1962. 264 p.

Problem of Scientific and Technological Terminology in Indian Languages. 1961.

Programme of the Education Commission and Its Task Forces and Working Groups: September-December, 1965. 1965. 104 p.

Progress of Education in India: 1937–47, Vol. I, II. A decennial review. 1949.

Review of Education in India: 1947–61. A reprint of a chapter of *First Yearbook of Education.* 1961.

Higher Education

Aims and Objectives of University Education in India. 1954.

Correspondence Courses. 1963. 16 p.

Development of Higher Technical Institutions in India (Report of the Sarkar Committee). 1946.

Directory of Institutions of Higher Education in India. Published for 1951–52; annually for 1953 to 1959; biennially thereafter.

Education in Universities in India. An annual statistical survey from 1947–48.

Facilities for Technical Education in India. 1948.

Facilities for Technical Education in India. Vol. I: *Diploma and Certificate Courses.* Vol. II: *First Degree and Post Graduate Courses.* 1965. Respectively 443 p. and 227 p.

General Education—Report of the Study Team. 1957. 97 p.

General Information for Indian Students Going Abroad. 1959.

Government of India Scholarships for Studies in India. 1957.

Guide to Education in India—Facilities for Professional Studies in Education, Law, and Journalism. 1961.

Higher Education in India. Delhi, 1953.

Higher Education in India. A Handbook for Overseas Students. 1953.

The Indian Institute of Advanced Study. Memorandum of Association Rules and Regulations, Indian University Administration. 1958. 149 p.

Institutions for Higher Education in India, 1953 (Publication No. 130). 1953. 60 p.

Living in India—A Pamphlet for Overseas Students (Revised edition). 1957.

National Council of Educational Research and Training Scheme of Assistance to Approved Research Projects in India. 1962.

Report of the Reviewing Committee on the Indian Institute of Technology. Kharagpur: 1961.

Report of the Three-Year Degree Course Estimates Committee. 1958.

Report of the University Education Commission (Radhakrishnan Report), Vol. I, II (Parts I, II). Delhi: Manager of Publications. 1st edition, 1950; reprint, 1962. 747 p.

Scheme of Assistance to Approved Research Projects in Education. 1962. 4 p.

Scholarships for Scheduled Castes, Scheduled Tribes, and Other Backward Classes: 1952, 1954, 1955, 1957.

Scholarships for Studies Abroad—Schemes Administered by the Union Ministry of Education (Revised edition). 1960.

Scientific Institutions and Societies in India. Delhi: Manager of Publications, 1949. 281 p.

Proceedings of the Regular Meetings of the All-India Council for Technical Education. From the first meeting in April, May 1946.

Propagation and Development of Hindi—A Review: 1956–57. 1958.

Report of the Banaras Hindu University Enquiry Committee. 1958. 44 p.

Report of the Committee of Members of Parliament on Higher Education. 1964.

Report of the Committee on "Model Act for Universities." 1964.

Report of the Expert Committee on Correspondence Courses and Evening Colleges. 1963. 16 p.

Reports of Inter-University Youth Festivals. Sponsored annually by the Ministry of Education.

Survey of Living Conditions of University Students—A Report. 1961.

UNESCO Project in India, 1953.

Rural Higher Education

Evaluation and Examination in Rural Institutes. 1960.

Proceedings of the First Meeting of the National Council for Rural Higher Education. 1956.

Report of the Rural Education Committee. 1959.

Rural Institutes—A Report of the Committee on Higher Education. 1955.

Physical Education

All-India Seminar on Physical Education for Principals of Physical Education Institutions. 1959.

A Plan for National Physical Efficiency Drive. 1960.

Report of the Ad Hoc Enquiry Committee on Games and Sports. 1959.

Reports on Coordination and Integration of Schemes Operating in the Field of Physical Education, Recreation, and Youth Welfare (Kunzru Committee). 1964.

Primary and Elementary Education

The Concept of Basic Education. 1956.

National Seminar on Compulsory Primary Education. 1961.

Orientation of Primary Education Towards the Basic Pattern—Report of the National Seminar. Held at Allahabad in May 1959. 1959.

174

Report of the Committee on the Relationship Between the State Governments and Local Bodies in the Administration of Primary Education (Kher Committee). 1954.
Seminar on Basic Education. 1957.

Secondary Education

Educational and Vocational Guidance in Multi-purpose schools. 1957.
New Pattern of Secondary Education. 1960.
A Plan for Secondary Education. 1955.
Reconstruction of Secondary Education. 1962.
Report of the Committee for the Integration of Post-Basic and Multi-purpose Schools in India. 1960.
Report of the Secondary Education Commission (Mudaliar Commission). From October 1952—June 1953. 1953.

Women's Education

Education of Girls and Women in India. 1952.
The National Council for Women's Education—Annual Reports. 1st, 1959–60; 2d 1960–61. Respectively, 1960 and 1962.
Report of the National Committee on Women's Education. From May 1958— January 1959. 1959.

II. Ministry of Food and Agriculture

Agricultural Universities in India. Report of the committee to advise State governments on legislation to establish agricultural universities in India. 1962.
Annual Report of the Indian Council of Agricultural Research. 1961–62.
The Forest Research Institutes and Colleges. 1949.
Progress Report on Agricultural Universities. 1962.

III. Ministry of Information and Broadcasting

Education for Democracy. 1952.
Independence and After. 1949.
India—A Reference Annual. 1964–1968.
India in 1952. A collection of articles. 1953.
Technical Assistance. 1952.

IV. Planning Commission

First Five-Year Plan: 1951–56. Delhi: Government of India, 1952.
Second Five-Year Plan: 1956–61. Delhi: Government of India, 1956.
Third Five-Year Plan: 1961–66. Delhi: Government of India, 1961.
Fourth Five-Year Plan: 1966–71. Delhi: Government of India, 1966.
Economic Development in Different Regions in India. 1962.
Report of the Working Group on Technical Education and Vocational Training. 1960.
Social Welfare in India. Delhi, 1960.
The Third Five-Year Plan Progress Report. 1963. 220 p.
The Third Plan Mid-Term Appraisal. 1963. 179 p.

V. University Grants Commission

Annual Reports. A report on December 1953—March 1957, and annually thereafter.

Basic Facts and Figures: 1963–64. 1964.

Centers of Advanced Study in Indian Universities. Delhi, 1964. 62 p.

Development Programmes Sponsored by University Grants Commission. 1964. 31 p.

Education as an Elective Subject at the Undergraduate Stage. 1966.

Evaluation in Higher Education. A report on the seminars on examination reform organized by the Commission under Dr. Benjamin S. Bloom. 1961. 272 p.

Handbook of Universities in India: 1963. 1964. 263 p.

List of Colleges Under Section 2 (F) of the U.G.C. Act as on 1st October, 1965. With *Addendum I.* 1965. Respectively 117 p. and 4 p.

M.A. and M.Sc. Examination Results: 1955–60. By subject. 1962. 69 p.

Medium of Instruction Report. By the Working Group appointed in 1959. 1961. 123 p.

Report of the Committee Appointed by the University Grants Commission to Examine the Problem of Medium of Instruction at the University Stage and to Recommend Ways and Means of Securing an Adequate Proficiency in English. Chairman Dr. H. N. Kunzru. 1959. p. 11. (Mimeo.).

Report of the Conference of Principles: May 1964. 1965. 55 p.

Report of the Conference on Problems of Teaching English. 1959.

Report of Seminar on National Integration: April 16–17, 1958. 1960. 127 p.

Report of Seminar on Post Graduate Teaching and Research in History. 1964. 70 p.

Report on Examination Reform. Delhi, 1962. 115 p.

Report on General Education. 1962. 89 p.

Report on the Problem of Student Indiscipline in Indian Universities. Delhi, 1960.

Report on Standards of University Education. Delhi, 1965. 282 p.

Review Committee Reports. Botany—1963; Bichemistry—1963; Chemistry— Education—1966; English—1965; Library science—1956; Mathematics—1962; Social work—1965.

Scholarships for Study Abroad and at Home. (4th revised edition). 1964. 218 p.

Social Work Education in Indian Universities. 1965. 100 p.

Some Facts and Figures. 1966. 23 p.

Three Studies in Examination Techniques. 1964. 33 p.

Universities Statistical Digest. I : 1 : 1–18. September 1962.

University and College Libraries. Delhi, 1965. 228 p.

University Development in India, Basic Facts and Figures: 1962–63. 1963. 69 p.

University Development in India, Basic Facts and Figures: 1963–64. 1964. 106 p.

University Development in India, A Statistical Report: 1961–62. 1962. 71 p.

University Grants Commission Act: 1956 (As modified up to January 1, 1963). Delhi: Manager of Publications, 1963.

VI. Other Commissions and Committees

Calcutta University Commission. *Report: 1917–19* (Vol. VI—Appendixes and Index). 1919.

Indian Education Commission. *Report.* 1882.

Indian Universities Commission. *Report: 1902.* Simla: Government Central Printing Office, 1902. 86 p.

Punjab University Enquiry Committee. *Report.* Lahore: 1933.

NONGOVERNMENT

AIYAR, C. P. RAMASWAMI. *Indian Universities, Retrospect and Prospects.* Annamalainagar: Annamalai University, 1965.

APPLEBY, PAUL H. *Public Administration in India.* Delhi: Manager of Publications, 1953. 66 p.

AVINASHILINGHAM, T. S. *Gandhiji's Experiments in Education* (Ministry of Education Publication No. 435). Delhi: Manager of Publications, 1960. 84 p.

—————. *The School and the Centenary.* (Swami Vivekanenda Centenary Series No. 2). Coimbatore District, South India: Coimatore Printers, 1961. 60 p.

BASHAM, A. L. *The Wonder That Was India.* New York: Grove Press, 1954.

BASU, A. N. *Education in Modern India: A Brief Review* (2d edition). Calcutta: Orient Book Company, 1947.

—————. *University Education In India—Past and Present.* Calcutta, 1944.

BHATTACHARJEE, JYOTI PRASAD. *Mechnization of Agriculture in India: Its Economics.* Sriniketan: Visva Bharati, 1949.

BOMBAY UNIVERSITY. *Handbook of the University of Bombay.* 1963.

—————. *Report of the Committee on the Medium of Instruction to be Adopted in the Bombay University.* Bombay, 1955.

—————. *Summary of Main Recommendations of the Bombay Reorganization Committee and Draft Bill for the Bombay University Act, 1951.* Bombay: 1951.

—————. *University of Bombay (1857).* Centenary Souvenir. Bombay: 1957.

BREMBECK, COLE S. and EDWARD W. WEIDNER. *Education and Development in India and Pakistan* (Education in Asia Series I). College of Education and International Affairs, Michigan State University. No date.

CALCUTTA UNIVERSITY. *Hundred Years of the University of Calcutta.* Calcutta: 1957.

CHANDIRAMANI, G. K. *Technological Education in India* (Ministry of Education Publication No. 239). Delhi: Manager of Publications, 1965. 20 p.

CHANDRAKANT, L. S. *Technical Education in India Today.* Delhi: Ministry of Scientific Research and Cultural Affairs, 1963. 67 p.

CHATTERJI, G. C., HELEN ADISHIAH, N. E. WILLIAMS, R. L. BARTHOLOMEW, and P. SPRALL. *My Idea of a University: A Symposium.* Delhi: Manager of Publications, 1957.

CIESLAK, EDWARD CHARNWOOD, JOHN TODD COWLES, and ANNA MARIE DROGOSITZ. *Examinations in Indian Higher Education.* Delhi: United States Information Service, 1959. 72 p.

Commonwealth Universities Yearbook: 1965. Annual directory and handbook. London: Association of Commonwealth Universities. 2,149 p.

Constitution of India. Delhi: Manager of Publications, 1951.

CORMACK, MARGARET L. *She Who Rides a Peacock.* A research analysis. Bombay: Asia Publishing House, 1961. 240 p.

"Crisis on the Campus." *Seminar.* No. 10, p. 10–43. April 1963.

DARUVALA, J. C. *Report on a Survey of the Attitudes, Opinions, and Personality Traits of a Sample of 1706 Students of the University of Bombay.* Bombay: Orient Longmans Private Limited, 1960. 77 p.

DAWES, NORMAN. *A Two-Way Street. Indo-American Fullbright Program: 1959–60.* Delhi: Asia Publishing House, 1962.

DAWOOD, H. R. and K. G. SAIYIDAN. "Relationship Between Secondary Schools and Universities." *Yearbook of Education, 1959: Higher Education.* New York: World Book Co., 1959. p. 484–93.

DEAN, VERA MICHELES. *New Patterns of Democracy in India.* Cambridge, Massachusetts: Harvard University Press, 1957.

DELHI PROVINCE POST GRADUATE TEACHERS' CLUB. *The Report of the Educational Gathering.* Delhi: The Club, 1950.

DESHMUKH, C. D. *Economic Development in India, 1946–1956: A Personal Retrospect.* Bombay: Asia Publishing House. 1957.

—————. *In the Portals of Indian Universities.* Convocation and other addresses. Delhi: University Grants Commission, 1959.

——————. *On the Threshold of India's Citizenhood.* Delhi: University Grants Commission, 1962. 392 p.

DEVADAS, RAJAMMAL. *Director of Home Science Institutions and Workers in Asia.* Home Science Association of India, 1962. 72 p.

——————. *Home Science Handbook for Teachers.* Delhi: Indian Council for Secondary Education, 1958.

——————. *Home Science in Colleges and Universities in India.* Ministry of Education, 1958.

DONGERKERRY, S. R. *A History of the University of Bombay: 1857–1957.* Fort Bombay: Bombay University, 1957. 300 p.

——————. *Memories of Two Universities.* Bombay: P. C. Manaktala and Sons, 1966.

——————. "The Problem of Student Indiscipline." *Journal of University Education.* 1:2:112–22. December 1962.

——————. *The Role of the University Teacher in a Changing Society* (Publication No. 50). Ahmedabad: Harold Laski Institute of Political Science, 1962. 16 p.

——————. *Some Experiments in General Education.* Bombay: Bombay University, 1955.

——————. *Thoughts on University Education.* Bombay: G. R. Bhatkal for the Popular Book Depot, 1955. 170 p.

——————. *Universities and National Life.* Bombay: Hind Kitabs Ltd., 1950. 115 p.

——————. *Universities and Their Problems.* Bombay: 1948.

DUTT, ROMESH CHUNDER. *Early Hindu Civilization, B.C. 2000 to 32 (based on Sanskrit literature)* (4th edition). Calcutta: Punthi Pustak, 1963. 285 p.

——————. *Later Hindu Civilization, A.D. 500 to 1200 (based on Sanskrit literature)* (4th edition). Calcutta: Punthi Pustak, 1965.

EDWARDS, MICHAEL. *The Last Years of British India.* Cleveland/New York: World Publishing Co., 1963. 235 p.

EMBREE, AINSLIE T., *ed. The Hindu Tradition.* New York: Random House, The Modern Library, 1966. 348 p.

Examination Reforms in Maharajah Sayajirao University of Baroda: 1950–57. Raopura Baroda: University of Baroda Press. No date.

EYDE, LORRAINE. "Indian Universities and Their Students." *International Review of Education.* 9:4:473. 1963–64.

FERSH, SEYMOUR. *India and South Asia.* New York: The Macmillan Co., 1965. 150 p.

Fullbright Program in India: July 1950—June 1962. A 12-year statistical survey. Delhi: U. S. Educational Foundation in India, 1962.

GANDHI, M. K. *An Autobiography or The Story of My Experiments With Truth.* Ahmedabad: Navajivan Press (Jivanji Dahyabhai Desai), 1st edition 1927; reprint 1948. 616 p.

GAUDINO, ROBERT L. *The Indian University.* Bombay: Popular Prakashav, 1965.

GOODMAN, LOUIS S. *and* ALFRED GILMAN. *The Pharacological Basis of Therapeutics* (3d edition). New York: The Macmillan Co., 1965.

Handbook of Indian Universities. Compiled by U.S. Educational Foundation in India. Delhi: Allied Publishers Private, Ltd., 1963. 339 p.

HANNAH, HAROLD W. Development of Agricultural Education and Research in North Central India. Urbana, Illinois: College of Agriculture, University of Illinois, *with* the International Cooperation Administration, 1958.

HARBISON, FREDERICK *and* CHARLES A. MEYERS. *Education, Manpower, and Economic Growth. Strategies of Human Resources Development.* New York: McGraw-Hill, 1964.

HARTOG, SIR PHILIP. *Some Aspects of Education, Past and Present.* Oxford University Press, 1939.

HUSSAIN, ZAKIR. *The Dynamic University.* Bombay: Asia Publishing House, 1965. 119 p.

India, A Study of the Educational System of India and Guide to the Academy Placement of Students from India in U.S. Educational Institutions (World Education Series). Committee on Foreign Students of the American Association of Collegiate Registrars and Admissions Officers in 1964. 1964.

Indian Medical Council Act. 1956.

INDIAN NATIONAL CONGRESS PUBLICATIONS. Dr. N. V. Rajkumar, *ed. First Year of Freedom.* Delhi: Acharya Jugal Kishore, 1948. 179 p.

——————. *Second Year of Freedom: August 1948—August 1949.* Madras: Madras Publishing House, 1950. 117 p.

——————. *Third Year of Freedom: August 1949—August 1950.* Delhi: All India Congress Committee, 1950. 106 p.

——————. *Fourth Year of Freedom: August 1950—August 1951.* Delhi: The All India Congress Committee, 1951.

INSTITUTE OF APPLIED MANPOWER RESEARCH. *Area Manpower Survey. Pilot Project Memorandum plus Annexures I—IV.* Delhi: 1963. 7 p.

——————. *Fact Book on Manpower.* Part II: *Education and Training.* Part III: *Scientific and Technical Manpower.* Delhi: 1963. Respectively 65 p. and 74 p. (Mimeo.)

——————. *Manpower Group Survey. First Round Engineering Manpower Survey.* Delhi: 1963. 7 p.

——————. *Memorandum of Association and Rules and Regulations.* Delhi: 1962. 14 p.

Institutes of Technology Act, 1961. Delhi: Manager of Publications, 1961.

INTERNATIONAL BUREAU OF EDUCATION (Geneva, Switzerland). *Review of Education in India.* An annual review for International Conference on Public Education.

INTER-UNIVERSITY BOARD OF INDIA AND CEYLON. *Handbook of Universities, 1951.* Also, *Supplement to the Handbook, 1951.*

——————. *List of Subjects in Arts and Sciences in which research was carried out in the universities and research institutions: June 1954—May 1958.*

——————. *Proceedings of Annual Meetings.* From 1925.

——————. *Universities' Handbook, India and Ceylon, 1964.* Delhi, 1965. 675 p.

——————. *University News.* Issued several times a year from February 1963 and monthly from January 1966.

JOSHI, G. N. *The Constitution of India* (Revised edition). Madras: Macmillan and Company, 1961. 466 p.

Journal of Association of Principals of Technical Institutions, India. Issued quarterly. Delhi: B. R. Sardana.

Journal of University Education. Published September, December, and March from September 1962. Delhi: Federation of Central Universities Teachers' Association.

KABIR, HUMAYUN. *A Programme of National Education for India.* Eastern Economist Pamphlets, 1953.

——————. *Education in New India* (2d edition). London: George Allen Unwin, Ltd., 1959. 230 p.

——————. *Indian Philosophy of Education.* Bombay: Asia Publishing House, 1961. 256 p.

——————. *Letters on Discipline* (Ministry of Education and Scientific Research Publication No. 334). Delhi: Manager of Publications, 1958.

——————. *Student Indiscipline* (Ministry of Education Publication No. 158.) (2d edition). Delhi: 1955.

——————. *The Indian Heritage* (3rd edition). Bombay: Asia Publishing House, 1962. 138 p.

KANUNGO, GOSTHA BEHARI. *The Language Controversy in Indian Education: An Historical Survey* (Comparative Educational Monograph No. 1). Chicago: University of Chicago Comparative Education Center, 1962.

KHER, B. G. *Aspects of Education.* A selection of addresses at various educational institutions in 1947. Bombay: Directorate of Publicity, Government of Bombay, 1948. 46 p.

KOTHARI, D. S. *Education and the Universities.* Address at the Vice-Chancellors' Conference at Delhi in October 1961. Delhi: University Grants Commission, 1962. 30 p.

——————. *Science and the Universities.* Delhi: University Grants Commission, 1965. 30 p.

_____. *Some Aspects of University Education*. Address at Vice-Chancellors' Conference in October 1962. Delhi: University Grants Commission, 1962. 30 p.

_____. *The Problem of Scientific and Technical Terminology in Indian Languages* (Ministry of Education Publication No. 549). Delhi: 1961. 7 p.

LAKSHMINARAYANA, T. A. *A Report*. To Dr. J. C. Hume, Chief, Health Division, Technical Cooperation Mission, American Embassy. Delhi: 1959.

LAMB, BEATRICE PITNEY. *India: A World in Transition*. New York: Frederick A. Praeger, 1963. 347 p.

LEWIS, J. P. *Quiet Crisis in India: Economic Development and American Policy*. Washington, D. C.; Brookings Institute, 1962.

Madras University Centenary Celebrations. 1957. 2 vols.

MAJUMDAR, RAMESH CHANDRA, H. C. RAYCHAUDHURI, *and* K. C. DATTA. *An Advanced History of India*. London: Macmillan and Co., Ltd., 1956. 1,122 p.

MATHAI, SAMUEL. *Indian Universities. For* Ministry of Education. Delhi: Manager of Publications, 1956.

McGILL, RALPH. "Report on India." *Atlanta Constitution*. November 21, 1951— January 8, 1952.

MEDICAL COUNCIL OF INDIA. *Conference on Medical Education: November 1961*. Delhi: Delhi Printers. 56 p.

_____. *Silver Jubilee Souvenir: 1934–1959*. Delhi: The Council.

MEHTA, ASOKA. *The Political Mind of India*. Bombay: Mahu Limaije *for* Socialist Party, 1952. 74 p.

MENON, T. K. N., *ed. Symposium: General Education*. Baroda: M. S. University of Baroda Press, 1960. 206 p.

MISA, ATAMANAND. *Educational Finances in India*. New York: Asia Publishing House, 1960.

MOOKHERJI, RADHA KUMUD. *Ancient Indian Education (Brahmanical and Buddhist)*. London: Macmillan and Co., Ltd., 1951. 610 p.

MUDALIAR, A. L. *Education in India*. Bombay: Asia Publishing House, 1960.

MUKERJI, S. N. *History of Education in India, Modern Period*. Baroda: Acharya Book Depot. 1955.

MUKERJEE, HARIDAS *and* UMA MUKHERJEE. *The Origins of the National Education Movement (1905–1910)* (1st edition). Calcutta: Jadavpur University, 1957.

MUKHERJEE, K. C. "Some Implications of the Robbins Report for Higher Education in India." *International Review of Education*. 12:1:47–57. 1966.

NAIK, K. C. *Agricultural Education in India. Institutes and Organizations*. (Series No. 4). Delhi: Indian Council of Agricultural Research, 1961.

NAIK, J. P. *The Role of Government in Indian Education (Educational Studies and Investigations,* Vol. 1). Delhi: National Council of Educational Research and Training, Ministry of Education, 1962.

_____ *and* SYED NURULLAH. *A History of Education in India (During the British Period)* (2d edition). Bombay: J. H. Collins *for* Macmillan and Co., Ltd.,

NANAVATI, SIR MANILAL *and* C. N. VAKIL, *eds. Group Prejudices in India, A Symposium*. Bombay: Voar and Co., Publishers, Ltd., 1951. 233 p.

NARAYAN, SHRIMAN. *On Education*. Delhi: Atma Ram & Sons, 1962. 103 p.

NEHRU, JAWAHARLAL. *The Discovery of India*. New York: The John Day Co., 1946. 581 p.

_____. *Glimpses of World History* (4th edition). London: Lindsay Drummond, Ltd., 1949. 971 p.

_____. *Independence and After. A Collection of Speeches*. Delhi: Publications Division, Ministry of Information and Broadcasting, 1949.

OWEN, ROWLAND. *India—Economic and Commercial Conditions in India. Overseas Economic Surveys*. London: Her Majesty's Stationery Office *for* Board of Trade Commercial Relations and Exports Department, 1953. 392 p.

PANANDIKAR, S. *The Teacher in India Today. For* Ministry of Education. Delhi: Manager of Publications, 1957. 22 p.

PARIKH, G. D. *General Education and Indian Universities*. Bombay: 1959.

Problems of Historical Writing in India. Proceedings of Seminar at Delhi, January 1963. Delhi: India International Center, 1963. 148 p.

Rao, V. K. R. V. *Special Committee for Commerce Education*. Ministry of Scientific Research and Cultural Affairs, 1961.

Rawlinson, Hugh G. *India: A Short Cultural History*. (4th revision). London: The Cresset Press, Ltd., 1952. 454 p.

Roots of Change. New York: Office of Reports, Ford Foundation, 1961. 52 p.

Saiyidain, K. G. *Education, Culture and Social Order*. Bombay: Asia Publishing House. 1st edition, 1952; reprint, 1963. 278 p.

—————. *National Service Scheme. A Report* (Ministry of Education Publication No. 541). Delhi: Manager of Publications, 1961. 79 p.

—————. *Problems of Educational Reconstruction* (3d edition). Bombay: Asia Publishing House, 1962. 296 p.

—————. *The Humanities in University Education*. Ministry of Education, 1957.

—————. "Universities and Social Responsibility." *Liberal Education* (Bulletin of the Association of American Colleges). Washington, D.C. 51–478–85. December 1965.

————— and H. C. Gupta. *Access to Higher Education in India*. A depth study of university admission procedures, for International Study of University Admissions, sponsored by UNESCO and International Association of Universities. Delhi: 1962. 76 p.

Sen, Gertrude Emerson. *The Pageant of India's History*. New York: Longmans, Green and Co., Inc., 1948. 406 p.

Sen Gupta, Padmini. *Women's Education in India*. Delhi: Ministry of Education, 1960.

Shrimali, K. L. *Presidential address*. At the Second Commonwealth Education Conference. 1962. 9 p.

—————. Presidential Address. At the 29th Session of the Central Advisory Board of Education. Delhi: Ministry of Education, 1962.

—————. *Problems of Education in India*. Delhi: Publications Division, 1961.

Singer, Milton, ed. *Proceedings of a Conference, Introducing India in Liberal Education*. At University of Chicago, May 1957. Chicago: University of Chicago Press, 1957. 284 p.

—————. *Sources of Indian Tradition*. New York: Columbia University Press, 1964. 2 vols.

Thacker, M. S. *Science and Culture*. Delhi: Planning Commission, 1963. 32 p.

Trumbull, Robert. *India Since Independence* (Headline Series, Foreign Policy Association, No. 105). New York: May—June 1954. 62 p.

UNESCO. *Humanism and Education in East and West*. An international round-table discussion organized by UNESCO. Paris: UNESCO, 1953. 199 p.

—————. *Interrelations of Cultures. Their Contribution to International Understanding*. Paris: UNESCO, 1953. 382 p.

—————. *World Survey of Education IV*. Paris/New York: UNESCO, 1966. 1,433 p.

Ward, Barbara. *The Rich Nations and the Poor Nations*. New York: W.W. Norton and Co., Inc., 1962. 159 p.

☆U.S. GOVERNMENT PRINTING OFFICE: 1970 O—356-543

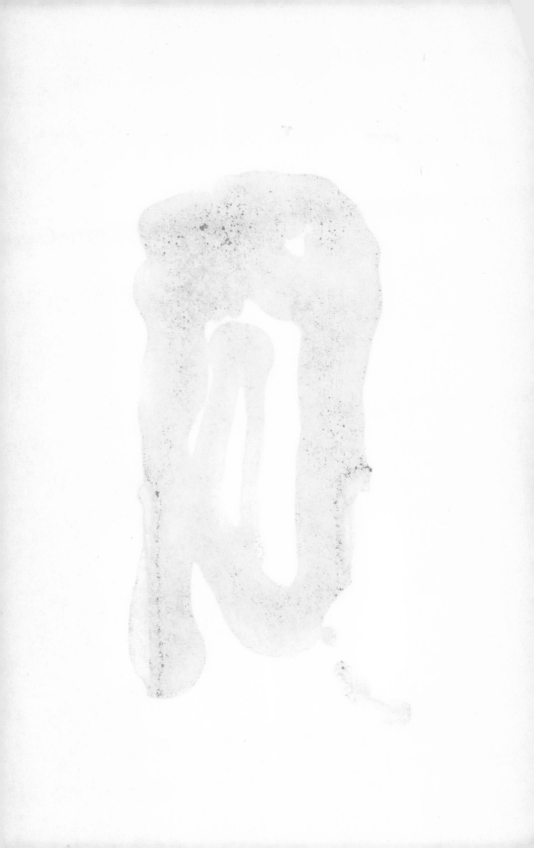